.... DISTRICT LIBRARY
.... AN 49045
O9-BHK-027

YOU MUST REMEMBER THIS

THE WARNER BROS. STORY

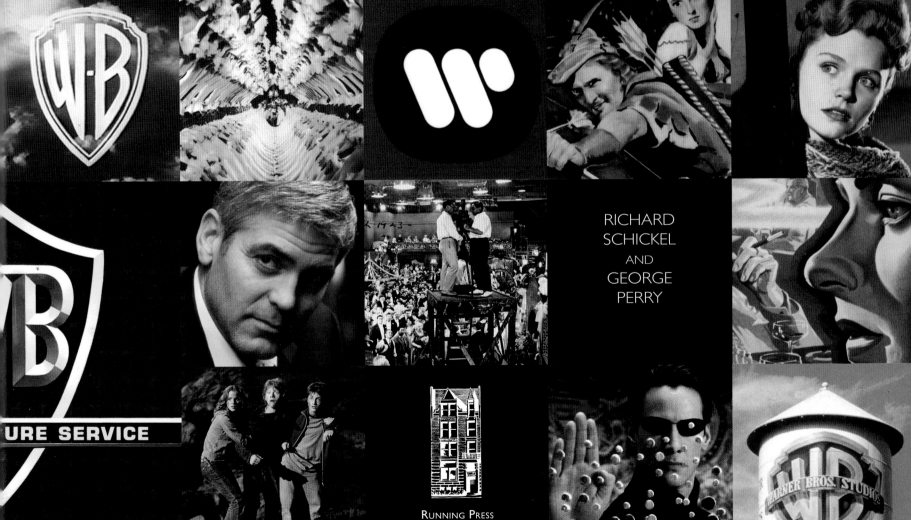

RICHARD
SCHICKEL
AND
GEORGE
PERRY

Running Press
PHILADELPHIA • LONDON

© 2008 Warner Bros. Entertainment Inc.

The views expressed in the book are those of the authors, not Warner Bros.

First published in the United States in 2008 under license by
Running Press Book Publishers

Printed in Singapore

This book may not be reproduced in whole or in part, in any form or by any
means, electronic or mechanical, including photocopying, recording, or by any
information storage and retrieval system now known or hereafter invented,
without written permission from the copyright owner.

9   8   7   6   5   4   3   2   1
Digit on the right indicates the number of this printing

Library of Congress Control Number: 2008926628

ISBN 978-0-7624-3418-3

Created and produced by
PALAZZO EDITIONS LTD
2 Wood Street, Bath BA1 2JQ, UK
www.palazzoeditions.com

Publisher: Colin Webb
Managing Editor: Sonya Newland
Art Director: Scott Erwert
Consultant Art Director: Terry Jeavons
Picture Editor: Patty Williams

Running Press Book Publishers
2300 Chestnut Street
Philadelphia, PA 19103-4371

Visit us on the web!
www.runningpress.com

CONTENTS

FOREWORD

I CAME TO WARNER BROS. IN 1971 TO MAKE ONE PICTURE, *DIRTY HARRY*. THAT BEGAN A RELATIONSHIP THAT HAS PER-SISTED TO THIS DAY, AND IN 1975 MY PRODUCTION TEAM MOVED INTO A LITTLE SPANISH-STYLE BUNGALOW (SOMETIMES REFERRED TO AS THE TACO BELL). TODAY, THIRTY-THREE YEARS LATER, WE'RE STILL THERE, THE OLD WRITERS' BUILD-ING TO THE RIGHT OF OUR FRONT DOOR, THE SITE OF THE OLD STUDIO TENNIS COURT—NOW A GARDEN—OUTSIDE OUR BACK DOOR. FROM IT YOU CAN LOOK UP AT THE WINDOWS FROM WHICH JACK WARNER KEPT AN EAGLE EYE ON THE STUDIO'S OPERATIONS—ESPECIALLY THOSE PESKY WRITERS, WHOM HE ALWAYS SUSPECTED OF GOOFING OFF.

I believe I've been on the lot longer than any other actor or director in its long history, though I've never had a long-term contract with the studio. We just go from picture to picture, trusting one another and liking one another. Through the years I've done films at other studios, but at Warner Bros. three different management teams have given me the freedom to make the films I've wanted to make—even sometimes when we all knew they would not be huge winners at the box office. It's a way of doing business that is, sadly, no longer common in the movie industry.

But, for me, another factor looms large in my relationship to the lot—that's the sense of living history that I breathe in when I stroll the studio's streets. They have been making movies here since 1926, almost three years before Warner Bros. acquired the lot and moved its headquarters from Hollywood to Burbank. Each of the thirty-four sound stages now carries a plaque listing the titles of the films made therein, from *Casablanca* to some of my own. "If these walls could talk" someone might say.

But I think that, in their way, they do. I can sometimes imagine a whispered line of famous dialogue emanating from these blank stucco walls, behind which they were first spoken. It's the same way with the standing sets. The stage across the street from my office was one of the studio's original stages, and the plaque on its wall tells us that sequences from *42nd Street, A Midsummer's Night's Dream, Mildred Pierce, White Heat,* and many others were made there. Brownstone Street, stretching between the Commissary and the Stephen J. Ross Theater (your picture never looks or sounds better than it does in that handsome venue) has been there since 1929. Edward G. Robinson was gunned down just inside one of its hallways by Humphrey Bogart in 1936's *Bullets or Ballots.* But the exterior of Murphy Brown's apartment was also here. Around the corner you can see the bookshop where Humphrey Bogart seduced Dorothy Malone in *The Big Sleep* (or was it the other way around?). A few yards from that is the exterior of a house built for *Kings Row,* which is also the house where James Dean lived in *East of Eden.*

Nowadays, if you enter some of the other buildings you will encounter what I believe to be the world's most extensive costume department—hundreds of thousands of outfits, all carefully arranged by historical epochs, some of which carry the names of Bogart or Cagney or Bette Davis, indicating their first use, sewn into their linings. If such a label is discovered, the item is set aside for the studio archive. Not far away is a drapery department that can offer you material first used in *The Jazz Singer.* In that same building you can find props that were used in Warner Bros. pictures from its first years in business. No other studio draws so extensively on its past to inform its present—and its onrushing future.

Yes, of course, newer structures are to be found all around the studio. But the core of this business continues to be located in the physical center of the lot, many elements of which date back so many decades. People sometimes speak of a Warner "DNA," something indefinable, yet palpable, that informs the films we go on making here. It's a romantic thought, and an unprovable one. Still, we know this studio has tended its past better than anyone else, making it available, in bits and pieces—a costume here, a lamp or a desk or a bit of drapery there—to its filmmakers every day. This book and the television series from which it derives, so reflective of the studio's eighty-five-year history, so evocative of the hundreds of movies that have been made just outside my front door, draws on that history. But extensive as both of them are, they are merely a sample of a great studio's riches. Even so, I think that film and this book will both renew and inform your memories of those movies which, in their mysterious ways, shaped you—and shaped the ideas, the society, the world that we share.

Clint Eastwood

INTRODUCTION

YOU COULD ARGUE THAT THIS BOOK, AND THE TELEVISION SERIES FROM WHICH IT DERIVES, HAS BEEN IN THE MAKING FOR SOMETHING LIKE SIXTY-FIVE YEARS. WHEN I WAS A KID, LIVING IN A SUBURB OF MILWAUKEE, THE NEIGHBORHOOD THEATERS NEAREST TO ME OBVIOUSLY HAD SOME SORT OF ARRANGEMENT WITH WARNER BROS. AND PLAYED MORE MOVIES FROM THAT STUDIO THAN FROM ANY OTHER. SOMEHOW, FOR REASONS I COULDN'T QUITE UNDERSTAND, THEY APPEALED TO ME MORE THAN ANY OF THE COMPETITION'S OFFERINGS. I DIDN'T KNOW EXACTLY WHAT A DIRECTOR DID, BUT I DO KNOW THAT I PARTICULARLY LIKED MOVIES SIGNED BY MICHAEL CURTIZ, HOWARD HAWKS, AND RAOUL WALSH BETTER THAN I DID THOSE OF OTHER FILMMAKERS; THEY WERE, I THINK, TOUGHER, GRITTIER, A LITTLE MORE DARKLY ROMANTIC THAN THEIR COMPETITORS. AND THEN THERE WERE THE STARS. I LOVED GALLANT ERROL FLYNN THE BEST, BUT JAMES CAGNEY AND HUMPHREY BOGART WERE CLOSE SECONDS. I EVEN LIKED BETTE DAVIS. LITTLE BOYS WEREN'T SUPPOSED TO CARE MUCH FOR "WOMEN'S PICTURES," BUT THERE WAS SOMETHING ABOUT HER—HER FEVERISH INTENSITY SOMEHOW TRANSCENDED HER GENRE.

What I'm saying, I guess, is that the studio had a character that I couldn't quite define, but was yet palpable and pleasing to me. Later, looking back at that period, it was the Warner Bros. films that I recalled first—*Casablanca,* of course, and *Yankee Doodle Dandy,* but also *They Died with their Boots On* and *Gentleman Jim,* and the wartime adventures like *Air Force* and *Destination Tokyo* and *Action in the North Atlantic.* I can discern now what I most treasured about these films. They were movies that to greater or lesser degree defined what it meant to be male for little boys who had many questions on that subject. They made imperatives out of the antithetical qualities of stoicism and rebelliousness, out of being alienated from the community, but eventually learning to reconcile with its values without loss of individuality.

Later, when I began working on television programs, the first two that I did revolved largely around Warner Bros. films. After that, when I began making television profiles of major American directors, many of them were about Warner Bros. directors—beginning with Raoul Walsh and continuing through Clint Eastwood. Through their careers, I forged a deeper identification with the studio—a sense that its story is crucial to the history of American movies, even to American social and cultural history—that is to me unbreakable. Which is why the opportunity to make a film about the long history of the studio seems to me the capstone of my career, the place to which it was all along heading.

This is not to say that there were no surprises for me as I worked on this project. I have come across wonderful movies—*The Hard Way, Roughly Speaking, The Damned Don't Cry*—that I had never seen and scarcely heard of—that have powerfully gripped me. I have re-examined movies (like *I Am a Fugitive from a Chain Gang*) and careers (like Doris Day's or the director Vincent Sherman's) that now seem greater than they formerly appeared to me. And I have also been able to delve into the fractious life of the studio, which often had all the logic of a cat fight in an alley. Out of this work—which has never seemed like work to me—a somewhat more sophisticated understanding of what the studio was doing, what its hold on me and others like me consisted of, has emerged.

It's perfectly obvious to everyone that in Hollywood's classic age, the 1930s and 1940s, Warner Bros. was the working-class studio. You can see that most obviously in its famously "tragic" gangsters, machine-gunning their way to power only to be gunned down not so much for their depredations but for their hubris, for daring to challenge the respectable and the law-abiding. Other studios made pictures of this type, but few of them matched the energy and fervor of this studio's movies. More important, these competing films did not emerge out of the context Warner Bros. supplied. Think *Baby Face,* about a sexually abused working-class woman who takes loveless revenge on bourgeois and upper-class men as she sleeps her way to the top of a banking empire. Or *Wild Boys of the Road,* about homeless children wandering the nation, endlessly harassed by the police as they search for jobs and a place to rest their heads. Or *Heroes for Sale,* in which a hardworking man loses everything—his family, his business—under the impress of the Great Depression, then simply disappears in the American vastness. Or *Black Legion,* in which a working stiff becomes the murderous tool of a Ku Klux Klan-like organization. Consider, as well, wartime Warner Bros. with its small, ethnically balanced fighting units bonding together in passionate defense of the American community, now threatened by external rather than internal forces. Again, other studios made films of this kind, but not with the conviction of Warner Bros.

One thinks, for example, of MGM, the most prosperous of the Hollywood studios. It was a place committed to glamorous stars and deluxe *mis en scenes.* But there was always something smug, self-satisfied about its pictures, something more purely escapist in its intentions. They didn't do social conscientiousness in Culver City. Or take Twentieth Century Fox, with its commitment to nostalgic sentiments and rural sweetness. Sure, it took up serious matters (see *The Grapes of Wrath* or *The Ox-Bow Incident*), but its more typical offerings headed toward the ameliorative ending. At Warner Bros. the hero or the heroine tended to end up dead, or at the very least marginalized or otherwise dismissed by polite society—and I'm not just thinking about all the doomed mobsters James Cagney played. I'm thinking about Bogart's romantic devastations in *The Maltese Falcon* and *Casablanca,* and the tragic conclusions of movies as disparate as *They Won't Forget* or *Dark Victory.* Or the misplaced passions of actors as disparate as John Wayne in *The Searchers* and Joan Crawford in *Mildred Pierce,* of the madness that attends the end of Bogart in *The Treasure of the Sierra Madre* or Cagney in *White Heat.* I'm thinking of the devastations that conclude *The Wild Bunch* and *Bonnie and Clyde* and *McCabe and Mrs. Miller,* of the existential chill, the air of fated hopelessness, that hovers over Stanley Kubrick's work for the studio. I'm even thinking of the *Dirty Harry*'s radical disaffection and loneliness and of William Munny's—well, all right—"dark victory" at the end of *Unforgiven* or the bleakness of the conclusions to more recent Eastwood films like *Million Dollar Baby* or *Letters from Iwo Jima.*

A studio as fecund as Warner Bros. makes many films in many different genres over the course of a long history that embraces several managements, diverse economic and social challenges—and, indeed, television, is admittedly slighted in this book. TV is vital to the continuing economic success of the studio and has been part of Warner Bros.' world since 1955, with stirrings and interest from the studio that date back to the late 1920s. That history deserves its own book of this size and scope, but that will be at another time and by another author.

But the best Warner Bros. tradition is a realistic one, scrappy, contentious, and not immune to doom. And if the logic of their stories demanded dismayed romance or diminished hopes or death itself, then the good Warner Bros. pictures went there—perhaps because the founding brothers always thought of themselves as outsiders, fighting their way in from the Hollywood fringe. They became successes, and as a result learned to live large. But they did not entirely forget their first-generation immigrant roots, never entirely abandoned the notion that most Americans live only a step or two away from economic disaster, are never invulnerable to those other devastations of fortune that plague even the most privileged of humankind.

Warner Bros. stars were never the prettiest or the most handsome. Indeed, you can't quite imagine a Cagney or a Robinson or a Bette Davis—oddballs all in looks and manner—building substantial careers elsewhere. And that says nothing of George Arliss. These were not people we envied or mooned over. These were people we identified with. Nor can you imagine another studio employing as many politically radical, personally disaffected writers. Or think of someone as angry, stubborn, and unpredictably gifted as Michael Curtiz making a thirty-year career anywhere else. You can't tell me that something of the dark and problematic tradition they established does not continue there. I think it's probably in the water that the tank—the studio's most famous landmark, decorated with its even more famous shield logo—supplies the place.

When writer-director Andrew Bergman, who had previously written a smart little history of 1930s Warner Bros., first drove on the lot (to co-write *Blazing Saddles*) he confesses to misting up. It was like coming home for him. I know what he's talking about. I never enter the gates of the studio without similar feelings. I've devoted more of my life to thinking about the movies than I care to admit, and most of my career to writing about them or making films about them. And this is the place where those feelings live most happily, most intensely. I hope some of that passion inhabits my history of Warner Bros., and informs and inspires both my film series and this book.

RICHARD SCHICKEL

WHEN WARNER BROS. OFFICIALLY CAME INTO EXISTENCE IN 1923 THE FILM BUSINESS WAS YOUNG, EXCITING AND PRECARIOUS, STILL IN THE PROCESS OF ESTABLISHING ITSELF AS THE MAIN PURVEYOR OF MASS ENTERTAINMENT IN A WORLD ENDEAVORING TO RECOVER FROM THE MOST CATACLYSMIC OF WARS. IN THE HOME, RADIO HAD BARELY BEGUN TO AUGMENT THE PARLOR PIANO AND THE VICTROLA, WHILE TELEVISION WAS SIMPLY A FANTASY OF FUTUROLOGISTS IN PULP MAGAZINES. OUTSIDE THE BIG CITIES THE CHOICE FOR AN EVENING OUT WAS EITHER A SILENT MOVIE OR A VAUDEVILLE SHOW. CHANGE, HOWEVER, CAME RAPIDLY. BY THE TIME TALKIES WERE SECURELY ESTABLISHED IN THE 1930S EVERY HOME HAD A RADIO, AND PHONOGRAPH RECORDS WERE SOLD IN THEIR MILLIONS, TO THE DETRIMENT OF LIVE PERFORMANCES, NOW SEEN AS OLD-FASHIONED AND ANACHRONISTIC.

Hollywood's reach was global, and American films dominated screens around the world. I was a child in the grimy, war-shattered Britain of the 1940s, when cinema was central to most people's lives—attended by eight times today's numbers—and recognized officially as having a therapeutic role in alleviating the privations of the times. Even as the bombs were falling people flocked to the movies, willingly sharing the commonality of danger in an ambiance that allowed them temporary respite from difficult circumstances. The wartime convoys that defied the Nazi U-boats to bring essential foodstuffs across the Atlantic also ensured a constant supply of new Hollywood movies. Someone high up had appreciated that morale was an essential component in the will to win. The fate of Rick and Ilsa in *Casablanca* would have resonated among all those who had endured the inevitability and pain of wartime partings.

Even when the Nazi menace subsided, the grimness remained after the war. The movie theater at least offered warmth, comfort, and temporary respite from the food lines, shortages and severe curbs on domestic heating. There were hundreds of theaters in London then, but the rationing of prints led to every release taking three weeks to filter across the city's many districts, a system that persisted until the 1960s. The main circuits were associated with particular studios. At the Odeon would be the sparky Betty Grable musicals from Fox and Paramount's Hope and Crosby comedies. ABC's Regal would play the high-gloss output of MGM and the well-crafted, dramatic movies from Warner Bros. in their characteristic shadowy Burbank lighting. There was a terrible postwar period when the depletion of dollar reserves led to excessive taxation of American films, followed by a boycott of the British market. After a few months of no new Hollywood films, agreement was reached and an accumulation of riches then swamped the screens.

The American industry had its troubles too. Antitrust legislation destroyed vertical integration, whereby the main companies could control the three arms of the industry—production, distribution, and exhibition. Warner Bros. was forced to relinquish its own theaters in the United States. Fortunately it did not extend abroad. In London the Art Deco Warner Theatre on Leicester Square, which had opened in 1938 with *The Adventures of Robin Hood,* remained to showcase the studio's films.

The next crisis was even more far-reaching. Television grew rapidly in the late 1940s, and by the 1950s audiences were declining, theaters closing, and retrenchment was taking place in production. A flurry of technological innovations, new screen shapes, and film formats, 3-D and enhanced definition were intended to fight back at the new medium by offering something that television was then incapable of emulating. Most quickly died out, with the exception of widescreen projection, CinemaScope, later Panavision, and new color processes that superseded the bulky and expensive three-strip Technicolor. It seemed that the only real way to beat television was to join and make the most of it. Warner Bros. Television was started in 1955, going on to originate scores of successful series such as *Maverick, 77 Sunset Strip, The Dukes of Hazzard, ER,* and *The West Wing* under its aegis. To tell the story of Warner television would require another volume, and here we are concerned only with the big-screen impact of a great Hollywood studio.

Today Warner Bros. Pictures is just one division of the world's largest media conglomerate, Time Warner, with magazine and book publishing, broadcasting networks, cable systems, home entertainment, digital services, online video, and the gigantic web portal of AOL among its many interests.

More than a century after the Warner brothers opened their nickelodeon, the first age of film is now drawing to a close. It will not be long before the very word will be an anachronistic misnomer when the presentation of visual entertainment becomes fully digital, and the physical transportation of cans of film from theater to theater goes the way of horse-drawn traffic and corner soda fountains. The future will bring changes that even now seem farfetched. Perhaps, for instance, the abolition of the screen altogether, with fully realized hologram images projected into a void, so that actors who are not actually there will appear to be moving around a stage as if they were. The use of CGI and other digital techniques will expand and develop, making movies ever more visually dynamic and spectacular. Yet we shall never lose the means to appreciate the wonderful talents of Cagney, Bogart, Davis, de Havilland, Crawford, Flynn, and the others in their black-and-white glory, watching them on our big-screen, high-definition TVs via Blu-Ray disks. Warner Home Entertainment will continue to draw on the magnificent accretion of films made in the last eighty-five years, many of them historical cinematic treasures and among the best ever made.

GEORGE PERRY

"YOU AIN'T HEARD NOTHIN' YET"

Al Jolson

ABOVE The four Warner brothers, c. 1920s, from left Sam
Warner, Harry Warner, Jack L. Warner, and Albert Warner.
PREVIOUS PAGE Placard carriers hired to promote the
serialization of *The Jazz Singer* story.

THE WARNER BROS. STORY

WARNER BROS. IS, OF COURSE, ONE OF THE GREAT HOLLYWOOD STUDIOS. IT HAS BEEN SINCE IT PIONEERED SOUND FILM PRODUCTION WITH *THE JAZZ SINGER* IN 1927—AND IT REMAINS AS POWERFUL AND PROFITABLE A PLAYER IN THE "NEW MEDIA" ERA AS IT WAS IN THE DAYS WHEN THE ONLY MEDIA IT HAD TO CONCERN ITSELF WITH WAS THE MOVIES. BUT FOR SOMETHING LIKE TWENTY YEARS, FROM THE EARLY 1930s UNTIL THE EARLY 1950s, WARNER BROS. WAS SOMETHING ELSE: A PRODUCTION ENTITY WITH THE MOVIES' MOST SHARPLY ETCHED PROFILE, THE PRODUCER OF TOUGH, VIOLENT, WISECRACKING, AND ABOVE ALL SOCIALLY CONSCIENTIOUS MOVIES THAT WERE UNLIKE THOSE OF ANY OF ITS COMPETITORS.

Many studios had identifiable house styles in those days. MGM movies, for example, had a kind of white telephone luxe (not to mention a raft of very handsome stars) and Paramount Pictures projected a kind of continental suavity in its offerings, but the characteristic Warner Bros. film, to quote a line thrown at James Cagney in *Jimmy the Gent,* "went down deeper, stayed down longer, and came up dirtier," than anyone else's. Its stars looked like mugs and floozies, its settings were grimy and the situations confronting its principals grim. Even its Busby Berkeley musicals generally featured chorus kids who, should their show fold, which they were often on the brink of doing, would be faced with the possibility of "doing things I wouldn't want on my conscience," as Aline MacMahon says in *Gold Diggers of 1933.* Berkeley himself clung to the belief that he was providing innocent Depression-era escapism with his giddily geometric musical numbers, but this was a guy capable of creating a dream sequence in which a "Broadway Baby" is killed when she's pushed off a terrace by a mob of heedless hedonists, and of staging "Remember My Forgotten Man," in which World War I soldiers move from the bread line into a lugubrious circular dream march offering no exit from their misery.

"The people who saw those pictures," Martin Scorsese recently reflected, "wanted to be entertained. They wanted to come in and forget their troubles. But at the same time … they wanted to see their troubles portrayed honestly. And they [Warner Bros.] were doing that." This was the niche no one else in Hollywood was filling. And though in the later thirties and in the forties the studio's style of fulfilling this need changed—the pictures became darker, more elegant, more romantic—the attempt to remain engaged in the issues of the day stayed constant—though beginning in the mid-thirties its concern shifted somewhat away from working-class life and problems, toward the rise of European fascism and toward American preparedness for a war Warners alone in Hollywood seemed certain was inevitable.

There is a mystery in all this. There was nothing in the history of the four Warner brothers that suggests a particular affinity for socio-historical sobriety. They were the sons of Polish Jews and Harry, the eldest of them, was born in Poland and was brought to the United States at an early age. The others—Albert (always called Abe), Sam, and Jack—were born in North America where the family moved about restlessly; from Baltimore to Canada (where Jack was born), then to Youngstown, a grim steel-making center in eastern Ohio, as the father Benjamin sought, without particular success, some share of the American Dream. At various times the family had butcher, bicycle, grocery, ice-cream and shoe-repair shops. Abe enjoyed a modest success selling soap, while Harry repaired shoes. Jack fancied himself a singer and had a little act with one of his sisters serving as his accompanist. None of the brothers had more than a grade-school education and though all of them had seen and liked movies, it was Sam, a bright and exuberant kid, the only one among them who was a reader, who was enchanted with them—especially their technology.

At one point Sam worked for Hale's Tours, an amusing, briefly profitable entertainment, which consisted of a rocking railroad car through the windows of which "passengers" could glimpse the projected images of various scenic wonders. His dad hocked his watch and the family horse to help buy him a used projector and soon enough the brothers had their first theater, the Cascade, in nearby New Castle, Pennsylvania, its chairs rented from an undertaker. Jack singing songs between their short pictures (and when the film broke), Sam cranking the projector. Thereafter they were in distribution with their Duquesne Amusement Supply Co., had a success touring a hand-tinted version of *Dante's Inferno* (Jack supplied primitive sound effects for it), and then in 1918, they produced *My Four Years in Germany*, based on James Gerard's account of his ambassadorial services in Berlin prior to America's entrance into World War I.

The picture was a hit—mostly showing the Huns being hateful as the ambassador looks on appalled. But the brothers did not build anything astonishing on its success. They just scrambled along like dozens of other marginal movie entrepreneurs, Harry and Abe in New York, Sam in Los Angeles, Jack in San Francisco. They were still scrambling when they formally incorporated Warner Bros. Pictures, Inc. in April 1923 and endured the hard times typical of all under-financed entrepreneurs: an early director was obliged to take a camera home with him to avoid it being repossessed; other employees remembered collecting paychecks on Friday but being told by Jack not to cash them until the following Monday. Jack's habit of prowling the lot, making sure the lights were turned off when employees left for the day, was born in these days—born, he said later, of necessity. The electric company had once turned off the studio's power for non-payment of its bill.

Yet despite these difficulties, in 1919 Warner Bros. moved out of its cramped Culver City headquarters into a fairly impressive new studio on Sunset Boulevard (the lot still stands, converted to a local television station's uses). In those early years, Warner Bros. made every kind of movie—comedies, costume dramas, romances of one sort and another—but nothing that prefigured the urban toughness of its films in the early sound years. Indeed, it must be said that many of its silent films bespoke ambition of another kind. To be sure, its first authentic star was a canine one, the immortal Rin Tin Tin, whose personality in a sense predicted those of the typical human stars of Warners' glory years—humble birth (in the German trenches where he was found after hostilities ended by his owner-trainer, Lee Duncan) and hard-working ways. Rin Tin Tin was naturally handsome, intelligent, and as Jeanine Basinger remarks, "like Joan Crawford among so many others, he seemed to know by instinct that stardom was a viable way out of bone-crushing poverty." Around the studio he was referred to as "the mortgage lifter." He was well rewarded for his efforts: his salary reached $6,000 a week, he was insured for $100,000, and according to Basinger, he had a valet, chef, limo and driver, ate only the best T-bone steaks, had eighteen stunt doubles, and an on-set orchestra playing music to get him in the mood for his thespian efforts. He also had a writer, the young Darryl F. Zanuck, whose gut instinct for popular filmmaking was unsurpassed and who, when he was made Associate Head of Production, would become instrumental in Warner Bros.' rise to major status in the industry.

People like to make comic capital out of the fledgling studio's reliance on a four-legged star for its initial success and, admittedly, he was not exactly Garbo—or even John Gilbert. But they reckon without seeing his movies, which were well-made and stirring little adventures. They also forget that as of 1924, Warner Bros. had a human star whose reputation exceeded that of any other movie player. That, of course, was John Barrymore, forty-two years old when he came to the studio just a year after its incorporation and two years after his legendary Hamlet on Broadway. He was still slender, reasonably athletic, and handsome in an old-fashioned matinee idol way. And he did not come cheap. His waywardness, cynicism, and alcoholism made him the anti-Rinty, but his prestige perhaps sent a signal to Hollywood—these guys were here to stay. And never mind that Barrymore's second Warner film, *The Sea Beast* (1926) imposed a happy ending on *Moby Dick*. Similarly, in this period Warner Bros. also had its first great director, Ernst Lubitsch, under contract, somehow managing to make sophisticated comedies like *Lady Windermere's Fan* (1925) and *The Marriage Circle* (1924) despite the inability of the silent screen to convey the kind of sly and rueful dialogue on which his great sound movies relied.

ABOVE Rin Tin Tin with trainer Lee Duncan on location in Monterey.
On the right is Major William Kneass, who signed the passport for
Rinty and his sister when they were brought from France in 1918.

John Barrymore

On the surface, perhaps, the studio remained a marginal enterprise for most of the 1920s. But, more or less quietly, it was laying the groundwork for its emergence. This was an era of consolidation in Hollywood. Through mergers and acquisitions the many producing entities were becoming fewer and fewer. By the end of the decade movies would be an oligopoly and Warner Bros. would be one of Hollywood's remaining seven major producer-distributor-exhibitors thanks to a friendship the brothers struck up with Motley Flint, a venture capitalist. Flint in turn introduced them to a still more prosperous financier named Waddill Catchings, who had access to the capital markets and, equally important, believed that in America it was only the fearless businessman who would succeed. In effect, he urged them to borrow their way to prosperity, which they did. In 1925 they acquired the Vitagraph operation, an industry pioneer that had fallen on hard times. This gave them, among other boons, an east coast studio and a group of thirty-four film exchanges. In 1928 they spent $100 million to acquire the Stanley Corporation of America chain of theaters, which greatly enhanced their clout as exhibitors. That company, in turn, was a major stock holder in First National Pictures, founded less than a decade earlier by a congeries of exhibitors who intended to distribute film it acquired from major stars and directors, bypassing the major studios in the process. Among other assets, Warner Bros. acquired the new studio that First National had built in Burbank, which, of course, remains Warners' headquarters to this day. Many Warner pictures were identified onscreen as "Warner Bros.-First National" productions until the 1950s.

But, of course, it was the sound film that made Warner Bros. a significant Hollywood presence. It was Nathan Levinson, who had worked with the government on radio matters during the war and was now advising the brothers about KFWB, the Los Angeles radio station they had started, who showed Sam the short sound film of a jazz band playing that stirred his spirit of technological adventure. He tricked Harry into attending a screening of the little picture, which excited him as well. But only within limits.

There had been previous experiments with "talking pictures," which had come to nothing because, Harry thought, they had been presented without showmanship. He also seems to have understood that most people within and without the industry were quite content with silent films. As several cinematic theorists would argue, all art is based on limits; paintings couldn't move, music couldn't create imagery, and so on. The conventions on which art depended were based on these limits, and the inability of the movies to speak was not generally perceived as a defect. An extremely sophisticated cinematic language, a unique method of communicating thought and emotion, had developed in the late teens and early twenties, which satisfied the needs of the intellectual community while in no way dismaying the popular audience. The frugal Harry also saw that sound production would exponentially raise the cost of producing and exhibiting movies (it would, for example, cost around $20,000 to wire a theater for sound). The one advantage of a soundtrack, Harry thought, might be in eliminating live musical accompaniment for films, which meant that he and the other exhibitors could dispense with live music in their theaters, saving a considerable amount in salaries. So he approved Sam's supervision of a series of sound short subjects.

Curiously, Sam did not particularly favor dialogue in the movies either. The one-reelers he produced consisted mainly of singers, both popular and operatic, warbling songs for the microphone-camera combination, though he did record a number of vaudeville acts (George Burns and Gracie Allen among them) doing comic dialogues. Their very limited audiences liked these films well enough, but their response did not constitute a groundswell of enthusiasm. Still, Warner Bros. decided in 1926 to add music and effects to *Don Juan,* starring John Barrymore and Mary Astor. It was quite a grand historical epic, had a full score, and most exciting to Sam, sound effects (he especially enjoyed the clink and clash of swords in the dueling sequences) but still no dialogue.

Don Juan, which could be shown quite effectively as a silent film, did well enough to encourage more sound features, and so the Warners acquired the rights to a hit Broadway show, Samson Raphaelson's *The Jazz Singer.*

OPPOSITE Matinee idol and "Great Profile," John Barrymore, fresh
from Broadway, where he had triumphed as Hamlet, c. 1925.

Again, no dialogue was planned, but its musical sequences would be recorded by Warner's Vitaphone system (huge phonograph discs that were synchronized with the picture). The story, about a cantor's son raised to succeed his father in the synagogue but drawn to the flash and glamour of popular music, would be carried by the intertitles.

The studio imagined that it would sign George Jessel to repeat the role he had originated in New York, but got into a contract squabble with him. It has been said that his friend and sometime vaudeville partner, Eddie Cantor, advised him that if the studio expected him to be heard on the screen he should ask for more

money, an idea rejected by Jack Warner in particular. Oddly enough, they ended up paying Al Jolson even more money to play Jackie Rabinowitz/Jack Robin. He was deemed worth his $75,000 fee, for he was the most famous Broadway performer of the moment, a man whose name was far more recognizable in the hinterlands than Jessel's was.

And so history was made. Jolson was an energetic attention seeker, and it was said that he simply could not prevent himself from speaking a few improvised and enthusiastic words during his performance of "Blue Skies" on screen. In the end, he and his fellow players spoke only about 850 words in the course of the movie. But, taken together with its songs, they were enough to energize the film. Somehow the rhythms of speech shook the movie out of its sentimental lethargy. As the critic Gary Giddens has observed, when Jolson launched into one of his upbeat numbers he was capable of shaking and shimmying in an electrifying manner that predicts Elvis Presley. And of blowing away—at least temporarily—any resistance to his sometimes annoying personality as he shamelessly begged the audience for its love. (The fact that he did some numbers in blackface went completely unremarked. So deep-rooted and persistent was that noxious showbiz tradition that many stars were still blacking up, including Doris Day in Warner Bros.' *I'll See You in My Dreams* as late as 1951.)

The Jazz Singer was a sensation when it was released in 1927, especially within the industry, where everyone immediately started to debate whether sound movies would prove to be a passing fancy or the wave of the future. To some degree this debate was fueled by the aesthetic issues we have already alluded to. Now that people could actually hear a movie talk, the rather banal dialogue of this one seemed to fulfill the worst fears of the nay-sayers. Looking back on it, and on the "talkies" that followed it, we can see what people at the time did not fully perceive—that the sound film utterly changed the nature of movies. They ceased to be a poetic medium and became a realistic one. Perfectly beautiful stars would, to some degree, give way to much more ordinary-looking actors, often enough appearing in settings that were much more intensely realistic than had previously been the case. The flowery rhetoric of the intertitles would be replaced by the vulgarisms of ordinary speech. Somehow, sound made bad movies seem much worse than they had when you could not hear people speaking. And that says nothing about how the camera being trapped in a soundproof booth (so its whirrings would not be recorded) briefly immobilized the movies' imagistic possibilities. It is not enough to say that sound "revolutionized" movies. It is more nearly correct to say that sound films are an entirely different medium than silent movies—one that works on its audience in a new way. New genres arose out of sound and old ones fell into disuse. Star styles and manner changed almost completely too, as did the way in which the studios functioned, adding layers of "supervisors" (latterly producers) to their executive ranks, their duties being mainly to fuss over scripts, which now had much more importance than they had in silent days.

ABOVE John Barrymore as Don Juan de Marana in disguise, and Mary Astor as Adriana Della Varnese in *Don Juan*, 1926. OPPOSITE One-sheet poster for *The Jazz Singer*, 1927. OVERLEAF Al Jolson during the production of *The Jazz Singer*—note the soundproof booth for suppressing camera noise on the left.

THE WARNER BROS. STORY

If you looked closely, you could see that much of what Warner Bros. was soon to become was predicted in *The Jazz Singer*. To begin with it was urban, contemporary, and lower class in its setting, which differentiated it from the movies more typical of the silent era, which were often set in small American towns or in a fancifully realized Europe and frequently told stories about the rich and the well-born, often enough functioning in historical settings. More important, perhaps, was the issue it explored. Jackie Rabinowitz aspired to secular stardom, as a singer of popular songs, on Broadway, on records, doubtless eventually in the movies. Put simply he wanted to be—yes, a jazz singer. His father, of course, wanted him to cling to sacred tradition, to a life of piety and poverty in the synagogue.

This was by no means an abstract issue. It was a problem faced by millions of children who were the sons of immigrants. It was, indeed, a problem that the Warner brothers themselves faced, though at the time it was less melodramatically stated in their family. As Neal Gabler, the historian of the Jews who founded Hollywood, puts it, Harry Warner, born in Poland, was a moral and moralizing man. He kept Kosher. He was a faithful husband and a good father. He believed that the movies should be something more than mere entertainment, that they should if possible serve some higher purpose. His youngest brother, Jack, was the opposite, a dapper, wisecracking gambler and womanizer, completely secular in outlook. He wanted everything that materialist, modernizing America could offer and was not particularly punctilious about how he achieved it.

As far as we can tell the two brothers disliked one another from their earliest days, and eventually Jack would find a way to betray Harry, strip him of his power within the studio, though that shattering incident was far in the future. For the moment they resolved their difficulties in private. And *The Jazz Singer* symbolically resolved their contentiousness. In the film Jackie fills in for his dying father, singing the Kol Nidre in temple on Yom Kippur, the highest of the Jewish holy days, but—and here the movie diverts from the play on which it was based—he also achieves Broadway stardom, with his mother beaming in the audience. We are left with the distinct impression that there are going to be very few kol nidres in his future.

Still, it achieved what would become known as a "Hollywood ending"—improbable happiness all around. Except for the moment it was one touched by tragedy. Sam Warner came down with a mysterious illness while he was putting the finishing touches to *The Jazz Singer*. His doctors were puzzled and forbade him from attending the world premiere of the film in New York, for which Jack set out alone. Midway in Jack's train journey Sam was hospitalized and the New York brothers, Harry and Abe, rushed westward by train, attempts to charter an airplane having failed. Jack also got off his train and headed back. En route they learned that Sam had suffered a stroke and was not expected to live. And he did not. He died twenty-four hours before the sensational premiere of the film, on October 6, 1927, at the Warners' Theater on Broadway, which none of his brothers attended.

There were, at the time, only about seventy American theaters wired for sound. *The Jazz Singer* had, perforce, a very slow rollout. But it achieved profitability in its initial release and the exhibitors rushed to prepare their theaters for sound films, even as Warner Bros. rushed to prepare a sequel, again starring Al Jolson, even as they and the other studios struggled to add sound sequences to the silent films in their pipelines. By the time the new Jolson picture was ready something like two thousand theaters were prepared to show it.

It was called *The Singing Fool* (1928) and is regarded by some as one of the worst major studio films ever made. It tells the story of a singing waiter achieving stardom (and temporary domestic misery in the course of his rise). His saving grace is his love for his child, and therein lies a tale. Jolson wanted a song to express his tender feelings for the lad and called up the acclaimed Tin Pan Alley songwriting team of Buddy DeSylva, Lew Brown, and Ray Henderson to request one. He needed it, he said, in a matter of hours. They were no fonder of "Jolie" than anyone else and they tossed off, in a matter of hours, a piece they thought summarized Jolson's most noxious quality, his sentimentality. But the star knew his audience. "Sonny Boy" became his greatest hit.

And *The Singing Fool* became his—and Warner Bros.—most successful movie to date, grossing more than five and a half million dollars, and remaining the biggest grosser in Hollywood history until *Gone With the Wind,* over a decade later. No one would ever again dismiss Warner Bros. as a fringe player, though fairly quickly its cumbersome Vitaphone system would fade from view. The industry standard would become the Movietone system, promoted by Fox, which placed a soundtrack directly on the film. Its quality was not, at first, as good as Vitaphone's, but it was easier, more flexible to use, especially for location shooting.

Curiously enough, for all its pioneering, Warner Bros. sound films were not necessarily better or more widely popular than those of its competitors. It had not yet found the genres and the stars that would, in a matter of just two or three years, typify its glory years. It was a movie that is remembered not for its content but rather for its technology that predicted the path Warner Bros. would soon be following. That was 1928's *Lights of New York.* Originally intended as a two-reel talking film about a chorus girl getting mixed up with mobsters, it was produced and directed by Bryan Foy, who was in charge of the sound short subjects. But it looked rather promising in this truncated form and Foy proposed expanding it to feature length and releasing it as the first "100 percent" talking picture. Darryl Zanuck, newly appointed Associate Executive in Charge of Production, was authorized to spend up to $75,000 on his own recognizance if Jack Warner was away from the office, so he spent the money on the expansion. Though the picture was deemed "100 percent crude" by *Variety,* it was a great commercial success, despite its lack of major stars and its pokey staging (especially in dialogue scenes where everyone spoke verrry slooowly, no overlapping permitted). Yet it had a couple of shadowy scenes that were almost *noir*ish in their lighting and, more important, it was full of big-city lowlifes, talking tough and acting rough. It was not the first movie ever about the underworld, but its success at the box office suggested that this was territory worth exploring.

As of 1929, the studio was prospering—it turned a profit in excess of $14 million that year, the last before the Depression settled in earnest upon America and the world. It would do about half as well the next year, then not attain a profit again until 1935. Yet it was beginning to make its unique mark in those years.

How exactly it did so is difficult to determine. Jack and Harry Warner were surely tough, no-nonsense guys and cheapskates to boot. Their studio was unquestionably the most parsimonious of the majors. They had begun their lives as small-town boys, aspiring to big-city glamour and wealth, but they were not in any sense attuned to the rhythms of urban life. The same might be said of the emergent Zanuck, a WASP from Wahoo, Nebraska, whose ambitions obviously exceeded his entry level screenwriting job. But there is nothing in his resume that suggests a predilection for big-city dramas, either. The main thing you must say about him was that he would prove to be a man of enormous social alertness and preternatural energy. But in 1929, his day was yet to come.

You could see this in *Noah's Ark* (1928), an epic production—possibly the most expensive the studio had yet undertaken. It was based on a story Zanuck had concocted, a World War I tale about romance and regeneration at the Front and the parallel Biblical story referred to in the title. The blend was uneasy, to say the least. But the climactic flood sequence, directed by the great Michael Curtiz, early in his long Warner Bros. career, was by the standards of the day (and even by modern standards), spectacular—literally thousands of extras (some say as many as two thousand of them) washed away by torrents of water. It was not a typical Warner (or Zanuck) film.

Indeed, if you look over the list of Warner Bros. pictures in the years just before and just after the decade turned, you cannot succinctly characterize them. They were still making every kind of movie, few of which featured stars whose names echo down the corridors of time. The one exception to that rule was a typical Warner oddity, George Arliss, who was sixty-one years old when he came to the studio to make *Disraeli* in 1929. He was a slender, unhandsome man, with a fairly florid acting style. He had been trouping the theatrical version of this property for years and had made it as a silent film in 1921. He played the great Prime Minister as a sly,

ABOVE The epic production of *Noah's Ark*—possibly the most expensive the studio had undertaken, 1929. OPPOSITE Doris Kenyon and George Arliss in *Alexander Hamilton*, 1931.

wise, humorous busybody, fixing up troubled romances among the juveniles even as he attended to the defense of the British Empire.

His pictures, even by the primitive standards of the early talkies, are awkward and stage-bound. But people liked him. There was a lack of pretense, a good nature about him that was appealing. And there was a certain honesty about him. His *Disraeli,* for example, openly dealt with anti-Semitism—a topic that would soon be banished from the screen—and his *Alexander Hamilton* (1931) revolves around an extramarital dalliance, openly admitted and then openly forgiven by no less than George Washington. His biopics gave way to more modern topics; typically he played rich and celebrated men who find ways of remaining useful and relevant when the world wishes to put them on the shelf. In *The Green Goddess* (1930) he even played the cruel ruler of a mythical Tibetan nation. For a few transitional

years he was as much of a mortgage-lifter as Rin Tin Tin had been. And every day at 4 p.m., work on his sets would cease for a half hour while tea was served to his casts and crews.

Very un-Warner Bros. was he. Except in these important respects: his pictures were entirely unlike those being turned out by the competition and, more important, he was a star completely unlike any other movie star—too old, too odd looking, too wedded to antique theatrical conventions. Yet audiences loved him; he was the foxy grandpa everyone either remembered fondly or wished they had known.

Perhaps more to the point he predicted, in his stagy, stodgy way, the kind of movies and stars that would come to dominate the Warner schedule in the early 1930s. To be sure, the later films would take up social issues that Arliss would not, could not, address, but they would do so in a similarly engaging matter, albeit with a rougher humor and a more bumptious manner, while retaining, in their choice and treatment of subject matter, something of his underlying seriousness. They would feature stars as unlikely as Arliss, unhandsome males like James Cagney, Edward G. Robison, and Paul Muni, curious-looking women like Bette Davis—people we cannot imagine achieving stardom at places like MGM or Paramount. If one loves what Warner Bros. did in the thirties and forties, it is because it was at once so consistently realistic, yet so determinedly eccentric, in comparison to what else was going on in Hollywood.

RICHARD SCHICKEL

EARLY DAYS

 Poland was the original homeland of the Warner brothers. Their parents Benjamin and Pearl were born in 1857 and 1858, and being Jewish suffered persecution under the Russian occupiers. They were denied a proper education, and relied on surreptitious instruction from a rabbi. Their first son, Harry, was born in 1881, followed soon afterward by a daughter, and in 1883 Benjamin left the ghetto, sailing to Baltimore on a cattle boat. A cobbler by trade, he started a shoe-repair business, and within a year had saved enough to send for his wife and children. Eventually Pearl gave birth ten more times, although in the harsh living conditions of the late nineteenth century, some of these children died in infancy. The four boys who were to become synonymous with the film industry were Harry, Albert (born 1884), Sam (born 1888), and Jack (born in London, Ontario, in 1892 during a period when Benjamin was trading furs and pelts in Canada). In 1896 the family moved to Youngstown, Ohio, where the sale of meat and groceries was added to the precarious shoe business.

As the boys grew older they took many different occupations. For a while Harry became a bicycle repairer, Albert a soap salesman, Sam a fireman on the Erie Railroad, and Jack an in-demand boy soprano. None amounted to a lifelong vocation. After an encounter with a new invention, the Edison Kinetoscope, Sam quit the trains and became a projectionist in Chicago. Excited by the possibilities of motion pictures, he went back to Youngstown and enthused the others. At nearby Niles, the Warners rented a store, bought a projector for $150, and showed films to excited audiences.

They had bought a copy of Edwin S. Porter's *The Great Train Robbery* of 1903, which—with its epic length of 12 minutes, a cast of 40, authentic-looking "western" locations in New Jersey, and a coherent narrative—was a beacon in the birth of the American fiction film.

They moved on to other towns. Soon they opened a small theater in New Castle, Pennsylvania, with ninety-nine seats, one short of the number that would have subjected it to strict fire regulations. They needed to buy more films to keep their audiences entertained, and Harry Warner devised a method for grouping theater owners so that prints could be distributed to several outlets in turn. The idea caught on and became America's first film exchange. Soon there were branches in several cities as thousands of small theaters opened up, clamoring for supply. Thomas Edison, concerned that so many were making money from what he considered to be his own invention, banded a number of production companies together to form the Motion Picture Patents Company—the notorious Trust—with the intention of collecting license revenue from each operator, and hiking rental rates. After uphill and expensive legal battles, the Warner brothers managed to sell their business to the Trust's General Film Company for $100,000. The only way they could now distribute pictures was by making them themselves. Their first efforts were undistinguished and unprofitable.

Carl Laemmle, who later became the founder and head of Universal Pictures, fought back at the Trust. He started the Independent Motion Picture Company (IMP) in 1909 and eventually won a court battle against the Trust. Encouraged by his action, the Warners decided to move to southern California, where Laemmle was based, and they were back in the exchange business. They bought films and released them under their banner, but with Europe in turmoil from war, business was slow.

It was the war that eventually gave them their break. The U.S. ambassador in Berlin, James W. Gerard, had written a bestselling book, *My Four Years in Germany* (1918), describing his efforts to divert the Kaiser from his belligerent path, and the brothers, beginning to get a feel for the film business, saw possibilities. It was bought for $50,000, heading off other bidders. Financing its production was difficult, but eventually it was made, mostly at the Biograph Studios in the Bronx, New York, under the direction of William Nigh. Graphic scenes of Prussian brutality, in accord with the anti-German sentiment that had brought America

into the war, were favorably received by the public, and the film grossed $1.5 million, leaving the Warners with a handsome profit. They were now firmly established as Hollywood film producers.

Mixing actual footage with reenactments, such as battles on the Western Front filmed on Long Island, and using distinguished Broadway actors to play contemporary leaders, *My Four Years in Germany* is an early example of docudrama, as well as a striking employment of the film medium to take an opinionated viewpoint on a serious issue. In that respect it prefigured many Warner Bros. films to come.

The box-office success enabled the brothers to stop renting a variety of studios, some of which had been of fourth-rate quality, and to settle on just one. Their Sunset Studios was created in 1919 when they bought part of the forty-acre Beesemeyer Ranch off Sunset Boulevard in Hollywood, and it was to become the Warners' West Coast production center.

OPPOSITE The Warner family celebrates the Golden Wedding Anniversary of Ben and Pearl Warner, patriarch and matriarch (seated center). ABOVE A young Albert Warner stands stands far right in front of the Bijou Theater in New Castle, PA, c. 1905.
LEFT Advertising art for *My Four Years in Germany,* 1918.

Meanwhile, Harry ran the Warner distribution office from New York. As treasurer, Albert looked after the financial side, and Sam and Jack were responsible for creative output. Postwar Hollywood was a flourishing, ruthlessly competitive environment, and the Warner brothers found the going hard, with Zukor's Paramount and Laemmle's Universal making the running. In 1920, the only Warner Bros. production was a fifteen-episode serial, *A Dangerous Adventure,* directed by Sam and Jack. It was a failure.

The company made three films in 1921, the only successful one of which was *Why Girls Leave Home,* adapted by Owen Davis from a play by Fred Summerfield, and directed by William Nigh, with Anna Q. Nilsson in the lead. She had drawing power, and demonstrated the new pressing need in Hollywood for stars—a commodity of which the Warners were desperately short.

UP AND RUNNING

At Sunset Boulevard and Bronson Avenue, on a ten-acre lot carved out of the Beesemeyer Ranch in 1919, the new Warner West Coast headquarters took shape. The distinctive façade in Greek Revival style, with its imposing colonnade of Doric columns, soon became established as a Hollywood landmark—and has remained so for nearly ninety years. Even when it became a bowling center for a period in the 1940s, Warner Bros. cartoons were still being made on the Sunset lot.

On April 4, 1923, Warner Bros. Pictures Inc. was incorporated, the formal birth date for Hollywood's distinguished and enduring production company. The new studio was big enough to shoot half a dozen films simultaneously, and among the initial production roster were some titles that would anticipate Warner Bros. product to come. For instance, *The Gold Diggers* (1923), from a Broadway success by Avery Hopwood, directed by Harry Beaumont, was about two chorus girls, played by Louise Fazenda and Hope Hampton, on the lookout for rich husbands—a plotline reused exhaustively when talkies came. Similarly, *Little Johnny Jones* (1923) had Johnny Hines playing an American jockey riding in England's premier horse race, the Epsom Derby. Based on George M. Cohan's

1904 stage musical, it lacked the songs. They came in an early talkie in 1929, but their biggest impact would come in *Yankee Doodle Dandy* in 1942. Gangster movies had already been foreshadowed by the tough urban drama *Heroes of the Street,* directed by William Beaudine and starring Wesley Barry, released at the end of 1922.

Sinclair Lewis's novel *Main Street* was directed by Harry Beaumont with Florence Vidor, Monte Blue, Louise Fazenda, and Alan Hale. F. Scott Fitzgerald's *The Beautiful and Damned,* actually filmed before Warner Bros. was incorporated, had Warner debut performances by Fazenda and Marie Prevost. They were both from the Mack Sennett comedy stable. It was released at the end of 1923.

The biggest new star, however, was not human, but a four-legged animal.

OPPOSITE TOP "On Tour with Dante's Inferno," the Warner's first picture road show, Atlantic City, 1910, Sam and Jack Warner on right. LEFT Sam and Jack Warner's Film Exchange newsletter, April 1909. ABOVE Sergeant Lee Duncan and Rin Tin Tin, the puppy he found on a French battlefield, destined for cinematic immortality.

DOG STAR

It was a dog that saved Warner Bros. from bankruptcy in the 1920s by becoming a canine superstar with a world following. The five-day-old pup was found in September 1918 in a bombed-out German kennel by Sergeant Lee Duncan, a doughboy serving in France, and was one of a litter of five. Duncan took the mother, Betty des Flandres, and her pups back to camp, earmarking a male and female for himself. They turned out to be the only ones who survived and he named them Rin Tin Tin and Nanette, after a couple of tiny French puppets that had been given to the soldiers.

1923

* *Time* magazine is launched
* Warner Bros. West Coast Studio is fully launched at Sunset and Bronson
* Warner Bros. introduces canine star Rin Tin Tin in his starring debut film *Where the North Begins;* his salary is $1,000 per week
* Calvin Coolidge succeeds Warren Harding as U.S. President after the latter dies in office
* *The Gold Diggers,* from a David Belasco produced stage hit, is the first Warner film featuring show girls looking for rich husbands—the beginning of an important subgenre
* *Little Johnny Jones,* based on the 1904 George M. Cohan musical but without its songs (it was a silent picture), anticipates *Yankee Doodle Dandy* two decades later
* Sarah Bernhardt dies
* The Hollywood sign is installed (as Hollywoodland, below)

"YOU AIN'T HEARD NOTHIN' YET"

Rin Tin Tin on set with his frequent co-star, June Marlowe, helping to promote wrist watches.

Many
years
ago
Rin Tin Tin

OPPOSITE Darryl F. Zanuck, Jack L. Warner and director Alan Crosland with Rin Tin Tin at Sunset Blvd. Studios, *c.* 1924. ABOVE Advertisement from a brochure promoting Warner Bros. films, and Lee Duncan directing Rin Tin Tin in *The Night Cry,* with Herman C. Raymaker behind the camera, 1926.

Within two months the war was over and Duncan began training the dogs. Impressed by their skills, he sought out the captured kennel master in his prison camp and learned about the breed, the German shepherd, unfamiliar to Americans. The Kaiser's army had trained these strong, agile, and intelligent animals for military duties.

Granted permission to take the young dogs back to the United States, Duncan embarked on a troopship, but during the fifteen-day voyage to New York Nanette caught distemper, and died before Duncan could reach his home in Los Angeles. He went back to work in a hardware store and exhibited Rin Tin Tin at various dog shows. A cameraman, Charles Jones, saw the dog in action, jumping a fence nearly twelve feet high, and offered Duncan $350 to put him on film. Duncan saw the possibilities and wrote a film scenario, *Where the North Begins.* In spite of hawking it around to several studios nobody was interested. Rinty's break came when a location movie crew (not Warner Bros.) was trying without success to film a sequence with a wolf. Duncan argued that Rin Tin Tin could do the scene in one take, and was finally believed when Rinty performed to perfection. He was kept on for the rest of the film, *The Man from Hell's River. Where the North Begins* (1923) Rin Tin Tin's star debut, soon followed.

The public was intrigued and impressed, and the soaring box-office takings staved off the financial disaster Warner Bros. had been facing.

Rinty became a huge star, receiving ten thousand fan letters a week. Eventually he even had his own weekly radio program. He made nineteen films for Warner Bros., most of which have been lost. With titles such as *Clash of the Wolves* (1925), *Hills of Kentucky* (1927), *A Dog of the Regiment* (1927), they were formulaic in plot. Rinty always saved the day and routed the bad guys, using intelligence and physical skills beyond the range of mere humans. Making his name by writing stories for the dog was Darryl F. Zanuck, aged twenty-two when he was hired by Warner Bros. in 1924.

His success in tapping such a handsome mother lode led to his rapid ascendancy to Associate Executive in Charge of Production to Jack L. Warner.

Lee Duncan stood by with Rin Tin Tin, caring for him to such a degree that at one time his wife sought divorce, citing the dog as co-respondent. In August 1932 the canine star died, allegedly in the arms of Jean Harlow who lived close by, and although Rinty was succeeded by his son, Rin Tin Tin II, it could never be the same. Duncan died in 1960, but the line through careful breeding still persists, and Rin Tin Tin IX only met his end in 2007. Rin Tin Tin X is his heir with a pedigree directly traceable back to Betty des Flandres. The first Rin Tin Tin is buried in the dog cemetery at Asnieres, France.

OPPOSITE The façade of the Warner Bros. Sunset Blvd. Studios, c. 1936.
ABOVE The New York premiere of *The Night Cry*, featuring Rin Tin Tin.
BELOW On the set of *Go Into Your Dance,* where Al Jolson is having makeup applied; director Archie Mayo talks on the phone, 1934.

1924

* John Barrymore's first Warner Bros. film, *Beau Brummel,* is a big hit, securing him a three-year contract and making a star of seventeen-year-old Mary Astor

* Woodrow Wilson, twenty-eighth U.S. President, dies

* Ernst Lubitsch's *The Marriage Circle* wins critical acclaim but fails at the box office

* J. Edgar Hoover is appointed to head the newly formed Federal Bureau of Investigation

* Edith Wharton's novel *The Age of Innocence* is filmed by Wesley Ruggles

* Rin Tin Tin's second Warner Bros. Film, *Find Your Man,* is written by twenty-two-year-old Darryl F. Zanuck and makes money in a lackluster year for the studio

* The Olympic Games are staged in Paris

* Marie Prevost stars in *Being Respectable, Three Women,* and *Cornered*

THE GREAT PROFILE

Before World War I, the silent screen had lured John Barrymore, the most renowned American stage actor of his time whose defining portrayal of Hamlet was a Broadway and West End legend, and in 1924 he made his auspicious debut at Warner Bros. in the title role of *Beau Brummel* opposite Mary Astor. She was then only seventeen, yet already a veteran of a dozen films; she became a star.

A member of America's greatest theatrical dynasty (his father was Maurice Barrymore, his mother Georgiana Drew, and his brother Lionel and sister Ethel were formidable stars of stage and screen), Barrymore had a charismatic appeal and a lively wit. He was quickly given a three-year contract by Warner Bros. Barrymore's luster was dimmed by his alcoholism, a self-destructive affliction that tragically rendered him almost unemployable, and his screen performances were viewed by some as erratic and ill-judged. He died in 1942 at the age of sixty, mourned not so much for what he was but what he might have been.

THE LUBITSCH TOUCH

Ernst Lubitsch arrived in Hollywood with a reputation for the films he had made in Europe. After directing his first American film, *Rosita,* for Mary Pickford at United Artists, he was engaged by Jack Warner to direct *The Marriage Circle* (1924), a marital comedy set in prewar Vienna, with Florence Vidor, Monte Blue, Marie Prevost, Creighton Hale, and Adolphe Menjou. The critics applauded, but the public hesitated. Lubitsch followed up with *Three Women* (1924), with Lew Cody, May McAvoy, Pauline Frederick, and Marie Prevost, again delighting reviewers but failing to ignite the box-office. In 1925 *Kiss Me Again,* with Prevost and Blue, satisfied them both, but is sadly a lost film. For *Lady Windermere's Fan* (1925) with Ronald Colman, May McAvoy, Bert Lytell, and Irene Rich, Lubitsch pulled off the extraordinary feat of capturing the humorous essence of an Oscar Wilde comedy without a word of dialogue. After the boisterous antics of *So This is Paris* (1926)—a sparkling summation of the Jazz Age—Lubitsch left Warner, but already "the Lubitsch touch" was formed and would transfer smoothly to the looming sound era.

ABOVE Carmel Myers embracing John Barrymore as *Beau Brummel,* 1924.

BREAKING THE SILENCE

Experimenting with sound went back to the earliest days of cinema in the 1890s, when Edison tried to synchronize his Kinetoscope to phonograph recordings. Many other hopeful pioneers tried but three problems defeated them. They had to ensure that the sound exactly matched the image on the screen. It needed to be powerful enough to be heard by a theater audience, and it needed to have good quality. Before electrical recording came in during the 1920s, amplification and fidelity could not be achieved. After years of struggle and legal battles over patents, the inventor Lee De Forest demonstrated his sound-on-film system in 1923. Eventually he secured the interest of Fox and it became the basis of their Movietone system.

Meanwhile, having acquired the Vitagraph Studios in New York and formed an association with Western Electric, Warner began to make shorts using a sound-on-disc system, Vitaphone. The sound quality was far superior to Fox's sound-on-film, which initially proved suitable for newsreels and not much else. Performers from the New York stage would go to Vitagraph and perform their acts before camera and microphone, and those shorts that survive are an extraordinary record of American vaudeville and musical theater in the 1920s.

Silent films were not actually played in silence. The humblest neighborhood theaters had live piano accompaniments, while the huge movie palaces that had sprung up in downtown areas of major cities would often feature a full orchestra. Sam Warner saw possibilities. Theaters unable to afford hiring an orchestra would be able to play films with a full orchestral accompaniment via Vitaphone. His brothers did not share his enthusiasm. Sam managed to place the score of an entire full-length feature on a disc for each reel, with occasional sound effects, and in August 1926, *Don Juan,* starring John Barrymore and directed by Alan Crosland (and at that time the most expensive film made by Warner Bros.) was premiered at the Warners' Theatre in New York. There was no dialogue. In the accompanying program was a spoken introduction by Will H. Hays, president of the Motion Picture Association of America (MPAA) and a selection of shorts featuring mostly classical pieces performed by the New York Philharmonic, stars of the Metropolitan Opera, and others.

The innovation was welcomed by the public, but had strained the fragile finances of Warner Bros., which was finding the going in the mid-1920s extremely tough. Persuading other exhibitors to install expensive equipment proved very difficult.

1925

✳ Lubitsch's *Kiss Me Again,* starring Monte Blue and Marie Prevost, is hailed as a masterpiece of romantic love

✳ Calvin Coolidge's presidential inauguration is the first to be broadcast

✳ Benito Mussolini assumes dictatorship of Italy

✳ Vitagraph Studios in Brooklyn, N.Y., are acquired by Warner Bros.

✳ Rin Tin Tin dons a disguise (a false beard) to foil the villain in *Clash of the Wolves*

✳ *Lady Windermere's Fan,* directed by Ernst Lubitsch, captures Wildean irony in spite of having no spoken dialogue

✳ *The New Yorker* is founded

✳ F. Scott Fitzgerald's *The Great Gatsby* is published

✳ Warner Bros. releases thirty features

ABOVE Ernst Lubitsch directs *Three Women,* 1923. This was Lubitsch's second Warner Bros. film.

45

Even Jack Warner was unconvinced that there was any future for the sound film, and the fact that there were competing systems heightened the uncertainty, with the major studios making an agreement not to plunge into sound until a consensual decision had been made on which one was to triumph. The Vitaphone shorts kept going in spite of doubts. Meanwhile, Fox was getting attention with sound newsreels, and a particular scoop was coverage of Charles Lindbergh's departure from New Jersey on the first solo transatlantic flight.

LEFT Vitaphone title card, 1933. BELOW Sid Grauman and Jack L. Warner standing in front of the truck containing the first Vitaphone sound equipment, to be installed in Grauman's Egyptian Theater in Hollywood, 1926.

HEARING IS BELIEVING

On October 6, 1927, *The Jazz Singer* opened at the Warners' Theater, New York. The day before, Sam Warner, who had championed its production as no other, suffered a cerebral hemorrhage and died in Los Angeles. His brothers were en route to California by train instead of attending the premiere. Although hailed as the first "talkie," *The Jazz Singer,* directed by Alan Crosland, was actually a silent picture laden with intertitles, the novelty being that the songs and orchestral accompaniments boomed out from the loudspeakers behind the screen. There are a few spoken words of dialogue, but they were ad-libbed by Al Jolson in musical numbers, and unintended. In particular his conversation with Eugenie Besserer, playing his mother, and her responses as he plays "Blue Skies" to her, was an inspirational touch.

The previous year, Jolson had appeared in a Vitaphone short, *The Plantation Act,* in which, in full blackface and cotton-picking costume, he performed three of his most famous numbers and even uttered his catchphrase "You ain't heard nothin' yet." But in *The Jazz Singer,* his gigantic presence sold what was essentially a creaky, sentimental story about a cantor's son torn between following his orthodox father into the synagogue or achieving musical stardom on Broadway. On the night of his debut on the Great White Way his estranged father lies dying, his last wish that his son should sing "Kol Nidre" for the congregation.

The crowds flocked to this entertainment, anxious to hear as well as see. The film had cost $422,000 to make—a huge budget for the 1920s—but made a profit six times over.

1926

✴ Warner Bros. premieres the first feature-length synchronized sound film, *Don Juan,* starring John Barrymore, at the Warners' Theater, New York (above, with Mary Astor)

✴ The magician and escapologist Harry Houdini dies

✴ Fox Film signs up with Movietone and its patented sound-on-film system

✴ Warner creates Vitaphone with Western Electric to develop sound-on-disc

✴ Al Jolson makes his screen debut in a Vitaphone short, *The Plantation Act*

✴ Gertrude Ederle, an American, is the first woman to swim the English Channel

✴ Harry and Jack Warner import the Hungarian director Michael Curtiz from Germany to direct *The Third Degree,* the first of over ninety Warner Bros. films

✴ John Barrymore appears as Captain Ahab in *The Sea Beast,* from Herman Melville's *Moby Dick*

✴ *The Better 'Ole,* with Sydney Chaplin (Charlie's brother), is the second Vitaphone feature with a synchronized score

ABOVE Chorus girls pose in a Vitaphone short.

Hollywood looked on aghast. The dreaded moment had come when the silent movie era was over. Initially sound had been seen as an ancillary novelty, a way of spicing up films with musical interludes. Many of the industry's leaders (including Harry Warner), as well as influential filmmakers, saw no future in spoken drama, although Jack Warner idolized Sam and would have concurred with him about sound's full potential. In a sense they were right. By the mid-1920s the silent cinema had developed a visual sophistication and fluidity that was about to be lost. Early recording techniques anchored previously mobile cameras, which had to be stationed inside stuffy, soundproofed booths so that the noise of whirring mechanisms would not be picked up by the microphones. Performers' range of movement was limited by the microphone range. Eventually soundproof "blimps" would liberate the camera, and microphone booms would allow actors to move more freely.

In the early sound era, sound-on-disc had the edge over sound-on-film aurally. The equipment, while expensive, was marginally cheaper. The projector was equipped with a turntable on which special sixteen-inch phonograph records, rotating at 33⅓ r.p.m., would be played in synchronization with the screen image. The projectionist would align the needle against an arrow (the grooves running from the inside, in reverse of

ABOVE Cast and crew on location for *Children of Dreams*, 1931. RIGHT Margaret Shilling as Molly Standing and Marion Byron as Gertie from *Children of Dreams*, astride the Vitaphone motorcycle and sidecar. OPPOSITE The premiere for *The Jazz Singer*, New York, 1927.

1927

✳ Warner Bros. output reaches forty-three features, the studio's highest yet

✳ The first transatlantic telephone call is made from New York to London

✳ The third Vitaphone feature with a synchronized music score is *When a Man Loves*, John Barrymore's only screen appearance this year for Warner

✳ The comedian George Jessel appears in *Ginsberg the Great* and *Sailor Izzy Murphy*, but loses the opportunity to star in *The Jazz Singer*, his Broadway hit, by demanding too much money

✳ Charles Lindbergh flies solo across the Atlantic

✳ The Academy of Motion Pictures Arts and Sciences is founded

✳ The top Warner stars are Monte Blue, May McAvoy, Irene Rich, Ben Lyon, Dolores Costello, and Rin Tin Tin

✳ Jerome Kern and Oscar Hammerstein II's watershed musical *Show Boat* opens on Broadway

✳ Al Jolson plays the lead in *The Jazz Singer*, singing six songs and speaking 281 words of ad-libbed dialogue, effectively ending the silent era of movies

✳ Sam Warner, driving force of sound films, dies on the eve of the premiere

normal phonograph records) and would start the reel against a cue mark. Should the needle jump synchronization would be lost, and it was necessary for the operator to keep a lookout. Today when film breaks occur projectionists remove damaged frames and splice the broken bits together, resulting in a slight jump in the screen image. But with Vitaphone the projectionist would have to insert a strip of blank film to match the missing portion, otherwise the rest of the reel would be out of sync. Discs could not be edited, which presented serious problems during the making of sound films. Before multi-tracking it was

often necessary to have musicians on stage but off-camera, playing their accompaniment live while actors performed. The rival sound-on-film method produced a poorer sound definition. In 1928 the inferior variable density soundtrack was replaced by the much-improved variable area system, RCA Photophone, which eventually became the industry standard. Warner Bros. abandoned sound-on-disc in 1930, although for a long period, in order to placate exhibitors who could not afford to reinstall sound equipment immediately, their films were released in both formats.

"YOU AIN'T HEARD NOTHIN' YET"

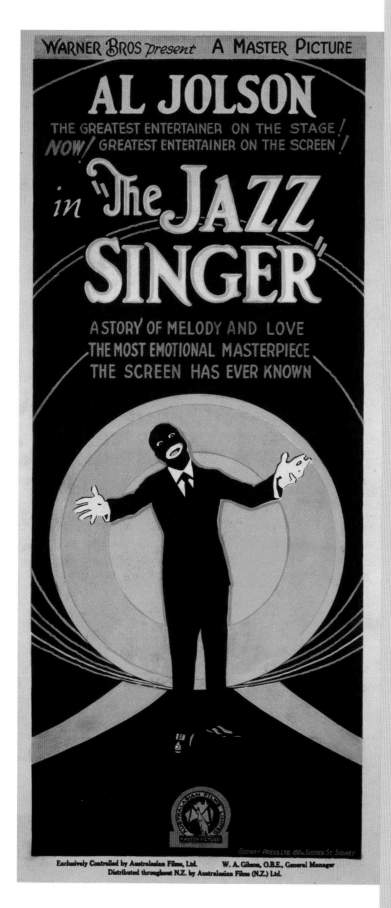

1928

* Warner Bros. releases *Lights of New York*, billed as the first one hundred percent "all-talking picture" with dialogue throughout

* In the U.S. over eight hundred theaters are equipped with the Vitaphone sound-on-disc system

* Warner Bros. takes over Stanley Corporation of America and 275 theaters, and also gains control of First National Pictures

* Jack Warner, as head of production with Darryl F. Zanuck as his number two, moves into First National's Burbank studios, wiring them for sound

* Al Jolson's follow-up to the success of *The Jazz Singer* is *The Singing Fool*, and is an even bigger hit, with the song "Sonny Boy" selling a record-breaking three million copies of sheet music

* Mickey Mouse appears for the first time in the silent animated short *Plane Crazy*, then is voiced by Walt Disney himself for his sound debut, *Steamboat Willie*

* Other studios, initially reluctant, are forced into producing sound films, and many nearly completed silent features are released with interpolated sound sequences

LEFT Poster for *The Jazz Singer*, 1927. ABOVE The recording room 1931, showing an early Western Electric film and disc recording machine. OPPOSITE Al Jolson with Jack and Albert Warner and Albert's wife Bessie.

AL JOLSON
Looking for the Bluebird

Al Jolson was not the first choice for *The Jazz Singer*. George Jessel originated the part on Broadway but wanted more than Warner Bros. was prepared to pay. Jolson was already past forty although the hero is meant to be his twenties, but such was his charismatic appeal it hardly mattered.

Asa Yoelson, born around 1885 in Lithuania, was raised in Washington, D.C. by his immigrant parents. His father, alleged by publicists to be a cantor like the father in *The Jazz Singer*, was highly religious and opposed to burlesque and vaudeville, but could not keep his son away. Young Al was stomping the grueling national circuits by his teens. In 1911 he was in a Broadway show, *La Belle Paree*, which he was soon stealing, enchanting audiences with his electrifying energy. His baritone voice already had the husky, vibrant tones that spawned a

million impersonations, and he quickly abandoned the conventional static singing postures of the time, bouncing kinetically around the stage making exaggerated arm movements, often addressing the audience directly. When he became a headliner he persuaded managements to build runways out from the proscenium, enabling him to physically relate to his public as no stage performer had before. He had discovered New Orleans syncopation as early as 1905 and developed a jazzy style that owed much to black music. His blackface routines are now often misunderstood: there was never any intent to patronize black people. In that Jim Crow era, Jolson was one of the first white entertainers to popularize black music to audiences that had been endemically conditioned to racial prejudice. The Jewish Jolson empathized with blacks, as anti-Semitism also prevailed on a horrifying scale.

"The world's greatest entertainer" was at his peak when Hollywood's call came. His ad-libbed dialogue in *The Jazz Singer* set in train the talkie revolution. Jolson's early sound pictures were huge successes, but then it became clear that

his talents did not suit the medium he had launched. Audiences tired of Jolson's *Red, Red Robins* and *Toot, Toot, Tootsies*, and *Dixie Melodies*, warming instead to the relaxed, intimate style of Bing Crosby. Jolson slowly faded from view, as did three of his four marriages. Wives failed to keep up with his ego and in the case of the third, Ruby Keeler, her career was ascendant as his slumped, a prime cause for marital disaster alongside his voracious appetite for gambling.

His revival came in the mid-1940s when Harry Cohn, head of Columbia, mindful of Warner Bros.' success with *Yankee Doodle Dandy*, decided to make *The Jolson Story*, with Larry Parks miming to Jolson's re-recorded songs. It was the hit of 1946, but lack of inter-studio cooperation meant no mention of Warner Bros.' part in his life. Jolson was once again the rage and there was even a sequel, essentially about his revival and the filming of *The Jolson Story*. He died in 1950, not long after his return from entertaining G.I.s in the Korean War, but he was a household name once more.

ALL-TALKING, ALL-SINGING, ALL-DANCING

Hollywood embraced the sound era by going into a tailspin. Films awaiting release were recalled and sound sequences were clumsily added. Projects awaiting production were reshaped for dialogue. The first all-talking feature film came from Warner Bros—*Lights of New York,* directed by Bryan Foy and originally intended as a sound two-reeler. Foy expanded the hackneyed story of a country kid finding the big city full of wickedness; although it was only fifty-seven minutes—a short running time for a feature—the creaky plot and labored acting made it seem much longer. Much of the dialogue was enunciated at dictation speed, including the first use in a sound film of the cliché "Take him for a ride." The film cost $23,000 to make and grossed nearly $1,160,000 in the United States.

Its success was modest in comparison with *The Singing Fool,* Al Jolson's follow-up to *The Jazz Singer,* directed by Lloyd Bacon. Jolson played a waiter who aspired to songwriting (and performed a string of numbers, including the lachrymose ballad "Sonny Boy" by Buddy G. DeSylva, Lew Brown, and Ray Henderson, the first song from a movie to sell a million copies of sheet music). Although intended as a parody of such sentimental songs, "Jolie" poured so much emotion into his rendering that the public fell for it as a straight number. Jolson was paid $150,000 for his starring role, and as the film took nearly $6 million the investment was a good one.

Talkies had raised Warner Bros. in the Hollywood pecking order, and they were able to buy the Stanley Co. of America (giving them 250 theaters) plus Skouras Brothers theaters and a third of First National Pictures, acquiring their theater chain, star lineup, and large studio lot at Burbank, on the other side of the Hollywood Hills. Jack Warner, head of production, with Darryl F. Zanuck as his number two, decided to concentrate future sound films there, and it became Warner Bros.' new home. The studio manager they appointed was Hal B. Wallis.

1929

✱ At the first Oscar ceremony, a special Academy Award goes to the studio for producing *The Jazz Singer* (above)

✱ Herbert Hoover becomes thirty-first President of the United States

✱ Warner Bros. releases eighty-seven features, forty-five of them bearing the First National logo

✱ *The Desert Song* with John Boles is the first Warner screen version of a Broadway musical with sound and dialogue, and is partly shot in two-color Technicolor

✱ Michael Curtiz directs *Noah's Ark,* a multi-narrative drama running at 135 minutes, although much of it is silent

✱ *On With the Show* stars Betty Compson in a backstage singing, dancing extravaganza "in one hundred percent natural color"

✱ The British actor George Arliss makes his talkie debut in *Disraeli*

✱ George M. Cohan's *Little Johnny Jones* is remade with songs

✱ *The Gold Diggers of Broadway* and *The Show of Shows* overwhelm audiences with spectacle, but revue-style movies begin to decline

✱ The Wall Street crash triggers a global economic depression

ABOVE Jack Warner with the Academy Award for *The Jazz Singer,* 1929. LEFT *Lights of New York* (1928), featuring Wheeler Oakman at the desk and Tom Dugan far right. OPPOSITE Looking southeast across Los Angeles river, toward the First National-Warner Bros. lot, c. 1932.

BEHIND THE CIGAR

Although small in stature, Darryl Francis Zanuck was possessed with dynamic drive and superabundant energy. His father was a night clerk in Wahoo, Nebraska, his mother the hotelier's daughter.

Their son was born on September 5, 1902. Underage and barely educated, he went to war for Uncle Sam in Europe, having lied his way into the U.S. Army. Much of his fighting was in the ring and among the multiplicity of postwar jobs—

cleaning cars, dishwashing in restaurants, sweeping up in barber shops—he tried his hand at professional boxing. He had a yen to be a writer, and after a few stories had appeared in print he started sending his ideas to studios. He grew a mustache to look older and to gain contacts he applied to join the Los Angeles Athletic Club; he was blackballed because they did not admit Jews. Zanuck proved he was not Jewish and reapplied, but hated their policy and would in 1947 make an Oscar-winning film, *Gentleman's Agreement,* in denunciation.

ABOVE From left to right: production manager William Koenig, Darryl F. Zanuck, Jack L. Warner, Al Jolson, and Sam Warner, at the Sunset Blvd. Studio in 1927. OPPOSITE Page from a Vitaphone sales brochure.

Nevertheless, he achieved his purpose, and found work with Carl Laemmle and as a gag-writer for Mack Sennett. Warner Bros. hired him as a staff screenwriter in 1923. They needed someone who could think up story ideas for Rin Tin Tin, and Zanuck excelled as the resulting films scored at the box office. Although only in his mid-twenties, he was a prolific scriptwriter with several noms-de-plume and he zoomed up the career ladder, becoming studio manager in 1928 and Jack Warner's second-in-command the following year. More than anybody, he imposed a distinctive signature on Warner Bros. product after the introduction of sound, and created tough and uncompromising gangster films such as *The Public Enemy* (1931) and *Little Caesar* (1931), social-conscience dramas based on reality such as *I Am a Fugitive from a Chain Gang* (1932), hard-boiled musicals such as *42nd Street* (1933) and *Gold Diggers of 1933,* which for all their frivolity had a serious edge. Unsurprisingly, using Jack Warner's fifty percent minimum eight-week pay cut from March 6, 1933, Zanuck left to run his own outfit, and in 1933 he joined forces with Joseph Schenck to form the company that two years later became Twentieth Century Fox, a new major studio.

1930

✶ James Cagney makes his screen debut in *Sinner's Holiday* (above)

✶ Scotch Tape, Twinkies, and Bird's Eye frozen foods are introduced to the public

✶ John Barrymore's first full-length talkie is *General Crack,* directed by Alan Crosland

✶ Al Jolson has a hit as a traveling minstrel in *Mammy,* directed by Michael Curtiz

✶ The first air stewardess flies with Boeing Air Transit, predecessor of United Airlines

✶ Howard Hawks directs *The Dawn Patrol* and is a box-office success

✶ Marilyn Miller reprises her Broadway success in the Kern-Hammerstein musical *Sunny*

✶ Edward G. Robinson makes his Warner Bros. debut as a bootleg king in *The Widow from Chicago*

MICHAEL CURTIZ
The Great All-Rounder

In Hungary Michael Curtiz (born Mihaly Kertesz in Budapest in 1888, died 1962) had been a stage actor and producer. He entered European cinema in 1912, first as an actor then as a director, and briefly served in the Hungarian army in World War I. Discharged early in the war, he returned to filmmaking in Budapest. When the industry was forcibly annexed by Bela Kun's communists in 1919 he left to work in German and Austrian studios, and very quickly acquired an international reputation as a prolific and reliable director. Hollywood duly took note, and in 1926 Harry Warner invited him to California to direct *The Third Degree*, the first of over ninety films he

would eventually make under the Warner banner. Curtiz allegedly spoke five languages, but none of them well, and his mangling of English was the stuff of legend, acknowledged by David Niven in the title of his autobiography *Bring on the Empty Horses¸* which was a Curtiz utterance during the shooting of *The Charge of the Light Brigade* when he wanted a few riderless mounts to pass the camera. Actors sometimes found him intractable and autocratic on set but Curtiz was one of the most accomplished, versatile, and successful studio directors, with an enviable array of hits including *Captain Blood* (1935), *Angels with Dirty Faces* (1938), *Casablanca* (1942), *Yankee Doodle Dandy* (1942), and *Mildred Pierce* (1945). In a sense his wide-ranging embrace of almost every genre, from thrillers to westerns to romantic dramas to musical spectaculars, has made it difficult to characterize a Curtiz style and denied him a place in the pantheon of great directors.

GEORGE ARLISS
Breath of the Past

Long before the birth of the movies George Arliss was acting on the English stage. Born in London in 1868, he had become an actor by the age of eighteen, and in 1902, after treading the West End boards in many productions, he toured the United States in a company led by Mrs. Patrick Campbell. Finding the atmosphere to his liking he stayed, with appreciative American audiences delighting in his carefully enunciated, declamatory style. He played many historical figures on Broadway, including Disraeli, Voltaire, and Richelieu, all of whom he would later portray on screen. He was already fifty-three when he made his film debut in 1921 in *The Devil,* repeating his 1900 appearance in a Molnar play, followed by the first version of *Disraeli,* his most famous role. That and three other of his six silent films have not survived, but the 1929 sound remake of *Disraeli,* for which he won an Academy Award, has. Arliss was granted the rare privilege of complete control of his ten Warner Bros. films, setting up his own production unit, and for *The Man Who Played God* in 1932—another talkie remake of his silent

picture—he insisted on casting a little-known actress as the female lead. She was Bette Davis.

Arliss was old, in his sixties, at the height of his screen career, and old-fashioned. He invested in his performances (the historical impersonations of Alexander Hamilton, Voltaire, the Duke of Wellington, and others) the weight of a Victorian actor delivering at full power. The more elderly members of his audience had pangs of nostalgia for the barnstorming days of nineteenth- and early twentieth-century theater, and warmed to his work. His face was prune-like, his makeup often gave him blackened lips like a silent-screen diva, and even though each role would provide him with a different wig or eyeglass he was always recognizable. His days at Burbank ended when Zanuck left to create Twentieth Century. Arliss went with him. He was a unique, huge, and unlikely star who retired to London as World War II approached, remaining through the bombing, to die in 1946.

GEORGE PERRY

OPPOSITE Hal Mohr, Errol Flynn, and Michael Curtiz on the set of *Captain Blood,* 1935. ABOVE George Arliss as Benjamin Disraeli in *Disraeli,* 1929.

2

"THE HEADLINES OF TODAY ARE THE MOVIES OF TOMORROW"

HARRY WARNER

DARRYL FRANCIS ZANUCK WAS, NO LESS THAN THE MYSTERIOUSLY REVERED IRVING THALBERG, AN AUTHENTIC BOY GENIUS OF HOLLYWOOD. OTHER THAN SMALL STATURES, OBSESSIVE WORK HABITS, AND THE FACT THAT THEY WERE BOTH RUNNING MAJOR STUDIOS BEFORE THEY WERE THIRTY YEARS OLD, THE TWO MEN HAD LITTLE IN COMMON. ZANUCK WAS A ROUGHNECK, WILLING TO ENFORCE HIS WILL WITH HIS FISTS IF NECESSARY; THALBERG WAS SMOOTH AND GENTLEMANLY. ZANUCK WAS A FEROCIOUS ATHLETE, A GAMBLER AND A WOMANIZER OF LEGENDARY PROPORTIONS. THE SICKLY THALBERG WAS A FAITHFUL HUSBAND (TO NORMA SHEARER) WITH NO KNOWN BAD HABITS. ZANUCK HAD BEGUN HIS CAREER AS A WRITER, A MAN WHO COULD DELIVER A SHOOT-ABLE SCENARIO FOR A QUICKIE MOVIE AFTER A WEEKEND'S WORK. THALBERG HAD BEGUN HIS CAREER AS A READER—HE WAS CONFINED TO BED FOR A YEAR AS A BOY AND DEVELOPED A TASTE FOR CLASSIC FICTION IN THAT PERIOD, THE MANNER OF WHICH, WHEN HE TOOK OVER AT MGM, HE TENDED EITHER TO ADAPT OR TO APE. PUT SIMPLY, PEOPLE FEARED THE EXPLOSIVE ZANUCK WHILE THEY RESPECTED THE SOFT-SPOKEN THALBERG.

Put another way, it may be that it was Zanuck's misfortune that F. Scott Fitzgerald never worked for him. For it is the conflation of the real Thalberg and his fictional alter ego, Monroe Stahr, in the unfinished, gaseously romantic *The Last Tycoon* (1976), on which his posthumous reputation largely rests. But, in truth, Zanuck was by far the more interesting figure of the two, and the corporate author of the more interesting body of work.

Born in 1902, he was three years younger than Thalberg and his story is at least as entertaining. His father was a hard-drinking hotel desk clerk, his mother a woman with a reportedly restless sexual nature. Essentially he became a runaway at age fifteen, lying about his age in order to enlist in the army, seeing European service in World War I (though he was never under fire), and returning home with the notion that he ought to be a writer. That did not work out too well; he drifted to Los Angeles, sold a few stories to the pulps, then found work as a gag writer for Mack Sennett and some of the major silent comedians. He even managed to sell a scenario to Thalberg when he was running Universal. Mainly Zanuck felt that the movies could absorb his demonic energy in a way that sitting alone hunched over his typewriter never could. His good fortune was to see, with the director Mal St. Clair (another Sennett refugee), a 1923 Warner Bros. picture *Where the North Begins* that featured a dog named Rin Tin Tin. It was they who thought the dog could be developed, talked the Warners into that notion, and in 1924, when Zanuck was a mere twenty-two years old, he began writing the scripts that made Rinty an authentic star.

But he could not confine himself to a dog. Using three pseudonyms he wrote every kind of picture, one year grinding out no less than thirteen scenarios for the studio, only six of which were credited under his real name. He was fast, good at structure, and a fount of ideas. He was Jack Warner's kind of guy and Jack was heard to say, around this time, that if Zanuck had only been Jewish he would be prepared to add his name to the studio's logo. That was probably just talk, but one has to think that, for a few years, Zanuck was close to being a surrogate brother to Jack, so many habits of mind (and raffish recreational habits) did they share.

Zanuck didn't have much to do with *The Jazz Singer* (1927), but by the time that groundbreaking movie was released he was Associate Executive in Charge of Production at Warner Bros. and the man whose sensibility stamped every bit of film the studio turned out—very profitably—in the last years of the wildly prospering twenties. In those years Warner Bros. had no particular character. The studio made every kind of movie, with musicals—it was the height of the "All Talking, All Singing, All Dancing" craze in the theaters—being predominant in the genre mix. It was not until 1931 that the kind of movies we think of as typical of Warner Bros. in the first full decade of sound production began to dominate its schedule.

PREVIOUS PAGE A scene from *Heroes for Sale,* 1933.
OPPOSITE Edward G. Robinson and James Cagney
in *Smart Money,* 1931.

"THE HEADLINES OF TODAY ARE THE MOVIES OF TOMORROW"

Here the question of intention arises. How much of what the studio turned out in those years represented a conscious decision on Zanuck's part to make a particular kind of film: tough, fast-moving, urban, wised-up. How much of this product was arrived at accidentally, a more or less instinctive response to conditions at the studio (especially the talent it had under contract) and to conditions in Hollywood and the world at large?

About Zanuck, who was still well under thirty years old when Wall Street laid its notorious egg, we can say that there was nothing in his record at that time to indicate that he was a particularly compassionate or socially conscientious citizen. On the other hand, he had recently known, first-hand, the pain of scrambling for a few dollars in hard-scrabble territory so he may have had a certain rough sympathy for the unemployed, whose

numbers reached at least 12.5 million and possibly as high as 18 million by 1932 (no one is quite sure to this day, labor statistics being a primitive science in the early thirties). And someone was hiring the performers (Edward G. Robinson, James Cagney, Paul Muni, Barbara Stanwyck, Joan Blondell, Bette Davis), the directors (William A. Wellman, Mervyn LeRoy), and the writers (tough-minded journalists and Broadway characters, not high-toned literary names) who could make the kind of pictures Warner and Zanuck liked.

It took Zanuck a couple of years to position his studio for the Depression era. But in 1931 Warner Bros. essentially started the gangster cycle with *Little Caesar* and *The Public Enemy,* starring its new plug uglies, Edward G. Robinson and James Cagney. The former was ponderous, the latter lively as a cricket, but both in some ways sociologized their criminal antiheroes, showing them to be products of a society that was radically out of whack. But it's a mistake to see Warner Bros. as a studio devoting itself to anatomizing the criminal element. Over the next two or three years it took up a huge variety of social problems, all of which portrayed fairly ordinary American citizens coping with the greatest and most heartbreaking domestic crisis since the Civil War.

To name just a few of these films, there was *Three on a Match* (drug addiction), *Baby Face* (a cold-eyed portrayal of a sexually exploited woman turning on her exploiters), *Heroes for Sale* (a veteran loses his family and the business he has built up, and becomes one of the dispossessed), *Employees' Entrance* (working women viciously

ABOVE AND OPPOSITE Poster art for *Smart Money* and
Little Caesar, both 1931.

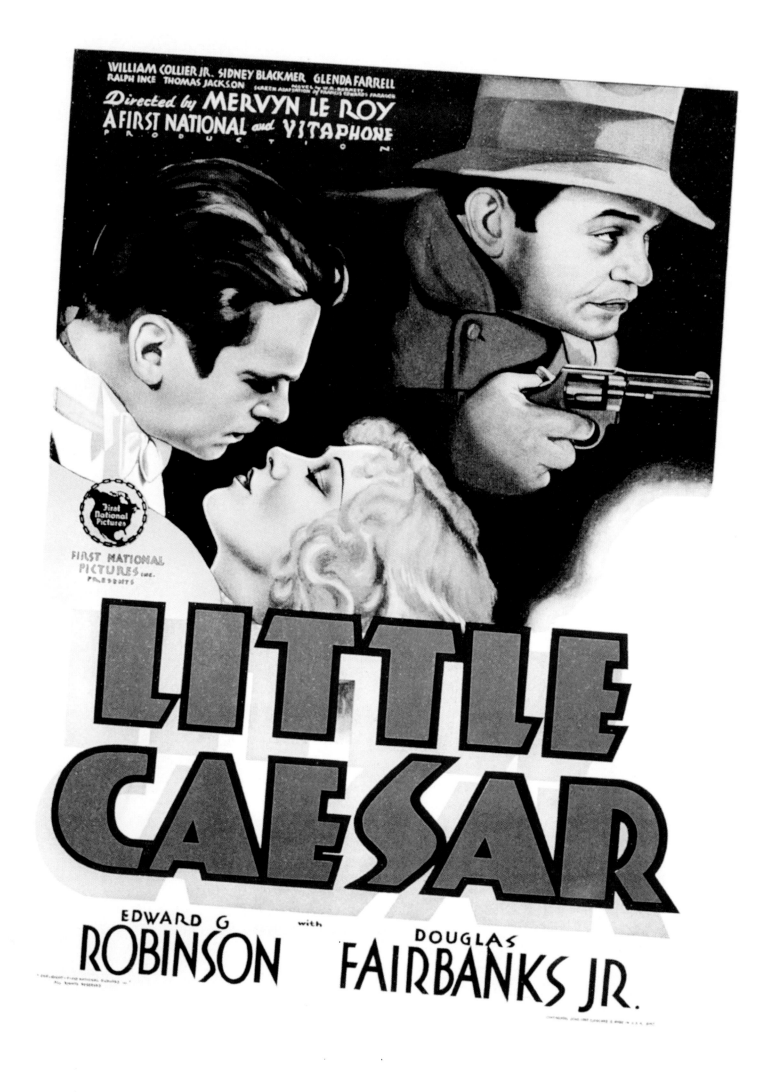

used by their unscrupulous boss), *Wild Boys of the Road* (teenagers ride the rails in a dangerous, desperate search for work). Best of all, there was *I Am a Fugitive from a Chain Gang,* possibly the best American film of the era, in which an innocent man is imprisoned in the eponymous southern prison system. It is a film of Kafkaesque hopelessness and one that suggests that in the America of its moment the possibility of even rudimentary justice was nearly nonexistent.

If one were to look only at the movies mentioned above, one would gain a picture of a great nation brought to its knees by economic and social calamity more vivid than anything available in the newsreels or the written histories of this terrible time. And that was only the top of the Warner Bros. line. There were, for example, the brass knuckle James Cagney comedies, in which the greatest star of the era used his wit and hardness to survive all sorts of marginal jobs. There were newspaper dramas (*Blessed Event,* 1932, is the best of them) that pioneered

criticism of mass media corruption. There was the not-so innocent hedonism of the Busby Berkeley musicals, which were never as escapist as their dance director claimed they were. In a dream sequence in one of them a "Broadway Baby" plunges to her death from a skyscraper terrace while her lover sips a cocktail, not even registering surprise at the occurrence. In another, the "forgotten men" of the era— the veterans of World War I—march in a vast anonymous circle, going nowhere, while a lugubrious tune plays.

The historian Neal Gabler believes that Zanuck self-consciously perceived a "niche" in the movie marketplace that no one else was filling and that he moved purposively to fill it. This is a thought Martin Scorsese expands upon when he remarks that the Warner Bros. audience wanted escape and entertainment, yet at the same time "wanted to see their troubles portrayed on the screen honestly." In other words, Warner Bros., unlike the other studios, was offering the audience impure as opposed to pure escapism. The national mood was down and dirty and, at least for a time, the audience was open, if not to down and dirty movies, then to intensely realistic ones. The hard cases making Warner Bros. movies at this time were not the initiators of the proletarian novels or the socially conscious plays that dominated the culture of the moment, but they were aware of those trends and talented enough to imitate them.

In their way. For there was something bracing in that realism, often enough something chipper and even cheeky about it. It somehow proposed that American inventiveness and energy would see us through. You could see it in the studio's attitude toward the fatuous censorship of the time. Official Hollywood, under pressure from the Catholic Church, had promulgated a production code in 1930 that forbade realistic onscreen portrayals of

OPPOSITE Busby Berkeley, in white by camera, directing Ruby Keeler and chorus girls in *Dames,* 1934. ABOVE Paul Muni and convict extras in *I Am a Fugitive from a Chain Gang,* 1932.

everything from strong language to openly lustful sexuality. But for the next four years, during the erroneously named "pre-code" era, its strictures were rarely enforced and Warner Bros. movies in particular showed men and women talking and behaving in ways readily familiar to their audience. The verbal air of a Warner film in those years was blue with innuendo (though never with four-letter words) and visually it was always clear who was sleeping with whom. At Warner Bros. the assumption was that no woman would be ruined by a *double entendre,* no man turned into a lustful beast by the sight of a chorine in dishabille. The films offered nothing that would not today be acceptable on primetime television, but they did treat their audiences as if they were grown-ups, capable of accepting dialogue and situations that accurately imitated life as most people experienced it. Even its unlikeliest star, the now almost-forgotten George Arliss, an aging English actor who played both historical characters (Disraeli, Voltaire, Alexander Hamilton) and foxy grandpas in contemporary dramas, frankly took up topics like anti-Semitism and extramarital love affairs in his films and people adored him—though his great-est historical service to the studio was probably bringing Bette Davis, her career in crisis, to the studio to play opposite him in *The Man Who Played God* (1932).

Within three years Davis's febrile energy had brought her first Oscar (for *Dangerous*), though by that time Zanuck was suddenly, shockingly gone. In 1933, as Franklin D. Roosevelt was about to take office and as the Depression reached its depths, the Hollywood studios, many of them unable to make their payrolls, decreed across the board salary cuts: fifty percent for its top earners, twenty-five percent for the working stiffs. At Warner Bros. Jack, who spent his life avoiding confrontations, decreed that Zanuck would make the announce-ment of the cuts, due to last for eight weeks, which he did. Then Jack and his brothers went back on their word, extending the hiatus. Infuriated, Zanuck, on his own, restored the cuts (which, incidentally, had not extended to the top executives). Now it was Jack's turn for fury and, in its face, Zanuck resigned. There's a school of thought holding that this was pretty much play acting on his part, that he had by then seen that he would never be taken into full partnership with the brothers and that he needed some excuse to break his employment contract with the studio. No matter. In days he had formed a partnership with Joe Schenck to found Twentieth Century Pic-tures, which in turn became Twentieth Century Fox, over which Zanuck presided off and on until the 1970s.

It is possible that he perceived that his era at Warner Bros. was ending, that a new kind of film—more finished, more elegant—was now in order. Certainly that was the kind of film his replacement, Hal Wallis, started making. Wallis was a large, phlegmatic-seeming man who had been at the studio for years, overseeing publicity. He was also, in his way, every bit as shrewd a showman as Zanuck had been, though never as conten-tious. The master of the firm, calm memo and a very shrewd reader of the dailies, he was never as close to Jack Warner as Zanuck had once been, but he was well liked by his writers and he had a sense that the world, and the Warner brothers themselves, were ready for a new kind of picture.

That was particularly true of Harry Warner. He and Jack were nominally Republicans, though they had supported Roosevelt in 1932 and maintained close ties with his administration. Most people thought of Warner Bros. as the New Deal studio and, surely, the pictures they made in the early thirties implicitly shared the sociopolitical assumptions of the New Deal. But among his other duties Harry was in charge of the studio's international distribution, and he grew increasingly alarmed by the rise of Hitler in Germany. As early as 1933 the Nazis issued an edict requiring all American studios operating in Germany to dismiss their Jewish employees and, rather than comply, Harry closed operations there—the first American company to do so by many years. In that very same year Warner Bros. made the first anti-Nazi film, an animated short called *Bosko's Picture Show,* which boldly satirized Hitler. In the later 1930s, when the Motion Picture Code's censors fought all attempts by the studios to make anti-fascist films, Warner Bros. did its best to speak its warnings in metaphors. In a curious way this suited the kind of pictures Wallis was beginning to produce.

OPPOSITE **Bette Davis** in a publicity pose for *Dangerous,* 1935.

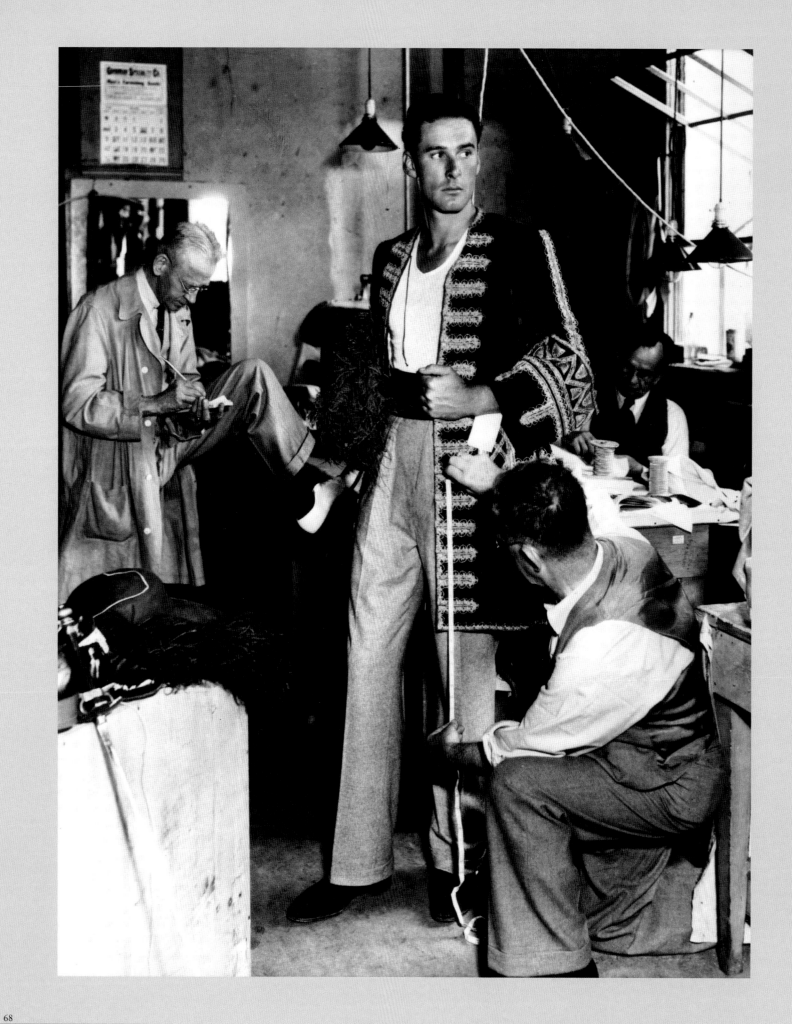

THE WARNER BROS. STORY

They tended to be more expansive, both romantically and historically, than Zanuck's films had been, much richer in their visual tonalities. Cagney had briefly left the lot, but its new queen, Bette Davis, liked the grandeur of the past—not to mention its costumery—and the new male star it had discovered, Errol Flynn, was seen to wonderful advantage in such swashbuckling adventures as *Captain Blood* (1935), *The Sea Hawk* (1940), and, of course, *The Adventures of Robin Hood* (1938). This new mode also suited the soaring symphonic tastes of the music department, led by Erich Wolfgang Korngold, Max Steiner, and Franz Waxman. Almost all of Flynn's films in this period permitted the studio to show him leading bands of democratically inclined outlaws against troops of the dictatorially inclined. Something similar occurred in the biopics that also became a studio specialty in these years. You could see Edward G. Robinson stand up to the racial prejudice of Imperial Germany in *Dr. Ehrlich's*

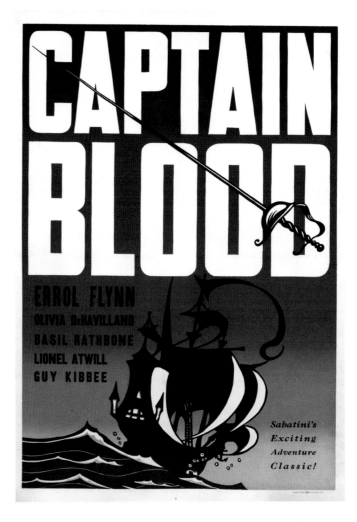

Magic Bullet (1940) or Paul Muni fight to free Captain Dreyfus in *The Life of Emile Zola* (1937), which, although it only briefly mentioned the anti-Semitism mobilized against that faithful soldier, nevertheless won the studio its first Best Picture Academy Award. Similarly, in *Juarez* (1939), Claude Rain's foppish Napoleon III goes on an anti-American, anti-democratic tirade that might have done Hitler proud. The studio was doing its best to alert America not to the dangers from within, but to those from without.

Not that it went completely silent about domestic disturbances. In 1937, *Marked Woman,* which signaled Davis's return to the lot after her dramatic attempt to flee its jurisdiction, was the sort of film Zanuck had once "ripped from the headlines," the fictionalized story of crusading district attorney Thomas E. Dewey's prosecution of the Murder, Inc. mob in New York. Better still, was *Black Legion* (also 1937), in which a simple man (Humphrey Bogart in his first good performance at the studio), passed over for promotion on the factory floor, is enlisted in a nativist organization patterned on the Ku Klux Klan, eventually committing murder at its command. "What Cagney was to the thirties, Bogart was to the forties," the critic Andrew Sarris has remarked. He was the actor that somehow symbolized the nation's mood in a particular era, and he would begin to achieve that status as the 1930s turned into the 1940s, when he stopped playing gangsters who were merely tough and permitted his romantic rue, his sense of old-fashioned, slightly disappointed principles to shine through, as he did when he played Roy Earle, the gangster "rushing toward his doom" in *High Sierra* (1941) and the witty yet rather radio-ish John Huston version of *The Maltese Falcon* that same year.

But we are perhaps getting slightly ahead of our story. For as Bogart was beginning his rise, Warner Bros. was, unlike the other studios, beginning to speak quite directly to the external threats it perceived to the nation as a whole. This was the era of the "America First" movement, during which something pretty close

OPPOSITE Errol Flynn in a costume fitting for *Captain Blood, 1935.*
ABOVE Advertising art for *Captain Blood.*

ABOVE Title lobby card for *Marked Woman,* 1937, featuring Bette Davis. OPPOSITE Humphrey Bogart as Roy "Mad Dog" Earle in a publicity shot for *High Sierra,* 1941.

to an American majority was demanding that the country stay out of European entanglements. It was a movement that contained a strong anti-Semitic bias, and it was one Harry Warner, in particular, was determined to oppose. The studio embraced a slightly fatuous slogan, something about combining "good citizenship with good filmmaking," but Harry was deeply serious about it. In 1939 a group of German espionage agents were tried and convicted in New York of spying for the Fatherland. These were headlines that Harry was determined to rip a story from. This was a story Joseph Breen, the Motion Picture Code administrator, was equally determined not to permit on the screen. Among the code's many bylaws was one preventing the making of films that held any foreign nation up to criticism, so when the script for *Confessions of a Nazi Spy* was submitted to him he replied furiously. Steven J. Ross, a University of Southern California historian who has studied this period intensely, summarizes Breen's astonishing views this way: "To portray Hitler only as a screaming maniac when he's done so much for the German people and has accomplished so much throughout Europe is really a travesty. And it's an unfair portrayal of the man." He added that Warner Bros.—all the studios—did much business in Europe and given Hitler's growing influence there this movie would probably do irreparable harm to the entire industry.

"In effect, Harry and Jack told him to go screw himself," says Ross, and they went ahead with the picture, though Hitler was seen in it only in a few newsreel clips. They had trouble casting it; many players feared appearing in it because they had relatives in Europe against whom the Nazis might take reprisals. And they had trouble releasing it: there was picketing by the German-American Bund, even the bombing of a theater in Milwaukee. They also had trouble making a gripping movie out of a story that was essentially a police procedural in which the bad guys posed no murderous threat to anyone.

But it was done. And the Warner brothers were not done either. Three years later they were back with a rather more entertaining comedy-drama about German spies in New York, *All Through the Night* (1941), in which Bogart plays a small-time gambler who gathers a group of underworld figures to fight a nest of Nazi agents. In this period the studio also addressed the need for preparedness. In the two most significant films of this type, World War I provided a convenient stand-in for the second world war the brothers were convinced was coming. In *The Fighting 69th* (1940) Cagney plays a loudmouthed and cowardly slacker who is almost cashiered from what was the eponymous and perhaps most famous combat unit of the first war (it was commanded by "Wild Bill" Donovan, latterly the founder of the OSS) for his repellent behavior but then redeems himself in action, martyring himself in the process by falling on a live grenade and saving the lives of his comrades.

In this film Cagney was an obvious surrogate for America—selfish, unpatriotic, refusing to acknowledge the seriousness of a totalitarian threat, only belatedly coming to heroic consciousness of the deadly issues the country faced. *Sergeant York* (1941), for which Gary Cooper won an Academy Award in 1941, takes up similar issues in a more sobering context. Based on the true story of a famous American hero of World War I, it presents York as a back-country conscientious objector, prepared to die for his country but not to kill for it, until he and his unit are surrounded by German machine gunners and he uses his sharpshooter's skill to wipe out many of the enemy troops and capture their survivors. He later tells his commanding officer that he felt he had to take many

ABOVE James Cagney in *The Fighting 69th*, 1940.
OPPOSITE Half-sheet poster art of Gary Cooper in *Sergeant York*, 1941.

lives in order to save still more lives among his comrades. "The fury of a patient man," the historian Leo Braudy correctly defines this act. In effect the movie is saying that eventually decent, well-meaning, isolationist America, like Sergeant York, will be pushed too far by a bullying world and will fight back—furiously.

In this period Harry Warner was heard to remark that "the headlines of today are the movies of tomorrow," a thought that had obviously occurred a decade earlier to Darryl Zanuck, a thought that had motivated many Warner Bros. movies throughout the 1930s. With war about to engulf the nation at last, the studio would find the lead time between headlines and movies shortening dramatically. But that was a circumstance Warner Bros. had long dealt with. More than any other studio it was ready, perhaps even eager, for the trials it and the nation were about to endure.

RICHARD SCHICKEL

HOODLUMS & HOOFERS

Two key Warner Bros. debuts occurred in 1930. Edward G. Robinson (born Emmanuel Goldenberg in Bucharest, Romania in 1893, in America from the age of nine) was a Broadway stage actor recruited by Hollywood with the introduction of sound, and appeared in films for Paramount, MGM, and Universal before making *The Widow from Chicago* (1930) at Burbank. Small and thickset, he could inject by voice and gesture an air of dangerous menace into his performances. He was soon typecast as gangsters and psychopaths, attaining stardom as the Capone-like hoodlum in *Little Caesar* (1931). During the 1930s he was one of Warner Bros.' most stalwart, reliable stars. He was equally adept at gentler, more sympathetic roles and, in a long career lasting more than forty years, he alternated between tough guys and social reformers with total credibility. In real life he was cultured and sensitive, a considerable art collector, unjustly targeted by the House Committee on Un-American Activities for being too liberal in his support of patriotic causes in World War II. He died in 1973, shortly before the Academy was to present him with an honorary Oscar.

James Cagney, born in New York in 1899 to an Irish father and Norwegian mother, grew up on the Upper East Side (acquiring fluent Yiddish), and was on stage on Broadway and in vaudeville for more than ten years before going to Hollywood, having started out as a chorus boy in a musical. He was playing New York leads by 1925. Teamed with Joan Blondell in *Penny Arcade*, he caught the eye of Al Jolson, who bought the show, selling it on to Warner Bros. with the proviso that they both repeated their roles on film. Cagney and Blondell made their movie debuts in *Sinners' Holiday* (1930), as the film version was retitled. Short, lithe, belligerent, anti-authoritarian, and self-assured to the point of cockiness, Cagney proved to be charismatic on screen, projecting a persona that exactly met the public mood following the Wall Street crash. He soon topped the Warner Bros. hoodlum roster, following his outstanding performance in *The Public Enemy* (1931).

By the time James Cagney hit the screen he had learned to be a song-and-dance man in the hard school of vaudeville touring. Earlier than that his childhood and youth in the working-class Manhattan neighborhood of Yorkville had given him plenty of opportunities to cultivate the streetwise persona he displayed in so many of his films. He learned to be a fast talker, use his fists, and dodge trouble even though some of his youthful friends ended up in the penitentiary. His real-life experience gave an edge to his screen performances, and he had the magnetic appeal of a born star, the ability to project a dynamic energy that forced his audience to sit up. His stardom was assured with *The Public Enemy* and the point at which, bored with her breakfast prattle, he smashed a grapefruit into Mae Clarke's face, was the defining moment. To some the brutal spontaneity of the gesture (apparently a joke between them that was never intended for the final cut) was shocking and unacceptable, while others relished its bravado.

Cagney's star shone over Burbank for many years. He played hoodlums and hobos, convicts and playboys, do-gooders and ne'er-do-wells, with total reliability. Too few of his films were musicals in which he danced a cocky, straight-limbed strut, but the best were *Footlight Parade* (1933), in which he was a hard-driving Broadway producer, and *Yankee Doodle Dandy* (1942), for which he won his only Oscar as the proud personification of the all-Irish-American George M. Cohan, the showman born on the Fourth of July.

OPPOSITE Edward G. Robinson as *Little Caesar* (alias Rico). ABOVE James Cagney in *The Public Enemy,* 1931. RIGHT James Cagney in the famous grapefruit scene with Mae Clarke in *The Public Enemy.*

"THE HEADLINES OF TODAY ARE THE MOVIES OF TOMORROW"

Edward G. Robinson as Rico in *Little Caesar.*

ABOVE One-sheet poster art for *Footlight Parade*, 1933.
RIGHT Cagney's first major starring appearance in *The Public Enemy*, 1931, pictured here with Jean Harlow.

1931

✱ *Little Caesar* propels Edward G. Robinson to stardom and begins a cycle of social-conscience crime films

✱ Jack Warner signs Barbara Stanwyck, who is then a hit in *Night Nurse,* a William Wellman thriller

✱ Thomas Alva Edison dies

✱ William Dieterle's *The Last Flight* looks at the lost generation of air veterans who stayed in Europe after the Armistice

✱ The Empire State Building is completed in New York

✱ Sound-on-film becomes the standard system for talking pictures

✱ Edward G. Robinson plays a muck-raking newspaper editor in *Five Star Final*

✱ Warner Bros. takes control of Teddington Studios, London, to make films mainly for the British market

✱ James Cagney becomes a megastar in *The Public Enemy,* playing a vicious Prohibition mobster (below)

BARBARA STANWYCK & JOAN BLONDELL
The Great Dames

Ruby Stevens, born in Brooklyn in 1907, was orphaned at four, raised by a sister who was a dancer, and then worked in menial jobs. She trained herself to dance and became a chorus girl at fifteen. In the speakeasy era she worked her way from burlesque to the *Ziegfeld Follies of 1930*. She had the lead in a Broadway play called *The Noose,* and changed her name to Barbara Stanwyck. Hollywood beckoned but it was a false start and she returned to Broadway. With the advent of sound she appeared in both talkie and silent versions of *Ladies of Leisure* for Columbia, and was signed by Warner Bros. for *Illicit*.

In the cast was Joan Blondell, and in *Night Nurse* (1931) they shared the female leads with Clark Gable playing a smaller part as a heavy. Born in New York in 1906, Blondell came from a theatrical family: her father Eddie was a vaudeville comedian and Joan was performing on stage as a child, touring the world with her parents. On Broadway she was teamed with James Cagney in *Penny Arcade*, and both of them were signed up by Warner Bros. for the film version, *Sinners' Holiday*. Although never a first-rank star, she played opposite Cagney in seven films, more than any other actress. Wide-eyed, blonde, and sardonic, she excelled in "Girl Friday" roles. She could deliver barbed lines with sassy relish, such as in *Footlight Parade* when she boots a rival out of the door: "Outside, countess. As long as there's sidewalks you've got a job."

ABOVE Joan Blondell (left) and Barbara Stanwyck in *Night Nurse,* 1931.

"THE HEADLINES OF TODAY ARE THE MOVIES OF TOMORROW"

PAUL MUNI

The city of Paul Muni's birth has changed countries several times and is currently Lviv in the western Ukraine, but before that it was Lvov in the Soviet Union, Lwow in Poland, and when he was born in 1895, Lemberg, Austria. His name was Meshilem Meier Weisenfreund and he was the offspring of Jewish actors who emigrated to New York when he was seven. He became a prominent member of the Yiddish Art Theater, and did not make his English-speaking debut until 1926 when he was thirty-one. He made a couple of films in the late 1920s, even winning an Oscar for one of them, *The Valiant,* but his screen career did not really kick in with the public until 1932, when he appeared in the controversial Howard Hawks film *Scarface,* based on the notorious gangster Al Capone, followed by *I Am a Fugitive from a Chain Gang* (1932) for Warner Bros. It was directed by Mervyn LeRoy from the bestselling account of Robert Burns, who was unjustly sentenced to forced labor

in Georgia and escaped to another state to face extradition battles. The chilling last line, "I steal," uttered by the fugitive unseen in total darkness, thrilled audiences. Muni was nominated for an Oscar, and was signed to a long-term contract. He appeared in a number of Warner Bros. social-conscience films, but his specialty was the biopic, and he won an Academy Award for *The Story of Louis Pasteur* (1935). He also played the title roles in *The Life of Emile Zola* (1937) and *Juarez* (1939).

Muni's acting impressed, but was hardly naturalistic, and while he was exacting in matching makeup and voice to his roles they retained an aura of theater, of self-conscious acting at odds with the ascendancy of the more relaxed styles that emerged during the 1930s. Eventually his film roles became sparse, the stage proving to be his metier. He died in 1967.

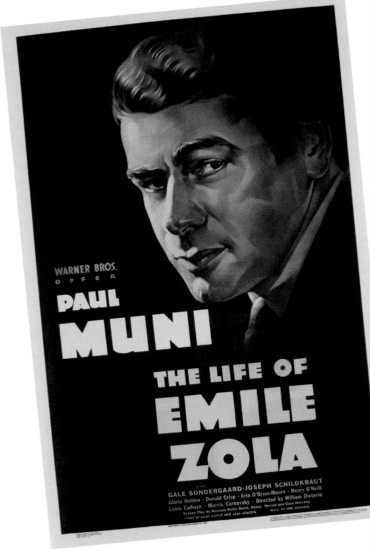

ABOVE One-sheet poster art for *The Life of Emile Zola,* 1937.

1932

* George Arliss stars in the remake of his silent success *The Man Who Played God* (above, with Bette Davis)

* In *The Crowd Roars* James Cagney plays a ruthless racing driver

* Cagney spectacularly quits Warner Bros. and takes his pay grievance to AMPAS and arbitration, returning with a hefty raise

* Rin Tin Tin dies aged sixteen in the arms of Jean Harlow

* The Olympic Games are held in Los Angeles

* *I Am a Fugitive from a Chain Gang,* based on a harrowing autobiography, is a box-office hit and a landmark in social criticism

* Barbara Stanwyck stars in the first sound version of Edna Ferber's Pulitzer novel *So Big!,* with William Wellman directing

* Warren William plays a lawyer who sends an innocent man to doom in *The Mouthpiece,* an indictment of legal corruption

* Jack Warner and Darryl Zanuck issue a memo to talent affirming the studio's complete control of script content

* Warner Bros. records a loss of $14.1 million

BUSBY BERKELEY

With the advent of sound, Hollywood discovered the musical—an unsurprising outcome. Many were made initially, and enjoyed considerable success. Apart from Jolson, who in early sound days was at the peak of his appeal, Warner Bros. had *The Show of Shows* as the answer to MGM's compendium of musical acts *Hollywood Revue of 1929* and *The Gold Diggers of Broadway,* a backstage story culminating in elaborate production numbers with seemingly hundreds of performers erupting in a spectacular all-singing, all-dancing extravaganza, as well as screen versions of Broadway hits such as *The Desert Song* and *Sunny.* Far too few musicals had coherent plotlines and audiences tired of the revue formula, especially as many of the films looked as if they had been photographed square-on from an auditorium. The early two-color version of Technicolor was often used for inserted sequences, and occasionally, as in *The Gold Diggers of Broadway,* for the entire film. In projection the red and green images reproduced enough of the spectrum to fool audiences into thinking that they were watching proper color, but its deficiencies became apparent with the introduction of Technicolor's three-strip process later in the 1930s. The public appetite for revue-style films eventually waned, and musicals began to fall out of favor.

William Berkeley Enos, born in Los Angeles in 1895, bucked the trend. As Busby Berkeley he gained a Broadway reputation as a dance director and choreographer, and was brought to Hollywood in 1930 by Sam Goldwyn to enliven some Eddie Cantor films. He moved to Warner Bros. in 1932 and applied his skills to *42nd Street,* a conventional backstage story about the unknown who replaces the star, with Ruby Keeler and Dick Powell. In wartime Berkeley had served in France, and during a checkered military career had at some time been in charge of drill displays, devising silent routines for the men to follow and the onlookers to admire. These were the principles he brought to his stage and film work, and his girls (chosen for shapeliness and beauty rather than dancing ability) glided through his intricate routines, forming kaleidoscopic patterns with their bodies. Berkeley's imagination was immense, and he used the camera as nobody before him, freeing the film musical from the proscenium mentality that had previously fettered it. He might show an audience settling in to watch the latest theatrical spectacle unfold before them, but once the show took off all manner of things would appear that could never occur on a Broadway stage. A famous specialty was the vertical overhead shot in which girls' limbs would be organized into intricate interlocking shapes. In one number he outlined violins in neon as the girls played them in the dark. In another he piled them high on a rotating pyramid emerging from a waterfall. He had them playing fifty-six pianos waltzing across a jet-black floor, and weaving in and out of starburst patterns on the surface of a pool. With shameless audacity Berkeley managed to inject into his work a degree of eroticism that seems far too obvious to have passed over audience's heads. The strengthening of the Production Code in 1934—the industry's self-imposed defensive policy in the face of a tide of hostility from churches and morality groups—tamed Berkeley, and after his 1933–34 flood of Warner musicals, including *Gold Diggers of 1933, Footlight Parade,* and *Dames,* his later work, his imitators by now legion, had a diminished impact.

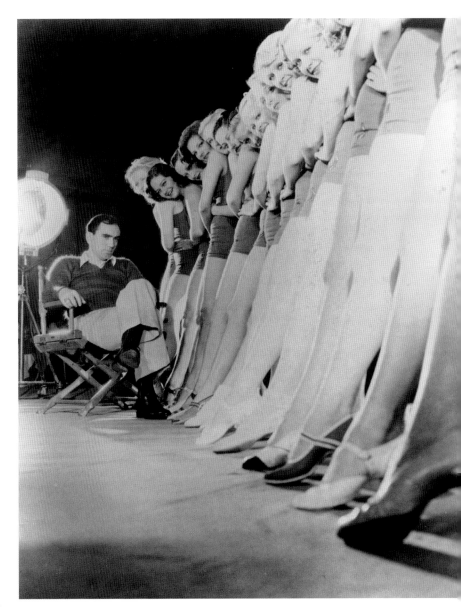

ABOVE Busby Berkeley directing dancers in *Footlight Parade,* 1933.

"THE HEADLINES OF TODAY ARE THE MOVIES OF TOMORROW"

ABOVE One-sheet poster art for *42nd Street*, 1933.
LEFT Ruby Keeler in the climactic title number in
42nd Street.

83

Half-sheet poster art for *Gold Diggers of 1933*.

Reproduction by Continental Litho. Corp.
Made in U. S. A.

DIGGERS OF 1933

WARREN WILLIAM
ALINE MacMAHON
JOAN BLONDELL
RUBY KEELER
DICK POWELL
GUY KIBBEE
NED SPARKS ★ GINGER ROGERS
DIRECTED By MERVYN LE ROY

A WARNER BROS.
AND VITAPHONE PICTURE

"COPYRIGHT—WARNER BROS. PICTURES, INC.
ALL RIGHTS RESERVED

1933

* *Gold Diggers of 1933* perfectly captures the public mood and is a massive hit (above and below)

* Adolf Hitler becomes German Chancellor

* With Busby Berkeley's exuberant choreography, *42nd Street* is a smash hit, ending the public's aversion to musicals

* Franklin Delano Roosevelt is sworn in as President

* Spencer Tracy, on loan from Fox, is hailed in *20,000 Years in Sing-Sing* after Cagney's refusal

* President Roosevelt initiates the New Deal program

* William Wellman's *Heroes for Sale* dramatizes post-war capital-labor conflict

* James Cagney and Busby Berkeley's spectacular numbers triumph in *Footlight Parade*

* The Roosevelt administration repeals the Eighteenth Amendment, ending Prohibition

* Over the year Warner Bros. posts a loss of $6.3 million

DICK POWELL

A former band singer from Arkansas, Dick Powell (1904–63) enjoyed two incarnations as a movie star. In the first he made his name as an engaging juvenile lead in a succession of Warner Bros. musicals, often teamed with Ruby Keeler or Joan Blondell, to whom he was for a while married. He was a round-cheeked crooner who often played apparent romantic indigents who would then turn out to be scions of well-heeled families. His popularity waned with the fading of his boyish charm, and the studio dropped him, but after playing Philip Marlowe in 1944 in *Murder, My Sweet* he was reinvented as a hard-boiled hero of *film noir*. The final phase of his career was as a major producer in the television world of the 1950s–60s.

RUBY KEELER

Keeler was born Ethel Hilda Keeler in Nova Scotia in 1910, but was raised in New York. On stage from teenhood, Ruby Keeler danced her way from speakeasies to a Ziegfeld musical, and at eighteen married "the world's greatest entertainer," Al Jolson, then forty-two. Her career went on the back burner until 1933 when she was cast opposite Dick Powell in *42nd Street*. Other Berkeley-choreographed musicals followed, among them *Gold Diggers of 1933, Footlight Parade, Dames,* and her only film with Jolson, *Go Into Your Dance*. Jolson fought with the studio and left in dudgeon, canceling her contract and effectively snuffing out her career. They divorced in 1940. She enjoyed a mature Broadway comeback under Berkeley's direction with a revival of *No, No Nanette* in 1971, and died in 1993.

ABOVE Ruby Keeler and Dick Powell in *Dames*, 1934.

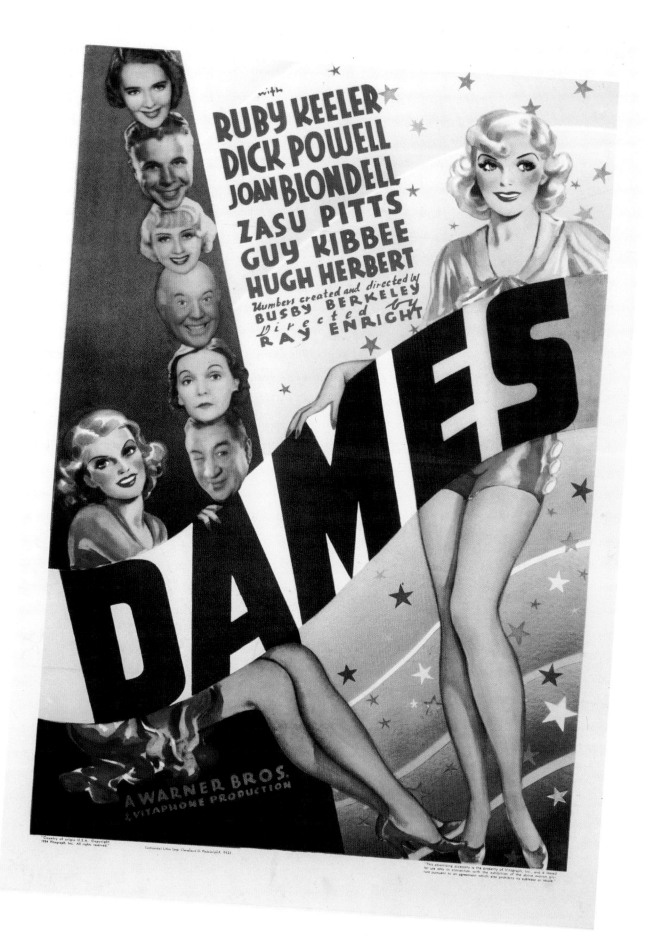

ABOVE One-sheet poster art from *Dames*.

ABOVE One-sheet poster art from *Dames*.

"THE HEADLINES OF TODAY ARE THE MOVIES OF TOMORROW"

1934

✳ A serious fire at the Warner Bros. Studios in Burbank destroys irreplaceable early negatives

✳ Calvin Coolidge's presidential inauguration is the first to be broadcast

✳ Bank robbers Clyde Barrow and Bonnie Parker are killed in a police ambush in Louisiana

✳ In Germany Nazi dictator Adolf Hitler is appointed Führer

✳ Bette Davis and James Cagney appear together in *Jimmy the Gent*, directed by Michael Curtiz

✳ Joel McCrea and Barbara Stanwyck are teamed for the first time in *Gambling Lady*

✳ *A Modern Hero* is the only American film ever to be directed by G. W. Pabst, a master of German cinema

✳ Alan Crosland's *Massacre*, with Richard Barthelmess and Ann Dvorak, uniquely considers the plight of Native Americans

✳ Ruby Keeler and Dick Powell feature again in the Busby Berkeley musical *Dames*

✳ The Hays Office strengthens the Production Code Administration

ABOVE Kay Francis surveying the wreckage of the 1934 fire.
RIGHT Berkeley girls were chosen for their statuesque beauty rather than dancing skills: from *Dames*, 1934.

ERROL FLYNN
Action Man

Although his accent was pukka British, Errol Flynn was actually an Australian, born in Hobart, Tasmania, in 1909, the son of a distinguished marine biologist. His childhood followed an unsteady trajectory in which he was expelled from schools in England and Australia, and in his youth he worked for a Sydney shipping company, attempted growing tobacco and mining copper in New Guinea, and sailed the southern seas. He played Fletcher Christian in a semi-documentary, *In the Wake of the Bounty,* two years before Clark Gable's famous portrayal, and decided to try his luck at acting in England. A minor film made by Warner Bros.' British studio caught the attention of Hollywood.

Flynn's first starring role was the lead in the breathless swashbuckling yarn *Captain Blood* (1935), directed by Michael Curtiz. This was the first of a dozen collaborations between actor and director, and the first of seven films in which Flynn was paired with Olivia de Havilland—in one of the finest instances of chemical attraction between leading performers.

The Flynn of the 1930s—*The Dawn Patrol* (1938), *The Adventures of Robin Hood* (1938), *The Charge of the Light Brigade* (1936), *The Private Lives of Elizabeth and Essex* (1939), and others—was tall, dashing, athletic, graceful, and supremely handsome; he could also wear period costume better than anyone. Men envied, women swooned. It was too good to last. Age puffed his cheeks and licentious living blunted his reputation. With his looks going and his notoriety escalating, he faded, dead from heart failure at fifty.

ABOVE Errol Flynn in the thick of *The Charge of the Light Brigade,* 1936.
LEFT French poster art for *The Charge of the Light Brigade.*
OPPOSITE A fine hero in *Captain Blood,* 1935.

1935

✳ Errol Flynn plays in *Captain Blood,* the first of seven films with Olivia de Havilland, and is a sensation

✳ Dust storms lay waste to southwestern states, creating the "Dust Bowl"

✳ Max Reinhardt makes his astonishing version of *A Midsummer Night's Dream,* with Cagney as Bottom

✳ The Austrian composer Erich Wolfgang Korngold, hired by Reinhardt, stays to write some of the greatest film scores ever

✳ Led by Benito Mussolini, Italy invades Ethiopia

✳ Will Rogers and aviator Wiley Post are killed in a plane crash

✳ Al Jolson and Ruby Keeler co-star in *Go Into Your Dance,* their only film together, but he spurns a sequel

✳ Louisiana senator Huey Long is assassinated in Baton Rouge

✳ Warner Bros. ends the year with a modest profit as the Depression continues

ABOVE Berkeley dancers promote *Gold Diggers of 1935* at the beach. ABOVE LEFT On the set of *Captain Blood,* director Michael Curtiz, Errol Flynn, and Jack L. Warner, with others, considering the effectiveness of knives and swords.
LEFT Errol Flynn in *The Charge of the Light Brigade.*

ERICH WOLFGANG KORNGOLD
Musical Exile

Erich Wolfgang Korngold (born 1897 in Moravia, now the Czech Republic, died 1957) was a child prodigy who became one of Austria's most eminent composers. He was invited to Hollywood in 1934 to orchestrate Mendelssohn's music for Max Reinhardt's film *A Midsummer Night's Dream* for Warner Bros. then composed an original score for *Captain Blood*. More followed. Korngold returned to Hollywood in 1938 to write a score for *The Adventures of Robin Hood*. While he was there Germany annexed Austria, and with the Nazis in power the Jewish population had its assets seized and civil rights removed. Korngold stayed in America, and among his outstanding film scores that followed were *The Private Lives of Elizabeth and Essex* (1939), *The Sea Hawk* (1940), and *Kings Row* (1942). His rich, romantic themes set a benchmark for film composing, and he won Academy Awards for *Anthony Adverse* (1936) and *The Adventures of Robin Hood*.

LESLIE HOWARD
Howard's End

To Americans Leslie Howard represented the quintessential romantic Englishman: charming, gentle-mannered, diffident, intellectual, a passive observer of the decline in the human condition. His parents were actually Hungarian Jews who had emigrated to London, where he was born in 1893, and his family name was Steiner. His acting reputation was cemented on the stage in London and New York. One of his theatrical successes, the mystical *Outward Bound,* was filmed by Warner Bros. in 1930, marking his debut in talking pictures.

He flitted between films and theater on both sides of the Atlantic, and after a run of Robert Sherwood's *The Petrified Forest* on Broadway, in which a desert wayside service area is held hostage by a dangerous escaped criminal, he was signed to repeat his role as the poetic dreamer caught up in the siege. Warner Bros. wanted Edward G. Robinson to play the gangster, but Howard insisted that an actor who had been his Broadway co-star should have the role. For that Humphrey Bogart was eternally grateful to him. Howard was one of very few Hollywood figures to die at the hands of the enemy. In 1943 his unarmed airliner, en route from Lisbon to London, was shot out of the sky by the Luftwaffe—a propaganda coup for Dr. Goebbels.

ABOVE TOP Erich Wolfgang Korngold playing the piano with director Max Reinhardt. ABOVE Humphrey Bogart as Duke Mantee and Leslie Howard in *The Petrified Forest,* 1936, reprising their Broadway roles.

BETTE DAVIS
Cousin Betty

Ruth Elizabeth "Betty" Davis was born in Lowell, Massachusetts in 1908, and later changed the spelling of her diminutive, modeling it after Balzac's *La Cousin Bette*, although she retained the childhood pronunciation. She decided to be an actress at high school, and in spite of her unconventional looks faced up to the odds and eventually pushed her way to Broadway. Her crisp New England diction gave her an edge in talkies and led to a few films for Universal, although when she arrived by train the publicist sent to meet her failed to spot anyone who looked like a potential movie star, and she was left high and dry. She made her Warner Bros. debut in 1932 in *The Man Who Played God,* at the specific request of George Arliss, and she always acknowledged her indebtedness. This was followed by many routine roles. Only after her loan-out to RKO for John Cromwell's *Of Human Bondage* did the studio appreciate that she was a serious actress of some depth. Some better roles followed, including *Bordertown* (1935), *Dangerous* (1935) and *The Petrified Forest.* Eventually Davis felt she was being slighted, and accepted an offer to film in England in breach of contract. A lawsuit was heard in a London court, but she failed to attract public sympathy when she claimed to be a slave on $1,350 a week. She lost—although the publicity was valuable—and on her return she succeeded in her purpose, in 1938 winning her second Academy Award for *Jezebel.*

HAL WALLIS SETS THE TONE

After Darryl Zanuck's departure Hal Wallis, initially a publicist, then studio manager, took over as Associate Executive. Although less flamboyant in personality, he was shrewd, forthright, and immensely efficient, and presided over one of the most outstanding periods of sustained successful output in Hollywood history. In Zanuck days he had stamped his imprint on the "torn from the headlines" crime films, particularly those made by Mervyn LeRoy, such as *Little Caesar, The Public Enemy, Five Star Final,* and *I Am a Fugitive from a Chain Gang.* Wallis favored historical biopics of heroes against the system, men such as Pasteur challenging medical orthodoxy, Zola the bigotry and injustice of the French military caste. Under his aegis a slew of "Merry England" films were made, often with Errol Flynn, effectively mythologizing the glories of past ages to make vivid entertainment. The studio signature of Warner Bros. was never clearer than it was during the Wallis years, which continued until 1944, when he moved on.

OPPOSITE Bette Davis and Leslie Howard in *The Petrified Forest.*
ABOVE Michael Curtiz and Hal Wallis here following a game of polo, *c.* 1934.

1936

✳ *Life* weekly picture magazine is launched (above)

✳ Leslie Howard insists Humphrey Bogart appears with him in *The Petrified Forest,* repeating their Broadway triumph

✳ Bette Davis loses against Warner Bros. in a breach of contract lawsuit heard in London

✳ Germany reoccupies the Rhineland, violating the Versailles treaty

✳ The spectacular hit *The Charge of the Light Brigade,* starring Errol Flynn and directed by Michael Curtiz, costs $1.2 million

✳ Berlin hosts the summer Olympics under Nazi swastika banners

✳ The Spanish Civil War begins

✳ *The Green Pastures* has an all-black cast with Rex Ingram as "De Lawd"

✳ William Randolph Hearst sways Jack Warner into teaming Clark Gable with Marion Davies in *Cain and Mabel,* but it still fails

✳ British king Edward VIII abdicates to marry U.S. citizen Mrs. Wallis Simpson

"THE HEADLINES OF TODAY ARE THE MOVIES OF TOMORROW"

ANTI-FASCISM ON THE MARCH

Even though Hollywood was largely founded and run by Jews, a blind eye was deliberately turned on events in Europe in the 1930s. Nazis and anti-Semitism were given no place in the cinema and Hitler was for the most part ignored. The Production Code Administration (PCA), under the control of Joseph Breen, actively prevented confrontation, mindful that a large market for Hollywood product continued to exist in Germany.

1937

✶ *The Life of Emile Zola* with Paul Muni (above) wins Warner Bros. its first Best Picture Oscar

✶ Franklin D. Roosevelt begins his second term as U.S. President

✶ Bette Davis returns to the studio with *Marked Woman,* based on the downfall of the gangster "Lucky" Luciano

✶ The German airship *Hindenburg* crashes and burns on arrival at Lakehurst, New Jersey, with heavy loss of life

✶ *Black Legion* with Humphrey Bogart attacks bigotry and xenophobia in heartland America

✶ Lavishly adapted from Mark Twain's novel, *The Prince and the Pauper* with Errol Flynn evokes sixteenth-century London and is released to coincide with King George VI's coronation

✶ Inspired by a real case, Mervyn LeRoy's *They Won't Forget* indicts southern prejudice, legal corruption, and lynch-law

✶ Amelia Earhart disappears on her attempt to fly round the world

Yet as early as 1933, the year that Adolf Hitler was sworn in as Chancellor and the Nazi Party gained control, an edict had gone out that all Jews working for American film companies in Germany were to be fired. Shamefully, most complied. Harry Warner decided that rather than subscribe to such injustice it would be better for Warner Bros. to close its Berlin offices and withdraw completely.

In the isolationist climate that prevailed in America, the Warners felt that the threat of fascist infiltration was strong. They lobbied President Franklin D. Roosevelt, who while appreciating the urgency of their arguments, was politically boxed in and powerless to take strong action. Unable to make films directly denouncing the Nazis, Warner Bros. attacked fascism in other ways, through films such as *The Life of Emile Zola*, *Black Legion*, and even *The Adventures of Robin Hood*. From 1936 it made a series of historical Technicolor two-reel featurettes, that used figures in history as diverse as Abraham Lincoln, Bill Cody, and Clara Barton to promote the democratic ideal. One, *Sons of Liberty,* directed by Michael Curtiz, showed how a Jewish banker, Haym Solomon played by Claude Rains, helped to finance the American Revolution.

In the face of Breen's opposition Warner Bros. pursued its policy of ripping stories from the headlines by making a film based on a case in which J. Edgar Hoover's FBI had unearthed a Nazi spy ring using the German-American Bund as a cover. One of the G-men involved, Leon G. Turrou, wrote a bestseller, and the rights were bought by the studio. Jack Warner defied Breen's advice and *Confessions of a Nazi Spy* was made, with Edward G. Robinson as the Turrou figure. Some stars refused to appear on the grounds that their families in Europe might be persecuted. The film is propagandistic and as a sop to the PCA it never mentions Nazi atrocities against the Jews. It was banned in many European and Latin-American countries, and even in America was regarded in some quarters as Jewish propaganda. Will Hays, the head of the Motion Picture Producers and Distributors Association, reinforced the diktat that anti-Nazi films were not to be made, and the ban remained in place until four months after the war in Europe had started. The House Committee on Un-American Activities (HUAC) had been monitoring films for anti-fascism, regarding it as a form of Communism, and was particularly interested in anything that smacked of communist propaganda, sometimes discerning it in the most unlikely places. Their investigations were brought to a sudden halt by Pearl Harbor.

OPPOSITE Special one sheet poster art for *Black Legion*, 1937.

DEATH TO SQUEALERS

THAT'S THE LAW OF THIS DEVIL CULT— the midnight mobsters who'll sell you the privilege of killing your neighbor for thirty pieces of silver—thirty dirty dollars and a mortgage on your soul!

BLACK LEGION

THE SCREEN BLASTS IT WIDE OPEN in this volcanic dramatization of the most terrific headline sensation since Warner Bros. "G-Men" and "I Am a Fugitive from a Chain Gang" thundered across the screen!

HERE'S THE FIRST ACTUAL STORY of the Black Legion's reign of terrorism, real, absorbing, fearless! A feature that rips the black shirts from the backs of the hooded hoodlums and bares a yellow streak a yard wide!

NOW SEE IT ALL—just like the cornered killer told it to beat the rope—the whole amazing story filmed by

Warner Bros.

Midnight Justice

Man-bait

HUMPHREY BOGART

The killer of "Petrified Forest" in an even more dynamic role... Heading this all-star cast—

DICK FORAN · ERIN O'BRIEN-MOORE ANN SHERIDAN ROBERT BARRAT Helen Flint · Joseph Sawyer · Addison Richards · Eddie Acuff Directed by Archie Mayo A Warner Bros. Picture

"Country of origin U.S.A. Copyright Vitagraph, Inc. All rights reserved"   CONTINENTAL LITHO. CORP. CLEVELAND, O.   W-2131

This advertising accessory is the property of Vitagraph, Inc. and is leased for use only in connection with the exhibition of the above motion picture.

FLYNN IN COLOR

Three-strip Technicolor raised production costs but brought big box-office returns when used well. In 1938 *The Adventures of Robin Hood,* directed by William Keighley (who was replaced halfway through by Michael Curtiz), cost an astronomical $2 million to make, but was an outstanding hit. Errol Flynn proved to be an immensely popular hero, whose battle for the oppressed against the authoritarian rule of Prince John, played by Claude Rains, was seen by some as a stand against fascism. Flynn was less assured in Bette Davis's only color film at the studio, *The Private Lives of Elizabeth and Essex,* again directed by Michael Curtiz, and like *Robin Hood* accompanied by a brilliant Korngold score.

In Curtiz's *Dodge City,* Flynn's first western, he cut a fine dash as the hero who brings law and order to the corrupt frontier. And the screenplay did seem to incorporate every known cliché of the sagebrush epic, from the monumentally destructive saloon fight to the flag-bedecked locomotive clanking into town as the symbol of a new civilization. Technicolor was the icing on the cake and audiences loved it— and Olivia de Havilland too. A Dodge City junket train, laden with stars and publicists, trundled from California to Kansas in one of the most classic promotional stunts of all time.

ABOVE A color test for Olivia de Havilland as Maid Marian in *The Adventures of Robin Hood,* 1938.

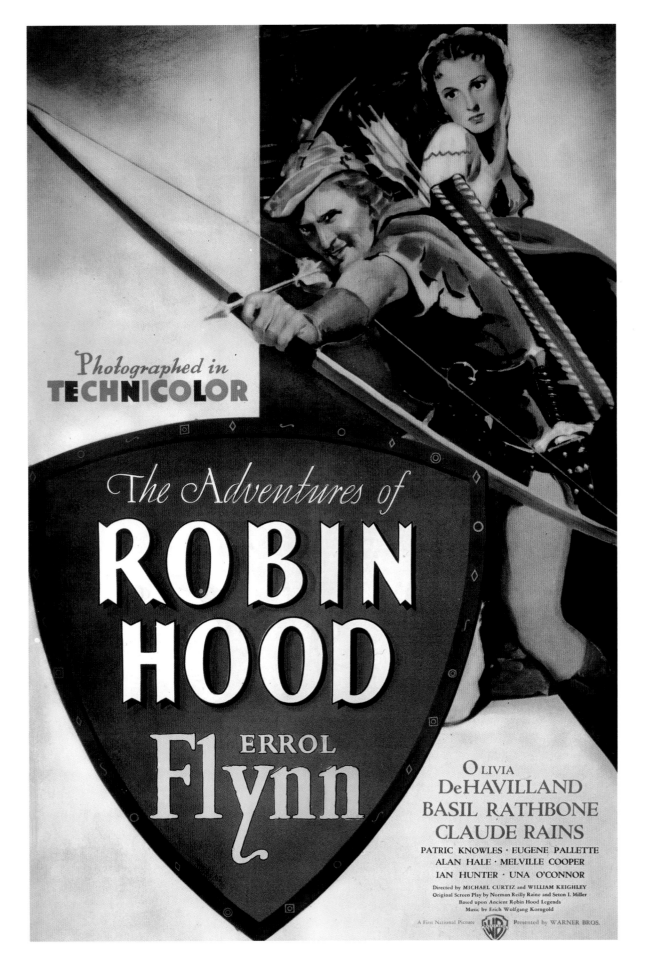

ABOVE Re-release one-sheet poster art for *The Adventures of Robin Hood.*

1938

* James Cagney and Pat O'Brien are teamed in *Angels With Dirty Faces* as slum kids who grow up on opposite sides of the law

* The year's biggest Warner Bros. hit and most expensive film to date is *The Adventures of Robin Hood* with Errol Flynn, shot in sumptuous Technicolor

* The first *Superman* story is published in *Action Comics No. 1*

* Bette Davis gives an Academy Award-winning performance in *Jezebel* as a headstrong southern belle

* Germany annexes Austria

* *The Dawn Patrol* is remade with Errol Flynn, David Niven, and Basil Rathbone

* European nations acquiesce at Munich to the Nazi takeover of Sudetenland

* Warner Bros. posts a loss of nearly $2 million

ABOVE Belgian poster art for *Angels With Dirty Faces*, 1938. RIGHT Bette Davis in *The Private Lives of Elizabeth and Essex*, with Errol Flynn, 1939. OPPOSITE A publicity shot of Bette Davis for *Fashions of 1934*.

DAVIS AT FULL STRETCH

By the late 1930s Bette Davis had reestablished herself at Burbank as the principal diva. The bruising she had received from her management battles had accorded her new respect, and meatier roles. In *Marked Woman* (1937), she was the leader of a group of call-girls (or hostesses, as the PCA insisted) that takes on the gang leader who runs them. In *Jezebel* (1938) she played a willful southern belle who scandalizes the neighborhood at a society ball. A second-rate Broadway flop with Miriam Hopkins, this story was transformed by the painstaking director William Wyler, who overran schedule and budget profligately, but scored at the box office, with Davis winning her second Oscar. She co-starred with Errol Flynn in *The Sisters* (1938), a turn-of-the-century drama, and played a rich girl stricken by terminal illness in *Dark Victory* (1939). In *The Old Maid* (1939) she appeared with Hopkins, her rival in real life, who in the film raises her illegitimate daughter. This was followed by her very effective portrayal of Queen Elizabeth in *The Private Lives of Elizabeth and Essex,* where she made no concessions to Hollywood glamour. Then came another period role, the tear-jerking *All This and Heaven Too* (1940), and Somerset Maugham's torrid vengeance melodrama *The Letter* (1940) under William Wyler's direction, plus more melodrama in Edmund Goulding's *The Great Lie* (1941) and a loan-out to Sam Goldwyn to play the ruthless Regina Giddens in *The Little Foxes* (1941). In order not to typecast her in high-powered drama, the studio gave her a screwball comedy written by Julius and Philip Epstein, *The Bride Came C.O.D.* (1941), with James Cagney as a smalltime aviator hijacking a society bride-to-be on her father's orders. It follows the idea of *It Happened One Night* without the panache, but nevertheless won the public's approval.

ABOVE Bette Davis in *The Old Maid*, 1939.
LEFT Henry Fonda and Bette Davis in *Jezebel*, 1938.

"THE HEADLINES OF TODAY ARE THE MOVIES OF TOMORROW"

LIFE ON THE LOT

During the 1930s the Warner Bros. Burbank studios greatly expanded. Many of the permanent sets on the back lot, such as the New York street, were built, as well as scenery workshops and other production buildings. The press mogul William Randolph Hearst personally financed the rebuilding of Stage #7, raising its roof to make it the tallest in Hollywood, so that spectacular Broadway settings could feature in *Cain and Mabel* (1936) the penultimate film to star his talented mistress, Marion Davies. A disastrous fire had ravaged the Burbank lot in 1934, and the studio fire chief, Albert Rounder, had a fatal heart attack after fighting the blaze. Many irreplaceable documents and films were destroyed.

The Sea Hawk, starring Errol Flynn, was another swash-buckling nautical adventure set in the days of Good Queen Bess (played this time by Flora Robson), with a stirring Korngold score. A new stage was built specially for the film, with a tank deep enough to enable two full-scale sailing ships to float opposite each other for convincing battle scenes. With characteristic thrift, the studio reused many of the costumes from the previous year's Flynn Elizabethan epic *The Private Lives of Elizabeth and Essex.*

1939

✱ Errol Flynn and Bette Davis are teamed in *The Private Lives of Elizabeth and Essex*, directed by Michael Curtiz in color, with a Korngold score

✱ In the face of opposition from the Hays Office, Warner Bros. releases *Confessions of a Nazi Spy,* made in a semi-documentary style

✱ Bette Davis makes her most successful film to date, *Dark Victory*

✱ The Spanish Civil War ends after Franco's forces take Madrid

✱ *Dodge City,* shot in Technicolor, is Errol Flynn's first western, a hit after a promotional tour by vintage train

✱ Paul Muni plays the title role in *Juarez,* with Claude Rains as Napoleon III

✱ In *Each Dawn I Die* James Cagney plays a framed reporter sent to the penitentiary

✱ New York and San Francisco stage spectacular World Fairs

✱ Hitler invades Poland, and Britain, France, and the British Empire declare war

ABOVE Gary Cooper, dressed as Alvin York, visits Bette Davis on the set of *The Bride Came C.O.D.,* 1939. ABOVE RIGHT French poster art for *The Private Lives of Elizabeth and Essex.* OPPOSITE Bette Davis in a publicity shot for *Dark Victory,* 1939.

"THE HEADLINES OF TODAY ARE THE MOVIES OF TOMORROW"

1940

∗ A new, huge sound stage is used for Errol Flynn's nautical action adventure *The Sea Hawk,* with Flora Robson as Queen Elizabeth

∗ Bette Davis's *All This, and Heaven Too* and *The Letter* are Oscar-nominated but lose to Hitchcock's *Rebecca*

∗ France and many other European countries fall to Germany

∗ Winston Churchill becomes British Prime Minister

∗ Edward G. Robinson portrays the discoverer of a cure for syphilis in *Dr. Ehrlich's Magic Bullet*

∗ Robinson also plays the German founder of the celebrated news agency in *A Dispatch from Reuters*

∗ In *Knute Rockne: All American* Pat O'Brien plays the great Notre Dame football coach, with Ronald Reagan portraying a star player

∗ The Battle of Britain is fought by the R.A.F. over southeast England

∗ The Luftwaffe begins the Blitz, its heavy bombardment of London

RONALD REAGAN
The All-time Winner

In the 1938 Hollywood-based comedy *Boy Meets Girl,* with James Cagney and Pat O'Brien, a radio announcer waxes enthusiastically at the glittering premiere of Errol Flynn's latest. His manner is polished and professional, in spite of the attempts by a ditzy blonde played by Marie Wilson to take control of the interview. Latterly the young actor had indeed been on radio, mostly as a sports commentator. Born in Illinois in 1911, he was muscular, athletic, and good-looking, and after a spell at NBC affiliates had been signed up by Warner Bros. Ronald Reagan appeared mostly in B pictures, or as a support in main features—so much so that he became typecast in "best friend" roles. Not that there were no memorable moments. Eyes moistened for the football flag-waver *Knute Rockne: All American,* in which he played the Notre Dame halfback George Gipp who utters as he dies: "… win just one for the Gipper," a line that was to become Reagan's rallying cry. His film career was long, but he was increasingly drawn into politics, gradually turning from a Roosevelt liberal into an arch-conservative, who as President of the Screen Actors Guild, purged communists from its ranks. His path took him to the gubernatorial mansion in Sacramento and then to the White House, where he served two terms as President, an ascendancy never reached by another actor. He died in his nineties, all memories erased by Alzheimer's, in 2004.

ABOVE Ronald Reagan in *Knute Rockne: All American,* 1940.
OPPOSITE Bette Davis and, in a minor role, Ronald Reagan,
in *Dark Victory,* 1939.

"THE HEADLINES OF TODAY ARE THE MOVIES OF TOMORROW"

BATTLING BOGART

Born in 1899 to a New York surgeon and a famous illustrator, Humphrey DeForest Bogart had a privileged early life, was expelled from Andover, and at the end of World War I briefly served in the U.S. Navy. For ten years he was on stage type-cast, as he would later claim, in roles in which he would poke his head through French windows and say "Tennis, anyone?" When talkies triumphed he went to Hollywood along with many other Broadway actors tempted by the quadruple earnings. It took him almost another ten years to make his mark in films, and throughout the 1930s he appeared as convicts, gangsters, down-and-outs, wastrels, and occasionally as a crusading district attorney. Although he repeated his Broadway success as the notorious hoodlum Duke Mantee in *The Petrified Forest,* and was praised as the protagonist in *Black Legion,* the film that earned him stardom was *High Sierra,* directed by Raoul Walsh and scripted by John Huston along with the novelist W. R. Burnett. Bogart played a professional criminal, sprung from prison to perform a robbery, and keenly aware that in his years inside standards have fallen and he has become an anachronism. In a role rejected by Paul Muni and then George Raft, Bogart triumphed. He then appeared as Sam Spade in *The Maltese Falcon,* which Huston not only adapted from Dashiell Hammett, but also directed. Warner Bros. had filmed the story twice before, in 1931 and 1936, but neither of these early efforts came close to the new version in which the trench-coated Bogart with the downward fedora brim characterized the lonely world of the cynical private detective, beset by picaresque underworld drifters in search of an illusory treasure, with Mary Astor as one of the screen's greatest *femmes fatale.* By now Bogie was an unassailable star.

ABOVE Humphrey Bogart and Edward G. Robinson in *Bullets or Ballots,* 1936.

IF CAGNEY HAD BEEN THE FACE OF DEPRESSION AMERICA, **BOGART** COULD BE MADE INTO THE FACE OF WARTIME AMERICA— **DOUR** AND **DUTIFUL**, YET SOMEHOW UNDERNEATH IT ALL, A **ROMANTIC** WHO COULD BE RECRUITED TO FIGHT AGAINST FASCISM.

ABOVE Six-sheet poster art for *The Maltese Falcon*, 1941.
RIGHT Humphrey Bogart as Sam Spade in *The Maltese Falcon*.

THE WARNER BROS. STORY

COOP AT BURBANK

For Frank Capra, Gary Cooper had played Mr. Deeds, and returned in 1941 in the title role of *Meet John Doe*, which was shot on the Warner Bros. lot. A prescient film, it featured Barbara Stanwyck as a newspaper columnist under threat of dismissal, who saves her job by inventing an American everyman, one John Doe. Forced to produce him she lights on a down-and-out played by Cooper, who brilliantly and easily takes on the mantle of people's hero, rooting out corruption and espousing decent values. John Doe clubs mushroomed every-where and became a national craze, as well as a magnetic attraction for a would-be demagogue (Edward Arnold). The film is as much an indictment of fascism as it is of dubious media methods.

Cooper, born in Montana to English parents in 1901 and part-educated in England, was one of the greatest Hollywood stars to have entered films in the silent days as a cowboy extra. He appeared in more than a hundred movies before his death from cancer at the age of sixty. His laconic, understated, heroic style was the stuff of legend, as was his skill at attracting women, sometimes by the mere flick of an eyebrow.

With war raging in Europe and the United States officially still uninvolved, Hollywood was handicapped by the Neutrality Act and acutely aware that isolationist politicians in Washington were anxiously monitoring perceived violations. Cunningly Jack Warner set in train the production of *Sergeant York* under the direction of Howard Hawks. The story of a great American hero of World War I, Alvin York is a dirt-poor Tennessee hillbilly farmer who in spite of his deep-seated religious con-victions goes to war and kills Germans as if he is at a turkey shoot, after wrestling with his conscience and concluding that he must do so to save the lives of hundreds of his own men. The much-decorated sergeant had resisted the filming of his story for years, and only agreed to participate because of the new war and because the producer, Jesse L. Lasky, had given him the right to keep an eye on the production. His first stipulation was that his part should be played only by Gary Cooper. It was a shrewd judgment. The film was highly re-garded in 1941 and Cooper won the Oscar for Best Actor.

GEORGE PERRY

1941

✴ Frank Capra films *Meet John Doe* with Gary Cooper and Barbara Stanwyck (above)

✴ President Roosevelt signs the Lend-Lease Act to help Britain

✴ Edward G. Robinson stars in the fifth and best version of *The Sea Wolf*

✴ Germany launches a massive invasion of the Soviet Union

✴ James Cagney makes *The Strawberry Blonde* with Rita Hayworth, *The Bride Came C.O.D.* with Bette Davis

✴ Humphrey Bogart attains stardom in *High Sierra*

✴ John Huston directs first time, *The Maltese Falcon*, with Bogart

✴ Vitagraph Studios in Brooklyn is used to make wartime shorts

✴ Roosevelt and Churchill meet in Newfoundland and found the Atlantic Charter

✴ Gary Cooper plays World War I hero *Sergeant York*, winning an Oscar

✴ Japan attacks Pearl Harbor and America enters World War II

ABOVE Gary Cooper and Barbara Stanwyck in *Meet John Doe*.
OPPOSITE Gary Cooper as Alvin C. York, in *Sergeant York*, 1941.

ABOVE On the Stage 7 set of *Sergeant York,* filming the pacifist
York's crucial battle with his conscience on a Tennessee mountain.
OPPOSITE Gary Cooper in World War I uniform in *Sergeant York.*

CHAPTER **3**

"THE GERMANS WORE GRAY, YOU WORE BLUE"

RICK TO ILSA IN *CASABLANCA*

W ARNER BROS. HAD A GOOD WAR—POSSIBLY BECAUSE, TRUE TO WHAT IT HAD ADVOCATED IN THE PREWAR YEARS, IT WENT INTO IT WELL PREPARED. IT HAD, AS HISTORIAN LEO BRAUDY SAYS, "BEEN MORE SENSITIVE TO THE IDEA OF AN AMERICAN COMMUNITY, AN AMERICAN COLLECTIVITY. THERE WAS A KIND OF CONTINU-ITY TO THE FILMS OF THE THIRTIES AND THE FORTIES. BECAUSE THE SAME KIND OF CHARACTERS APPEAR IN THE WAR FILMS. THEY'RE THE ONES WHO ARE CAUGHT BETWEEN THEIR INDIVIDUALIST DESIRES AND THE NEEDS OF THE GROUP."

In picture after picture Warner Bros. had shown groups of ordinary (largely male) American citizens strug-gling to assert their rights and values against all manner of threats. It didn't matter if they were coal miners (*Black Fury*), truck drivers (*They Drive By Night*), electrical linemen (*Manpower*), or gangsters (*All Through the Night*), or indeed members of the armed forces (the series of military comedies that featured James Cagney and Pat O'Brien). Multi-ethnic, somewhat fractious, but essentially good-natured, these working stiff gangs would always eventually set aside personal needs and ambitions in order to further the greatest good for the greatest num-ber. The studio also developed a nice line in loners, volatile in the case of Cagney, more sardonic in the case of John Garfield; these were men who stood outside the developing group ethos criticizing its practical utility until, for one reason or another, they learned better. Something like *Dust Be My Destiny* (1939), in which Garfield plays a hobo tempted and threatened by domesticity, offers—until its reconciliatory ending—quite a radical critique of the unexamined bourgeois values of the American justice system.

Setting aside occasional gestures of that kind, you can see how these 1930s movies prepared the way for wartime Warner Bros. Here was something the studio—for that matter, most Americans—saw as larger, indeed more life-threatening, than any of the exigencies the Depression had imposed on the nation. And, more than any other studio, Warner Bros. was prepared for them. As film historian Jeanine Basinger says, "in some bizarre way, they were really films about class set to war."

Or perhaps we might say they were films in which, finally, class was seen to not count for much given the des-perate circumstances of the moment. To me, the most vivid such lesson was taught in the near-surrealistic, nearly forgotten *Hollywood Canteen* (1944). The place was largely the invention of Bette Davis, a gathering spot for servicemen on leave where they might eat, dance, and occasionally mingle with the stars and starlets. It fea-tures skinny, boyish, entirely naïve Robert Hutton as a soldier smitten by Warner contract player Joan Les-lie, who almost made it to stardom (until, upon asking for a raise, Jack Warner fired her). She lives in a sweet

PREVIOUS PAGE Ingrid Bergman as Ilsa in *Casablanca*. ABOVE "A radical critique of the unexamined bourgeois values of the American justice system" in *Dust Be My Destiny*. OPPOSITE Cinematographer Arthur Edeson shoots Humphrey Bogart as Rick Blaine and Ingrid Bergman as Ilsa Lund in the closing scene of *Casablanca*.

little house surrounded by a white picket fence, attended by her ordinary American parents. But this little romance is not really the point of the movie. Its point is to show that much more famous stars—Davis herself, Barbara Stanwyck, Joan Crawford—are utterly democratic, mingling casually, humanly with the G.I. contingent. Dane Clark, playing Hutton's more aggressive buddy, actually faints when he discovers that the woman he's dancing with cheek to cheek really is Joan Crawford. Later, in a dialogue with Hutton's "Slim," he voices the movie's moral: "Big shots talking things over with Little Shots like me—and being nice." He shakes his head in awe and wonder. The exquisite confusion of realms the movie sets forth, straight-faced, is of course never alluded to, in what must be one of the giddiest representations of the American "collectivity" ever offered.

Movies like *Hollywood Canteen* were not the studio's main line of business in these years. It had under contract the kinds of actors needed to populate the classic American platoon: farmers, city kids, WASPs, Catholics, even Jews (though the latter were never identified as such). It also had the left-leaning writers who could write that kind of material and the directors (Raoul Walsh, Michael Curtiz) who could set them going in suspenseful, eventually heroic action. As Basinger says, the platoon wasn't always composed of soldiers. They might fight in the air (*Air Force*), on or under the seas (*Action in the North Atlantic, Destination Tokyo*) as well as in occupied Europe (*Desperate Journey*) and the steaming jungles of Asia (*Objective, Burma!*). It didn't matter what the venue was or

what uniforms the actors donned, these movies were, as Basinger says, "a little grittier, a little tougher" than those of the competition.

And, one might add, a little crazier. Take for example *Passage to Marseille* (1944). In it Bogart plays a French newspaper editor unjustly imprisoned on Devil's Island—he's sort of a modern-day Dreyfus—for his opposition to neo-fascism in his native land. Eventually one of those Warner Bros. groups is assembled in captivity, make their escape via a small stolen boat, and are picked up by a tramp steamer flying the Vichy colors. So far, so narratively routine, aside from its structure, which comprises flashbacks piled on flashbacks. But then the ship is attacked by a German bomber, which it manages to gun out of the sky. Its crew is stranded on the wing of their plane, clearly indicating their desire to surrender, when Bogart seizes a machine gun and cold-bloodedly murders them. It is, not to put too fine a point on it, a war crime—and the sequence was removed from prints exported overseas.

It was also perhaps a measure of the slightly weird passions the war unloosed on the Warner Bros. lot. In *Air Force* an American pilot, ditching his plane and floating helplessly to earth, is machine gunned by a Japanese Zero's pilot. In *Objective, Burma!*—voluntarily

ABOVE Poster art for *Passage to Marseille*, 1944. OPPOSITE Cary Grant in *Destination Tokyo*. OVERLEAF The cast of *Passage to Marseille* takes a walk down a studio street (l–r) Peter Lorre, Humphrey Bogart, Charles La Torre, George Tobias, Sydney Greenstreet, Philip Dorn, Helmut Dantine, Claude Rains, Victor Francen.

withdrawn by Warner Bros. in Britain mainly because that theater of war was a largely British show, which the film failed to acknowledge—American scouts are captured by the Japanese and mercilessly tortured off-screen. When they are discovered dying, a newspaper man, accompanying the troops, goes ballistic, denouncing the Japanese as "moral idiots" and "stinking little savages," and demanding that they be "wiped off the face of the earth."

In *Destination Tokyo,* Cary Grant plays the commander of a submarine that downs a Japanese plane in a firefight. The plane's pilot survives and a sailor goes to rescue him from the icy waters of the north Pacific. For his troubles he is knifed to death by the flyer—an obvious reference to the "stab in the back," which is how the attack on Pearl Harbor was generally described in the American press. He is of course machine-gunned to death,

but then Grant gathers his crew and gives a little speech about roller skates, "the best that money could buy," that the American sailor bought for his son on his birthday. By contrast, he says, the enemy aviator doubtless bought a sword for his son on a similar occasion. By such wigged-out rhetoric and solemn yet humble metaphors were the war aims of America and her enemies, especially the Japanese, contrasted in Warner movies.

Curiously, and despite the Warners' longstanding anti-Nazism, Germany was more gingerly treated. They were, after all, white guys, and following the official government line the widely known facts about what would come to be known as the Holocaust were scarcely mentioned. The one Warner picture that does so, *Mr. Skeffington* (1944), was the soul of discretion on this matter. The picture starred Bette Davis, who had been suffering nobly, if often enough redemptively, for years in increasingly upscale movies (*Jezebel, Dark Victory, The Old Maid*). In this film she plays a ravenous social climber who marries a Jewish investment banker (Claude Rains) solely for his money. They naturally become estranged, their marriage largely kept alive by his patient, all-encompassing love for their daughter. He takes the young woman with him to prewar Europe where he must look after his "interests" and he is there imprisoned and ill-used by the Gestapo. He returns to New York broken and

THE WARNER BROS. STORY

blinded. But his wife, meantime, has lost her looks to an illness, so an O. Henry ending is conveniently arranged. He cannot see that she has lost her looks, but she now has his money—and a sudden access of decency—so they are allowed to settle down to a companionable marriage. It was sentimentally satisfying, dramatically unsatisfying, but at least—and only just this once—was "The Jewish Question" raised in a wartime Warner film.

The question of Communism was, to the studio's ultimate embarrassment, raised rather more openly. President Roosevelt himself asked Harry and Jack to make *Mission to Moscow*, the autobiography of Joseph E. Davies, the corporate lawyer whom Roosevelt appointed the first post-revolutionary ambassador to the USSR. FDR felt that after decades of anti-Soviet propaganda America required a more sympathetic treatment of a country that had suddenly become a wartime ally. Davies is played by Walter Huston as a perfect dupe—and dope. By the time the film is over it has, astonishingly, endorsed the Purge trials, the Hitler-Stalin Pact, and Russia's invasion of Finland. It has also shown Madame Molotov, wife of the Foreign Minister, as the chipper commissar of the cosmetic industry, cheerfully informing Mrs. Davies that "we discovered that feminine beauty is not a luxury." It also features a conversation between Davies and Stalin in which the former states his conviction that history will regard the latter

(the murderer, lest we forget, of twenty million Russians in his campaign to re-engineer their souls) as "a great humanitarian." Written by fellow traveler Howard Koch and directed with his usual, totally apolitical panache by Michael Curtiz, the film today plays as unconscious farce. But that's not the way it earnestly, soberly played upon its release in 1943. It is unquestionably the most blatant piece of pro-Stalinst propaganda ever offered by the American mass media.

It is perhaps all the more astonishing because Harry Warner's journey from fervent anti-Nazism to virulent anti-Communism had at this moment reached new heights. Two years earlier, on the eve of war, the producers had finally recognized the Screen Writers' Guild (as the union was then called) and a modest agreement on economic particulars had been reached—an eighty-five percent union shop and a minimum wage for writers of $120 per week. The deal was to be sealed at a gentlemanly dinner at the Brown Derby and the union's president commented that it seemed to be fair to both sides. At which point Harry exploded. According to Nancy Lynn Schwartz in *The Hollywood Writers' Wars,* he loosed a stream of expletives, calling the writers "dirty communist sons of bitches," accusing them of wanting to steal his studio and

OPPOSITE Bette Davis as Fanny Trellis Skeffington and Claude Rains as Job Skeffington in *Mr. Skeffington,* 1944.
RIGHT Walter Huston as Ambassador Joseph E. Davies in *Mission to Moscow,* 1943.

"THE GERMANS WORE GRAY, YOU WORE BLUE"

then screaming obscenities so vile that her witness to the occasion said he "wouldn't dare repeat" them. Two of Harry's fellow moguls half-carried him outside to the parking lot and then sent him home. The other studio bosses were so embarrassed by the outburst that they immediately signed the contract.

The scene seems almost anomalous given the studio's embrace of the nation's liberal-minded war aims. So many Warner Bros. pictures included a speech in which someone, generally the hero, expounded on how this war was not just about removing the deadly threat of fascism from the world but also about building a better world, a peaceable world, firmly based on international law and one which, implicitly, would require everyone—the United States included—to surrender some measure of its sovereignty in order to secure permanent peace. And to assure everyone that those who died in the war had not done so in vain, as the fighting men of World War I had done.

If Warner Bros.' wartime movies were a little more intense and passionate than those of its competitors, it must be said that it sometimes paid off. Wartime is rarely the moment for great moviemaking, especially

if, as in this war, the government is hovering over your shoulder urging the gaudy patriotic gesture, reluctant to endorse the more nuanced one and, in this instance, virtually requiring silence on the Holocaust. Even so, it was Warner Bros. that made the two truly memorable films of the era.

The first of them was *Yankee Doodle Dandy* (1942), the story of George M. Cohan and his showbiz family—warm, sentimental, and of course generously punctuated by the sentimental and patriotic songs its protagonist wrote. It did plenty of often literal flag-waving, but like a great many American films of the time, especially musicals and romantic comedies, it idealized the recent American past. Our history was short—nothing like England's, for example—especially when it came to the creation of cultural touchstones.

We had to make do with evocations of turn-of-the-century America: ice-cream socials, singsongs around the parlor piano, and in this instance a nostalgia for the simple values of vaudeville and Broadway musi-comedy.

It should have been a routine film, as most of its competitors were. What transformed it was Cagney's demonic energy as Cohan, the play of responses on his face—he seemed sometimes to be reacting, a little bit differently each time, to every word spoken to him. He had always been an actor of fiercely concentrated energy. Here, unmoored from his "hoodlum" (his word) persona, mobilizing his energy for unambiguous patriotism, he unleashes in us torrents of good feelings. And that says nothing about his dancing. Mostly he moves, loose-limbed, high-kicking, jaunty, from the waist down. He was a self-taught hoofer, so his dancing was unmediated by formal instruction. It seemed, especially here, to be the direct expression of something joyous in his soul—which freed an instinctive, answering joyousness in its audience. There are moments in *Yankee Doodle Dandy* that, no matter how often I see it, can bring me close to misting up. It has been said that Cagney, at the time a fiery liberal, made the film in part to silence right-wing accusations that he had embraced Communism, by demonstrating his forthright Americanism. But no matter—its rush and innocence sweeps away any political subtexts. His performance, everything about the film including the choice to make it in black and white, grounds

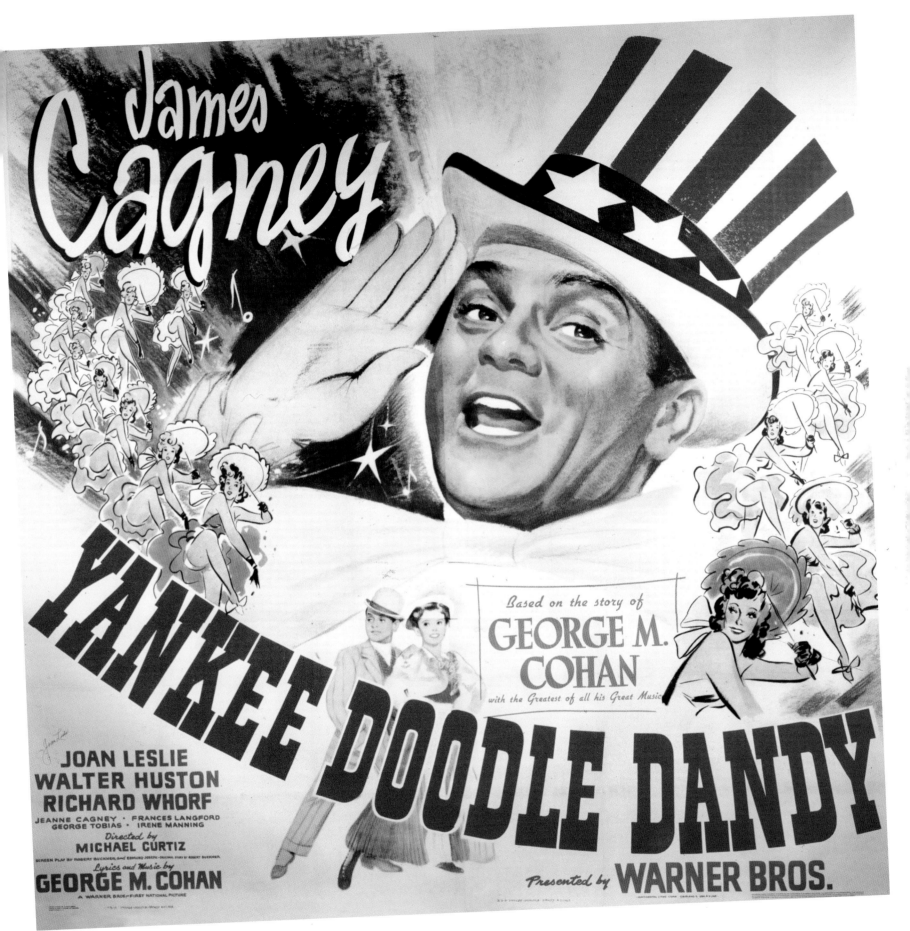

ABOVE Six-sheet poster art for *Yankee Doodle Dandy*, 1942.
OPPOSITE James Cagney as George M. Cohan in *Yankee Doodle Dandy*.

"THE GERMANS WORE GRAY, YOU WORE BLUE"

RIGHT "We'll always have Paris",
a champagne moment in *Casablanca*,
1942, with Dooley Wilson as Sam,
Humphrey Bogart as Rick Blaine, and
Ingrid Bergman as Ilsa Lund.

THE WARNER BROS. STORY

its giddiness in some sort of reality. In its way it is the apotheosis of everything that had been best in the Warner populist tradition over these many years.

A year later, Warner Bros. was back at the Oscars with an equally strong entrant—*Casablanca*. "The pacing for entertainment purposes that Curtiz and Warner Bros. pioneered in the early and mid-thirties culminated in *Casablanca* and made it the best audience film you can imagine," says Martin Scorsese, and he's right. Umberto Eco once wrote that the film succeeded mainly because it didn't miss a trick; it contained every cliché of its exotic-romantic genre. If it had omitted a single one, he said, it would have failed to attain its immortality. One of its writers, Julius Epstein, who with his brother Philip wrote many a memorable Warner screenplay, agreed with Eco. "Everything is concocted," he once said, "but this was really concocted."

Which, of course, it was. But who would deny that Bogart's Rick Blaine was the perfect variant on that standard Warner character, the slightly cynical, deeply rueful outsider who will find redemption only when he surrenders his individual desires to those of the group? Or that most of Warner Bros.' outstanding roster of character players (Paul Henreid, Claude Rains, Sydney Greenstreet, Peter Lorre) were perfectly deployed. Or that Ingrid Bergman was so meltingly vulnerable? Or that… But why go on? It sometimes happens that, almost by chance, all the elements required to make a memorable popular movie are accidentally assembled and that nothing happens in production to sour the mix. And that it arrives at its perfect moment in a troubled world when, as in this case, the larger issues hovering behind the story are in doubt, when people need to be reassured that the spirit of common decency can still assert itself against a gloweringly indecent world. You could see at the time what it meant to people, and even now when *Casablanca* plays as a period piece it retains the power, if only by analogy, to assert without embarrassment those simple values we all still like to believe are alive in the world, even if they're in hiding. Besides which, but never to be forgotten, the film's dialogue retains its snap, sass, and swoony romanticism.

Casablanca also precipitated a studio crisis. Hal Wallis's deal at Warner Bros. included the right to produce any picture he wanted and gave him first choice of all the "properties" that piqued the studio's interest. This included the unproduced play *Everyone Comes to Rick's,* which Jake Wilk, east coast story editor, brought to his attention. Wallis acquired it and set about producing it despite daunting script difficulties, casting problems, and finding the right director. Yet he persevered and triumphed, and at Grauman's Chinese the night of March 2, 1944, he had a right to a certain amount of confidence that the film would be named Best Picture (he was already down to receive the Irving G. Thalberg award for his producing career). But when the film indeed received the Best Picture accolade and Wallis rose to fetch his prize he was astonished to see Jack Warner—who had no association whatever with its production—darting forward to claim the statuette.

ABOVE Ilsa's note to Rick. OPPOSITE Bogart's portrayal of Rick Blaine, "the slightly cynical, deeply rueful outsider" and Ingrid Bergman, "so meltingly vulnerable."

He remembered Warner's family blocking the way from his seat to the aisle and settled back into his chair, furious and determined to leave the studio as soon as possible. A couple of days later the Academy mailed an Oscar to him, but the damage had been done. In a sense it was the Zanuck story all over again; no one but a Warner would have his name associated with the studio's highest triumphs.

By this time the tide of war was turning in America's favor, and *Casablanca* seemed to bode well for a postwar world that would maintain the nation's old values yet at the same time restore an optimistic and liberal-minded faith in the future. Within a year of the war's end, however, one could see in the developing history of this studio, of movies in general, of the country as a whole, something quite the opposite taking place, something that narrowed and diminished the American psyche.

This mood shift seemed to strike Warner Bros. with particular force. The war had not been over for two months when it, along with most of the other majors, was struck by a union styling itself the Conference of Studio Unions (CSU) that wished to replace the corrupt International Alliance of Theatrical Stage Employees

and Motion Picture Machine Operators (IATSE) as bargaining agent for most of their back-lot employees. It was ostensibly a jurisdictional dispute, but the CSU had strong connections with the communist left (its leader, Herbert Sorrell, was close to Harry Bridges, the communist head of the militant west coast dock worker's union, which supplied muscle for the CSU in picket lines. Sorrell himself was almost certainly not a party member, but it was not difficult for his opponents, themselves not exactly paragons of liberal-minded good will, to portray him as a Red). So there was a powerful ideological undertow to the strike. For unknown reasons the CSU decided to concentrate its most militant picketing on Warner Bros., perhaps the most paternalistic of the studios, and October 5, 1945, there was a riotous confrontation at its main gate. Clubs were swung, cars were overturned, fire hoses were turned full force on the strikers. The other movie unions, notably the Writers Guild and the actors, decided to cross the picket lines and an uneasy peace was established until the following fall, when Sorrell called another jurisdictional strike. Again there was violence at Warner Bros. and this time the strike dragged on for years before the CSU was finally defeated.

For the Warner brothers, though, the damage had been done. Their long flirtation with the left was ended and in the years ahead they would fully embrace the raging anti-Communism of the postwar years. In 1947, a year after their studio had been struck for the second time, Jack Warner joined most of the other moguls in testifying as

friendly witnesses before the House Committee on Un-American Activities at the hearings which produced the indictments against the soon-to-be famous Hollywood Ten. In his prepared testimony Jack said he and his brothers were prepared to "subscribe generously" to a "pest removal fund," designed to ship communists back to Russia, whence he asserted they must have come. It was not—shall we put it mildly?—very sophisticated testimony and Warner was unable to name any of his employees as communists, though a narrow majority of the Ten had in fact worked for him at one time or another.

According to opinion polls at the time most Americans sympathized with the Ten and had they not, under CP discipline, provoked a raucous confrontation with the committee's chairman, J. Parnell Thomas, they might have retained that sympathy. Indeed, a planeload of major Hollywood figures, among them Bogart, Lauren Bacall, Danny Kaye and John Huston, had organized a Committee for the First Amendment and had flown to Washington to support the embattled writers and directors. But once John Howard Lawson, the Hollywood Red's commissar, testified loudly, pompously, lecturishly, that support melted away. The studio imposed a blacklist on the left and the Age of Suspicion was born.

That was by no means the end of Hollywood's travails. In the late forties and early fifties the studios, having lost a federal antitrust suit, were obliged to divest themselves of their theater chains, seriously threatening their economic stability. Worse, by 1950 television had arrived in the United States and movie attendance dropped by

OPPOSITE In the 1945 labor strike between two opposing unions, three cars were overturned, and the police had to use fire hoses to break up the melee. ABOVE Bogart and Bacall lead the Committee for the First Amendment in October 1947. Behind them are June Havoc and Danny Kaye.

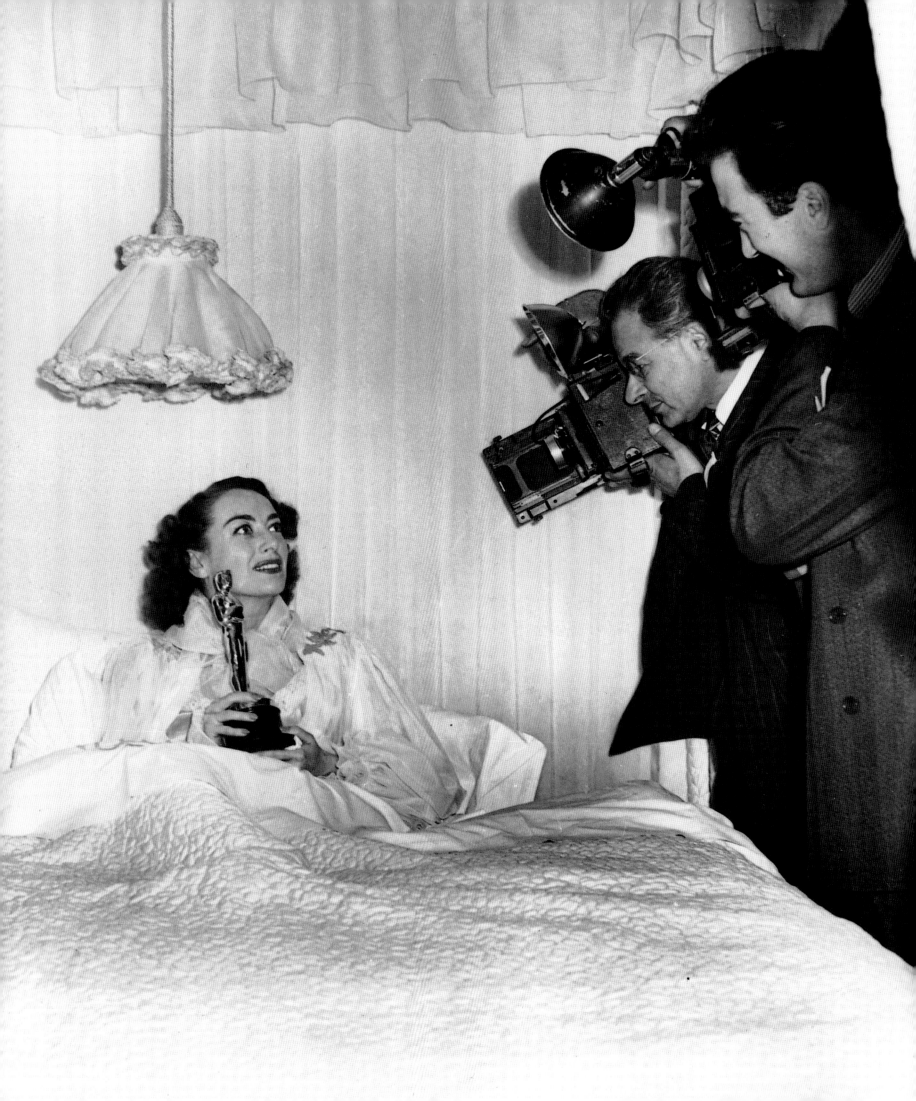

one-third; where once Hollywood could count on ninety million customers per week, it now had only sixty million, heading downward to the roughly twenty million it was playing to in the late sixties. Warners did not cut its production as radically as the other studios did, but like them it began trimming long-term employees—hiring talent only as needed—and generally tightening its belt. It would not lose a lot of money in the fifties and sixties, but it would not return to fiscal health or indeed to something like the production standards of the thirties and forties until Steve Ross acquired the studio in the early seventies.

More to our interest, however, is the sudden and radical change in subject matter that struck the studio almost immediately after the war ended. Some of the films it made were very good, but they did not exhibit the communitarian values or the fundamental good nature of the old Warner movies. They tended to explore hurt, isolated, and mostly inconsolable individuals. One has to concede that they reflected postwar America very well: a country looking for suburban luxe, for a rather heedless individualism, and for love in all the wrong, *noir*ish places. *Mildred Pierce* set the tone in 1945. Her career in disarray, Joan Crawford had come over from MGM looking for roles like this and she took to Mildred with a sort of doomy relish. She starts out baking pies in her kitchen

for extra money and almost overnight becomes the millionaire owner of a restaurant chain. In the process she falls for the wrong guy (a louche Zachary Scott) and turns her mean-mouthed daughter (Ann Blyth) into a grasping slattern who first takes her man away from mom and then murders him. It's a woman's picture—lots of suffering—with *film noir* balls. It's full of grasping upward mobility and a heedless inability to predict the long-term consequences of the activities it portrays. Crawford made a number of similar films in the forties and early fifties, most notably the almost forgotten *The Damned Don't Cry* (1950), based loosely on the career of Virginia Hill, the gangster Bugsy Siegel's inamorata.

After her came a sort of deluge. John Huston was becoming the dominant Warner director in this period and although he cast himself as a colorful, almost piratical figure in Hollywood at the time he loved dark and cynical themes. He once told film critic Kenneth Turan that such subjects shone "like a black opal" to him. He also loved

OPPOSITE Joan Crawford the morning after the Academy Awards, March 8, 1946, holding the Oscar she received for her role in *Mildred Pierce*. RIGHT John Huston discusses a scene with Humphrey Bogart and Lauren Bacall on the set of *Key Largo*, 1948.

exotic settings, the sheer adventure of getting a cast and crew into rough country, and seeing how the attendant difficulties would impact the story he was telling. His *Key Largo* (1948), in which a mobster (Edward G. Robinson) and his entourage invade a shuttered resort on an island off Florida was such a picture—though it was largely, claustrophobically, a studio shoot. In an odd way it's a regressive kind of film, with the gangster seen as a kind of fascist and Humphrey Bogart playing a Rick-like character, a war hero trying to opt out of action against the sadistic Robinson, but ultimately triumphing over him. The difference between this film and the classic Warner crime films is that it is much more bleakly and intricately psychological in its workings. And a lot more talkative, as Huston's films tended to be when compared with those of Raoul Walsh, for example.

His *The Treasure of the Sierra Madre* in 1948 was much more a classic Huston film: a small group of men invading harsh country intent on wresting a "treasure" from it, but falling into deadly difficulties (represented by Bogart's growing paranoia, at first comical, later murderous). In this film, as in others of the time, the cash nexus is less significant as a motivator than it was formerly. Now it is human perversity that sets the film's bitterly ironic tone.

Even when the studio addressed a socially conscious theme, as it did in *Storm Warning* (1951), about the Ku Klux Klan dominating a southern town, it did so in a new spirit. The writers, Richard Brooks and Daniel Fuchs, actually borrowed their basic situation from Tennessee Williams' *A Streetcar Named Desire*. Young wife (Doris Day, rather good in a serious role) is in sexual thrall to brutish Brandoish husband (Steve Cochran), while visiting older sister (Ginger Rogers) stirred up trouble between them. This time, though, the main issue is more political than sexual. He's a member of the KKK and she accidentally witnesses him committing murder. The film is shot in an admirably *noir*ish manner by Stuart Heisler, and it ends powerfully with the Klan flogging Rogers for her refusal to bend to its will. Again, this is a charged-up variant on a standard Warner trope, modernized, somewhat sensationalized for the postwar audience as the studio groped for relevance in a changing world.

It was undoubtedly *White Heat* in 1949 that offered the most powerful effort in that regard. It was Cagney returning to his gangster roots, but as filmmaker-historian Andrew Bergman remarks, somehow more menac-

ing now that he had gained weight (in both senses of the word) and his fundamentally anarchical spirit was touched by middle age. "Let's make him nuts," Cagney claims to have said as he contemplated the role. In other words, let's not rationalize Cody Jarrett's murderous behavior as the result of poverty or other sociological causes. It was wonderfully liberating to Cagney; if his behavior was the product of some loose genetic screw he was not obliged to take responsibility for his depredations. He was free to plunk himself down in his mother's lap for comfort when his blinding headaches rendered him impotent to lead his Dillinger-like gang. He was free to abuse Virginia Mayo's gang moll or idly pump bullets into anyone who had the misfortune to cross his path. He is finally free for self-immolation when, cornered by the cops, he climbs to the top of an oil storage tank (conveniently shaped like a globe) and blows himself up in a mushroom cloud of smoke.

The atomic-age symbolism was obvious. So was the fact that this was beloved James Cagney, the star who had best symbolized the spirit that had made the studio great, who was destroying himself. In effect, *White Heat* said that all the old star and generic bets were off, that the studio would henceforth grope for an authentic voice in which to speak to a new, less predictable, less idealistically defined world.

RICHARD SCHICKEL

ABOVE In *Storm Warning*, 1951, Ginger Rogers accidentally witnesses her brother-in-law, played by Steve Cochran, committing a murder as a member of the KKK. OPPOSITE Half-sheet poster art for *The Treasure of the Sierra Madre*, 1948. Human perversity set the film's bitterly ironic tone. OVERLEAF The last scene from *White Heat*, 1949 with James Cagney on the "top of the world."

THE ATOMIC-AGE
SYMBOLISM WAS OBVIOUS.
SO WAS THE FACT THAT
THIS WAS BELOVED
JAMES CAGNEY, THE
STAR WHO HAD BEST
SYMBOLIZED THE SPIRIT
THAT HAD MADE THE
STUDIO GREAT, WHO WAS
DESTROYING HIMSELF.

ALMOST AT WAR

By 1941, as war raged, much of Europe had been seized by Germany, British cities were under constant aerial bombardment, and Russia was engaged in fierce fighting against the Nazi invaders, but until December the United States was officially non-belligerent and neutral. Hollywood was constrained to maintain the restrictions imposed by the Neutrality Act and not engage in hostile action against Germany. Isolationists were highly vocal, and Charles Lindbergh, their leading celebrity figurehead, had testified before Congress, urging that a pact be negotiated with Hitler ensuring peace. The Naval Air Corps assisted in the production of *Dive Bomber*

(1941), a Technicolor tribute to the service and America's readiness, with Errol Flynn as an air medic working on the problem of pilot "blackout" during crash dives. Ronald Reagan as an Atlantic ferry pilot in *International Squadron* (1941) joins the Royal Air Force. Brash, cocksure, and irresponsible, he redeems himself in combat. The same fate befalls James Cagney in *Captains of the Clouds* (1942), his first film in Technicolor, in which he is a self-confident Canadian bush pilot who signs up for the Royal Canadian Air Force. Although it was made while neutrality prevailed, it was not released until after Pearl Harbor. Before then Warner Bros. also distributed the British documentary *Target for Tonight* (1941)

JAMES CAGNEY

"CAPTAINS OF CLOUDS"
in Technicolor

DENNIS MORGAN ★ BRENDA MARSHALL

ALAN HALE · GEORGE TOBIAS · REGINALD GARDINER · REGINALD DENNY

Directed by
MICHAEL CURTIZ
Country of Origin U.S.A.

Presented by
WARNER BROS.

directed by Harry Watt, reconstructing a bombing mission over Germany by the crew of an R.A.F. Wellington, F for Freddie, and it was effective propaganda in winning sympathy for beleaguered Britain.

Made before Pearl Harbor but released early in 1942 was *All Through the Night,* directed by Vincent Sherman, which made fun of the Nazis yet at the same time demonstrated that the American homeland was vulnerable. Humphrey Bogart plays a gambler who, while trying to find how his favorite cheesecake maker has been murdered, stumbles into a fifth-column plot to blow up a battleship in New York harbor, with Conrad Veidt as chief spy. By the time of its release America had joined the war, but was more than ready to laugh at this comedy thriller. In the cast was Phil Silvers, who was also teamed with Jimmy Durante in *You're in the Army Now* (1941), the precursor of many crass rookie comedies.

The espionage formula would also become a staple of wartime filmmaking, and in the month of Pearl Harbor, John Garfield was a hospital intern who thwarted a Nazi agent posing as a clinical psychologist in *Dangerously They Live* (1941), a modest melodrama typical of many others to come.

OPPOSITE Olympe Bradna and Ronald Reagan share a toast in *International Squadron,* 1941. ABOVE Half-sheet poster art for James Cagney's first film in Technicolor, *Captain of the Clouds,* 1942. BELOW John Garfield as Dr. Mike Lewis in *Dangerously They Live,* 1941.

1942

✱ In *Kings Row* Ronald Reagan loses both legs (above)

✱ Carole Lombard dies in an air crash on a war-bonds tour

✱ James Cagney makes his Technicolor debut in *Captains of the Clouds*

✱ The U.S. Navy engages the Japanese in the Battle of Midway

✱ Bette Davis makes *In This Our Life* and *Now, Voyager*

✱ Errol Flynn as a downed flier escapes across Germany in *Desperate Journey*

✱ The Guadalcanal landings are the first U.S. Marine offensive attack of the war

✱ James Cagney triumphs as George M. Cohan in *Yankee Doodle Dandy*

✱ The Siege of Stalingrad begins

✱ Gasoline is rationed in the United States

✱ *Casablanca* has its premiere in New York

ABOVE Ann Sheridan as Randy Monaghan, holding Ronald Reagan as Drake McHugh, who has suddenly realized that he has lost both his legs, in *Kings Row*, 1942.
RIGHT Humphrey Bogart as Alfred "Gloves" Donahue and Jane Darwell as "Ma" in *All Through the Night*, 1942.

THE YANKEE DOODLE BOY

In World War I the Broadway showman George M. Cohan composed "Over There," which would become the unofficial anthem of the doughboys who sailed to France in 1917. The 1942 film biography of Cohan, *Yankee Doodle Dandy,* reprised the song and once again it symbolized American soldiers at war. The Warner Bros. film was a spectacular musical, a patriotic flag-waver directed by the versatile

Michael Curtiz, with James Cagney playing the lead in a dynamic Oscar-winning turn.

Few actors have ever dominated a film as he did this. Taking a role of a great fellow Irish-American that had been rejected by Fred Astaire, he steamrollered his way through a tremendous musical with electric energy, the passion of his performance transcending all the implausibilities, contrivances, and clichés of the Hollywood biopic. At odds with the studio and renowned for his rebellious streak, Cagney had also

been fingered in some quarters for being too left wing, and even though the Soviet Union was now an ally of the United States, there was an entrenched fear of Communism. Cagney persuaded Jack Warner that only he could play Cohan, clearly aware that the Grand Old Flag, Born on the Fourth of July sentiments would enhance his status as a loyal American. Improbably—although in musicals such absurdities are forgivable and accepted—he bookends the film by calling at the White House for a one-to-one evening chat with Franklin D. Roosevelt, who has summoned him in the nation's hour of need to give him an honor. The showman narrates the story of life in the theater to the President in a flashback interspersed with exuberant musical numbers. At the conclusion he starts off down the grand staircase and bursts into a joyous, precisely timed dance. Cagney was actually less a dancer, more a hoofer who had learned his steps in the high-pressure world of vaudeville and musicals in the 1920s. He would bounce around the stage, stiff-backed yet agile, in a series of rhythmic jerks and rapid taps, his confidence and enthusiasm deceiving his audience into believing they were watching sublime stylishness. Nobody could wing it like Cagney.

OPPOSITE James Cagney as Little Johnny Jones in *Yankee Doodle Dandy,* 1942. ABOVE Cagney plays tennis on Jack Warner's tennis court in 1935.

"THE GERMANS WORE GRAY, YOU WORE BLUE"

IN LIKE FLYNN

If anyone could play a tarnished hero Errol Flynn had to be a prime contender. In *They Died With Their Boots On* (1941), directed by Raoul Walsh, he took on the role of George Armstrong Custer, progressing from a foppish, academically dim West Pointer to a U.S. Army general who, through a combination of reckless courage and hotheaded bravado, manages to lose the 7th Cavalry and his own life battling Chief Crazy Horse and his Sioux braves at Little Big Horn. Walsh substituted for Michael Curtiz, who had fallen out with Flynn, and the score—uplifted with the jaunty Irish air "Garry Owen" that became the 7th's marching song—was by Max Steiner.

As history it was as farfetched as most biographical accounts emanating from Hollywood studios, but as entertainment it was masterly, not least for the eighth (and final) pairing of Flynn with Olivia de Havilland, the wife who sees him off to battle. The timing of its release, when America had become engaged in a rather mightier conflict than the Indian Wars of the 1870s, added to its instant appeal.

Flynn excelled again as *Gentleman Jim* (1942), the humble bank clerk James J. Corbett from a pugnacious working-class background in San Francisco, who became renowned as a boxer, and was known as the "Father of Modern Boxing," he beat John L. Sullivan (Ward Bond) for the world's first heavyweight title. Walsh again directed, with Alexis Smith as his society love interest.

In between he had played an Australian piloting an R.A.F. bomber shot down over Germany in *Desperate Journey* (1942), also with Walsh directing. Flynn and his crew, including Ronald Reagan as his number two, escape across Germany committing mayhem en route and outwitting the Nazis (who are singularly incompetent) at every turn. Eventually stealing a captured British aircraft from under the German noses, Flynn declares as they cross the English Channel "Now for Australia, and a crack at those Japs."

Flynn was unfit for military service, and when he tried to enlist was shown the door. In 1942, Flynn was charged with and acquitted of statutory rape, the case adding to his notoriety and introducing the mischievous phrase "In like Flynn.

OPPOSITE Errol Flynn as George Armstrong Custer in *They Died with Their Boots On,* 1941. ABOVE One sheet poster art for *Desperate Journey,* 1942, in which Flynn led a downed R.A.F. bomber crew escaping across Germany. ABOVE RIGHT Swedish poster art for *Air Force.*

1943

∗ Howard Hawks makes *Air Force,* centered on a B-17 bomber (above)

∗ Roosevelt and Churchill meet at Casablanca to discuss the war

∗ *Casablanca* and Michael Curtiz win Academy Awards for Best Picture and Best Director

∗ Olivia de Havilland wins the case against Warner Bros. for adding on suspension time to her contract

∗ *This is the Army* is a top moneymaker for Army Relief

∗ Leslie Howard dies in an airliner shot down by the Germans

∗ The Allies land in Sicily

∗ Bette Davis sings in *Thank Your Lucky Stars*

∗ Italy surrenders to Allied forces

∗ *Mission to Moscow* is made to sanitize American-Russian relations

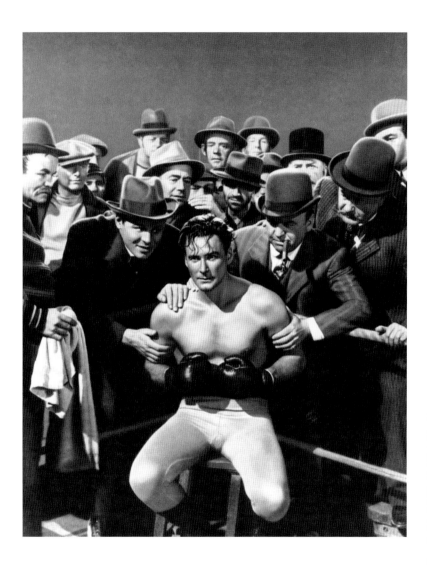

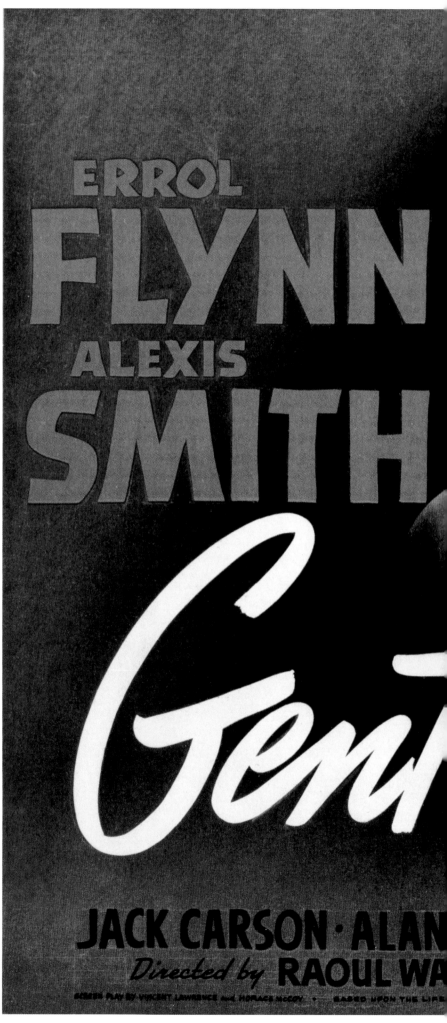

ABOVE Errol Flynn as world heavyweight boxing
title contender James J. Corbett.
RIGHT Half-sheet poster art for *Gentleman Jim*, 1942.

Ieman Jim

IALE
SH

MES J. CORBETT

Presented by
WARNER BROS.

A WARNER BROS. ~ FIRST NATIONAL PICTURE

"WE HAVE THE STARS"

Bette Davis, holding up well in a lackluster role as Monty Woolley's secretary in the film from the Moss Hart-George S. Kaufman Broadway hit comedy *The Man Who Came to Dinner* (1942) and stealing Olivia de Havilland's husband in John Huston's *In This Our Life* (1942), scored a spectacular success opposite Paul Henreid in *Now, Voyager* (1942) a great romantic tearjerker directed by Irving Rapper. He was the alternative to Michael Curtiz, who had been rejected by Davis. As Charlotte Vale she is a frumpy Boston heiress, repressed by her tyrannical mother (Gladys Cooper), and rescued from a breakdown by a sensitive psychiatrist (Claude Rains), who steers her transformation into an attractive, poised, and confident woman. She embarks on a hopeless affair with a married architect who is unable to leave his emotionally dependent wife. Eventually Vale becomes a surrogate mother to the less stable of his daughters, and as Max Steiner's poignant score swells and he asks her if she will be happy, answers, "Oh Jerry, don't let's ask for the moon. We have the stars."

Memorable was Henreid's way with a cigarette in an era when many people smoked in films without any notions of risk. He would light two cigarettes in his mouth and pass one to her, a courting trick that became standard for lovers everywhere the film was shown. In fact, this trick had been used in a Bette Davis film for First National ten years earlier, *The Rich are Always With Us* (1932).

Davis would fill another sympathetic role in *Watch on the Rhine* (1943), from Lillian Hellman's play, and in Vincent Sherman's *Old Acquaintance* (1943), from John Van Druten's play, she co-starred with Miriam Hopkins as her friend and rival across twenty years. Their real-life enmity is apparent on screen.

It was followed by *Mr. Skeffington* (1944), also directed by Sherman, in which she plays a selfish wife, with Claude Rains her unloved and long-suffering husband who returns blind, after internment in a wartime concentration camp. Unable to see that she has become hideous following an illness, he eventually makes the happy discovery that she now actually wants him.

OPPOSITE Paul Henreid as Jerry Durrance lights one for Bette Davis as Charlotte Vale in *Now, Voyager*, 1942.
ABOVE One-sheet poster art for the film.

"THE GERMANS WORE GRAY, YOU WORE BLUE"

WE'LL ALWAYS HAVE CASABLANCA

It was expected to be a routine love triangle, with a topical espionage background and an exotic setting that could easily be conjured up on a Burbank sound stage. Various contract players were announced and discarded—Ronald Reagan, Dennis Morgan, and Ann Sheridan among them. George Raft lobbied for the male lead but it went instead to Humphrey Bogart, now riding high after his triumph in *The Maltese Falcon* (1941). His casting opposite Ingrid Bergman presented problems. Taller than him, she had to be photographed carefully. The sexual chemistry between them was closely monitored by his jealous real-life wife Mayo Methot, who would

make unscheduled set visits to ensure nothing was going on. The polyglot cast assembled for the exacting Hungarian director Michael Curtiz was a veritable United Nations of involuntary exiles from the Nazis, with Bogart and his loyal aide, played by Dooley Wilson, almost the only Americans present. By some miracle of serendipity everything worked and *Casablanca* became one of the most popular films ever made, its lines memorized and recited by generations born decades after Rick and Ilsa parted on the tarmac in its celebrated final scene.

As the determinedly neutral American nightclub owner in the Moroccan outpost of Vichy France before Pearl Harbor, whose outward indifference masks a heavy emotional burden, Bogart was perfect casting. Rick's past is reawakened when Ilsa (Bergman), the former lover who left him in Paris the day

the Germans marched in, arrives suddenly accompanied by a husband, Victor (Paul Henreid)—an icon of the Resistance. The old passion is rekindled, observed by Rick's friend the local police chief Louis (Claude Rains), who has survived by charming both sides. Some commentators see Rick's crisis of conscience and his eventual abandonment of neutrality as a metaphor for America's decision to enter the war.

Casablanca was shot fast under strict wartime restrictions, often on recycled sets, The Desert Song providing the medina, Now, Voyager the Paris railroad station. Quaintly endearing mistakes were made in haste. Letters of transit signed by General De Gaulle, leader of the Free French, would have been of as much use under Vichy as a release from Colditz signed by Winston Churchill. The Germans in the nightclub should not have sung "Watch on the Rhine," banned by the Nazis, and only substituted for the "Horst Wessel Song" because the legal department could not clear the rights in South America. The Nazi overseer who arrives to represent the Third Reich is given an airport welcome worthy of a general, but is a mere major.

Unhappy endings are often regarded as bad for box office, but Casablanca totally rebutted this perception. The most common experience in wartime was the parting of loved ones, and perhaps the doomed romance of Rick and Ilsa, and Rick's noble sacrifice, offered solace for millions who had faced that reality.

OPPOSITE Off set Bogart and Bergman discuss a scene while ABOVE LEFT Bogart with his own camera records the action on the set of Casablanca. ABOVE RIGHT Claude Rains, Paul Henreid, Ingrid Bergman, and Humphrey Bogart publicize the movie. BELOW Bogart and Henreid play chess on set, watched carefully by Claude Rains on the left.

ABOVE Happier times in Paris. RIGHT "If you can play it for her, you can play it for me," Dooley Wilson as Sam placates Humphrey Bogart as Rick.

OPPOSITE French poster art for Casablanca. ABOVE "The problems of three little people don't amount to a hill of beans in this crazy world." Tension grips the airport as Heinreid, Bogart, and Bergman watch Rains handle the situation. RIGHT Bogart sees the love of his life leave with her husband.

A HARD ACT TO FOLLOW

The massive success of *Casablanca* had taken Warner Bros. by surprise, despite the fact that they had deliberately planned to reposition Humphrey Bogart as a romantic star. His film prior to it had been an action thriller with a war slant, *Across the Pacific* (1942), with Mary Astor and Sydney Greenstreet from *The Maltese Falcon* cast. Its climax was a Japanese onslaught on the Panama Canal (it was to have been Pearl Harbor but real events took over during preparation, although the geographically inappropriate title was retained). Bogart's character, court-martialed and thrown out of the army, plays a cover for some espionage on a Japanese ship. John Huston began the direction but left to join the Signal Corps, handing over the reins to Vincent Sherman without explaining how Bogart was to be extricated from an impossible situation at the hands of the enemy, and the end sequences show it.

After *Casablanca* came *Action in the North Atlantic* (1943), in which Bogart is number two to Raymond Massey, the skipper of a Liberty ship on the dangerous Atlantic run, forced by circumstance to take command. The Merchant Marine was unglamorous and unregarded, yet supplied the lifeblood to Britain and the Soviet Union, both suffering hideous losses from U-boat attacks. The Office of War Information (OWI) had prevailed on Jack Warner to have the film made, and it was directed by Lloyd Bacon, with uncredited backup by Raoul Walsh and Byron Haskin. The screenplay was by John Howard Lawson, and after the war it was used as evidence against him by the House Committee on Un-American Activities, finding the ecstatic reception of the battered convoy by the people of Murmansk unacceptable and repugnant propaganda.

After making *Sahara* at Columbia, playing a U.S. tank commander routing Rommel's Afrika Korps in the desert, with the aid of a United Nations motley of rescued stragglers,

ABOVE Half-sheet poster art for *Action in the North Atlantic*. OPPOSITE TOP Humphrey Bogart, Raymond Massey, and cast in the burning seas in *Action in the North Atlantic*. OPPOSITE Lorre, Dantine, Bogart, and Tobias on a freighter.

Bogart returned to Burbank for *Passage to Marseille* (1944), a reunion of a significant number of *Casablanca* alumni (Rains, Greenstreet, Lorre) under the direction of Michael Curtiz. The story, structured with flashbacks within flashbacks, has him as a French journalist banished before the war to Devil's Island on a trumped-up charge for infuriating the appeasers, escaping with others, and after being shipwrecked and rescued by a Vichy tramp steamer after days adrift, joining the Free French to fight the Germans. Based on a Nordhoff and Hall novel (the authors of *Mutiny on the Bounty*) it is less than satisfactory, rendered doubly confusing to today's audiences unaware of the muddled politics of France during World War II.

LUCKY STARS

One of the phenomena of wartime programming was the emergence of patriotic musical extravaganzas corralling as many stars as possible, sometimes in cameos or "blackouts," or performing unexpected party pieces, with a flimsy storyline providing some sort of link. They were by no means confined to Warner Bros. Paramount had *Star-Spangled Rhythm,* MGM *Thousands Cheer,* United Artists *Stage Door Canteen.* In some respects they were a throwback to the early days of sound, when musical revues were churned out until audiences tired of them.

In World War I the young recruit Irving Berlin had staged an army show at his training base, calling it *Yip Yip, Yaphank,* with his soldier's lament ("Oh, How I Hate to Get Up in the Morning") as one of its highlights. It was so successful that it transferred with its army cast to New York, the evening ending with the uniformed men singing "We're On Our Way to France" and marching offstage, up the aisles, and out of the theater. In World War II Berlin revived the idea. *This is the Army* played on Broadway and toured nationally, raising $2 million for Army Emergency Relief. Warner Bros. turned it into a Technicolor film directed by Michael Curtiz, and the minimal plot had a dancer, George Murphy, staging the show in World War I, and his son, played by Ronald Reagan, repeating the idea in World War II. With nineteen Berlin numbers, including Kate Smith's definitive rendering of "God Bless America," it was one of the war's considerable morale-boosting efforts, heightened by many stars giving their services free, and the box-office profits went to the Relief Fund.

1944

* *Hollywood Canteen* celebrates a starry wartime institution (above Bette Davis and John Garfield)

* Cary Grant stars in *Destination Tokyo* and *Arsenic and Old Lace,* the latter made in 1941 but held until the play closed on Broadway

* Bette Davis ages twenty-six years in *Mr. Skeffington,* with Claude Rains

* The two-year Siege of Leningrad ends

* Fredric March portrays Mark Twain in a vivid biography

* Humphrey Bogart's *Passage to Marseille* disappoints

* The Allies land in Normandy in the biggest invasion in history

* Paris is liberated

* *The Desert Song* is remade with Nazis as the villains

* London comes under fire from V1 and V2 missiles

* Glenn Miller disappears during a flight across the English Channel

SOOTHING MUSIC

Musicals were perceived as a welcome escape from the burdens, shortages, and anxieties of wartime, and often generated nostalgic yearnings for what were thought to be more innocent times some forty years earlier. In *Shine On Harvest Moon* Ann Sheridan (her singing dubbed by Lynn Martin) and Dennis Morgan played Nora Bayes and Jack Norworth, a husband and wife team who graced the Broadway stage of the 1900s, although their story was necessarily sanitized. Lacking too was color, reserved only for the title song.

The old warhorse, *The Desert Song*, was more fortunate, and starred Morgan and Irene Manning. Originally a Sigmund Romberg operetta, this was made into an early sound film in 1929. The version released in 1944 brought the story of oppressed Riffs and the heroic Red Shadow into a more topical context, in which the Vichy French government, with finance from the Third Reich, is using them as forced labor to build a railroad in Morocco. Directed by Robert Florey, it was filmed in desert locations in New Mexico. Problems with the OWI and the shifting midwar political position of France held up the release for a year but it was a box office success. It was filmed again in 1953, staring Gordon MacRae and Kathryn Grayson, but Florey's version is considered the best.

The background of *Thank Your Lucky Stars* was Hollywood itself, with S.Z. Sakall and Edward Everett Horton putting on a charity benefit that features such novelties as Errol Flynn singing, Ida Lupino, Olivia de Havilland, and George Tobias jiving, Alan Hale and Jack Carson performing a comedy song, "Goin' North," and most famously Bette Davis bewailing "They're Either Too Young or Too Old," a mordant song by Arthur Schwartz and Sammy Cahn, followed by a lively jitterbug.

In the movie *Hollywood Canteen* (1944), a couple of soldiers spend their last nights before embarkation to the South Pacific at the so-named establishment on Cahuenga Boulevard, which had been founded in 1942 by Bette Davis, John Garfield, and Jules Stein of MCA to entertain servicemen entirely free of charge. At the Hollywood Canteen stars performed for nothing, and also waited tables, washed dishes, cooked, and cleaned, alongside many other volunteers from the film and radio industries. The admirable institution welcomed nearly three million uniformed guests between 1942 and 1945. In the film one of the soldiers meets the young star Joan Leslie, on whom he has a crush, and the other finds he is dancing with Joan Crawford. With the Andrews Sisters, Jimmy Dorsey's band, Carmen Cavallaro's Orchestra, Joe E. Brown, Eddie Cantor, and many others taking the stage, it served to remind troops on active duty overseas that Hollywood was right behind them.

OPPOSITE Jane Wyman and Jack Carson perform in *Hollywood Canteen*, 1944. ABOVE In the same film, Bette Davis sings (sort of).
BELOW Dennis Morgan, Ann Sheridan, Marie Wilson, and Jack Carson wait backstage in *Shine on Harvest Moon*, 1944.

DEEP AND DARK

The two films that Cary Grant made at Warner Bros. during the war were in considerable contrast. In *Destination Tokyo* (1943) directed by Delmer Daves, he was a submarine commander charged with a difficult mission—to sneak into Tokyo Bay in order to prepare for General Doolittle's B-25 bombing raid from the U.S.S. *Hornet,* itself the subject of an MGM film *Thirty Seconds Over Tokyo.* Although overlong, the film builds its tension carefully, and particularly memorable is an improvised appendix operation on a crewman at an awkward time deep in enemy waters. Grant is calm and resolute as the captain of the usual assorted crew, including John Garfield and Dane Clark. It was the performance that served as the blueprint for Tony Curtis's sharply observed and hilarious Grant impersonation in *Some Like it Hot* fifteen years later.

Frank Capra's screwball black comedy *Arsenic and Old Lace* was actually filmed in 1941, but not shown until 1944. The reason for the delay was that the play by Joseph Kesselring enjoyed an unprecedented long run on Broadway, and by agreement the film release had to wait until it came off. In the film Grant, having just married Priscilla Lane, finds his honeymoon deferred when he discovers that his sweet, totally dotty aunts (Josephine Hull and Jean Adair) are in the business of bumping off men and having them buried in the basement by their younger brother (John Alexander), who believes that he is President Theodore Roosevelt digging the Panama Canal. In spite of the action being restricted to a house in Brooklyn, the edgy farce cracks along at a breakneck pace. Grant was later embarrassed by the degree of overacting he expended on his role. He gave his six-figure salary to the U.S. War Relief Fund.

ABOVE Cary Grant and Priscilla Lane walking down Ave. D to the set of *Arsenic and Old Lace* in 1941, although the film was not released until 1944. BELOW John Garfield and Cary Grant in *Destination Tokyo,* 1943. OPPOSITE Advertising art for *Arsenic and Old Lace.*

BACALL'S ELECTRIC DEBUT

While filming *Passage to Marseille* Humphrey Bogart was visited by the director Howard Hawks and introduced to a nineteen-year-old New York model whose face had been on the cover of the March 1943 issue of *Harper's Bazaar*. Hawks told him she would be playing the lead in Bogart's next picture, even though she had not acted in films before. *To Have and Have Not* (1944) was based on a lesser Hemingway novel in which Chinese immigrants were smuggled into Florida from Cuba. The plotline was changed by William Faulkner and Jules Furthman to take account of political sensitivities, and the "Good Neighbor" policy that Roosevelt had inherited from Hoover and enlarged to maintain good relations with Latin America.

Bogart played Harry Morgan, an American boat owner in Martinique soon after the fall of France, who ekes a living by taking visitors fishing and engaging in occasional gunrunning. The harborside is atmospheric in the best Burbank tradition, Hoagy Carmichael strums and sings in the waterfront bar, Walter Brennan is an amiable drinking companion. Like Rick in *Casablanca,* Harry initially wants to remain neutral and aloof from the war, but a mysterious, captivating young woman (Bacall) is persuasive in recruiting his assistance in smuggling

an underground leader from the Vichy-run island. He commits more rapidly than his predecessor, without the self-pitying equivocation that would have seemed less relevant by 1944.

Bacall's debut was conspicuous, swamping much of the rest of the action. Although less than half her co-star's age she approached him as a sexual equal with a predatory appetite, a sultry enchantress with a slow, husky voice, and one of the screen's most memorable come-hither lines: "You know how to whistle, don't you? Put your lips together and blow." To the delight of the public the sexual chemistry so apparent on screen erupted in reality and the pair became lovers, marrying soon after Bogart was able to divorce his wife Mayo Methot.

ABOVE On the set of *To Have and Have Not,* 1944, Bogart and Bacall play chess. RIGHT Three-sheet poster art for *To Have and Have Not.* OPPOSITE "The sexual chemistry so apparent on screen erupted in reality and the pair became lovers."

1945

✳ Joan Crawford triumphs in *Mildred Pierce* (above)

✳ President Roosevelt dies soon after the start of his fourth term

✳ Lauren Bacall makes her debut in *To Have and Have Not*

✳ Errol Flynn's *Objective, Burma!* creates controversy

✳ Hitler commits suicide in Berlin, Doenitz is named the new Führer

✳ The Allies defeat Germany and V.E. Day is celebrated

✳ George Gershwin is the subject of the lavish biopic *Rhapsody in Blue*

✳ Japan surrenders after the atomic destruction of Hiroshima and Nagasaki

✳ John Garfield brilliantly plays a blinded serviceman in *Pride of the Marines*

✳ The United Nations is founded

ABOVE Three sheet poster art for *Mildred Pierce*. RIGHT Walter Huston as Ambassador Davies and Vladimir Sokoloff as the Russian President in *Mission to Moscow*, 1943.

KEEPING THE LID ON

Hollywood output during the war years was subject to intense scrutiny and censorship, with Washington totally accepting the value of film as a propaganda weapon. One of the prime targets was negativity, the suggestion that American democracy was weak and ineffective against the Axis sledgehammer, and when the Office of War Information Bureau of Motion Pictures began its work in earnest in 1942, it viewed with alarm some of the movies that had gone out before it could exert its weight. Henceforth all screenplays were to be vetted before production, and at later stages desired changes would be enforced. Its seal of approval meant the granting of a license to export, and although much of Europe was no longer available, the Latin-American market, the British Isles, and the far-flung British Empire were sustained by a steady flow of American films.

The issues that concerned the OWI were not confined to military matters. Films critical of social policy were severely restricted, and regarded as not only bad for civilian morale but also showing the United States in a bad light internationally. References to racial tensions were deemed unacceptable. Some Warner Bros. films—such as *I Am a Fugitive from a Chain*

who had known little of Soviet politics beforehand, was denounced as a fellow traveler and hung out to dry.

Spiritual values were defended in *God is my Co-Pilot* (1945) with Dennis Morgan playing Colonel Robert Lee Scott of the Flying Tigers, with the hypothesis that a belief in the Almighty gave the strength to win. The film was released at the end of the war, and had a certain resemblance to *Sergeant York* in proposing divine justification for killing the enemy, but in this instance the religious proselytizing marred an otherwise straightforward war film.

Raoul Walsh's hard-hitting action film *Objective, Burma!* ran into serious trouble when shown at the Warner Theatre, London, in 1945. Errol Flynn was on peak form as the leader of a group of American paratroopers dropped into enemy jungle to knock out a radar installation, then enduring a desperate struggle to get out. It was tense, grim, and well made. What it lacked was an acknowledgement that Burma was mostly a British and Australian theater of operations. Uproar ensued, led by veterans of the Burma campaign, and the film was voluntarily withdrawn after only a few screenings. It was not shown again in Britain until the 1950s.

Gang or *They Won't Forget*—could never have been made in the wartime climate.

Perhaps the most notorious Warner Bros. film made during the war was *Mission to Moscow,* directed by Michael Curtiz and based on a book by Joseph E. Davies, a former U.S. ambassador to the Soviet Union. After Germany's invasion in 1942, America and Russia had by necessity become allies, but Washington was acutely aware that Stalin was generally perceived as a dictator as infamous as Hitler, and that communist doctrines were inimical to American democracy. Such peacetime attitudes were no longer relevant and something had to be done to make the Russians acceptable. The film, covertly urged by Roosevelt himself, and written by Howard Koch, was blatant whitewash, suggesting that the defendants in the notorious 1938 purge trials were traitors anxious to betray their country to the Nazis, and that Stalin was a trustworthy ally who had long recognized the threat from Germany even when America was disinterested. Koch and Curtiz, capable filmmakers, made the thesis look convincing in the context of 1943. After the war the film was seen as profoundly embarrassing and was hastily buried. Koch,

ABOVE LEFT One-sheet poster art for *God is My Co-Pilot,* 1945.
ABOVE Errol Flynn as Captain Nelson, trekking through the jungle in *Objective, Burma!,* 1945.

BEHIND THE WORDS

Lives of authors often provided material for films in the 1940s, particularly when the biography had significant relevance to the literary output. In *The Adventures of Mark Twain,* much of the life of Samuel Langhorne Clemens on the Mississippi and in the goldfields of California and Nevada provided the material for his writing, and the development of a humorous style that enabled the retention of his place as America's favorite author decades after his death. Irving Rapper's film, adapted by Alan Le May from the play by Harold M. Sherman, took such liberties with the facts that it integrated Twain into his own stories as a participant rather than an observer. Fredric March's performance was strong and, in the latter years of Twain's long life, poignant, rising above the sentimentality.

The Brontës of Haworth were the subject of *Devotion,* directed by Curtis Bernhardt, with Olivia de Havilland as Charlotte (*Jane Eyre*), Ida Lupino as Emily (*Wuthering Heights*), and Nancy Coleman as Anne (*Agnes Grey*). The tortured brother Branwell was played by Arthur Kennedy, Sydney Greenstreet delivered a magisterial Thackeray, and the score was by Korngold. The film was made in 1943, but came out in 1946 due to a glut of unreleased films as well as a consequence of Olivia de Havilland's row with the studio. It was her last Warner Bros. film, and she was given third billing as further punishment. A romanticization of the reality, the film may have been moderately entertaining, but was hardly worth the wait.

Sounder was *The Corn is Green,* the film of Emlyn Williams' play, directed by Irving Rapper, which became a vehicle for Bette Davis. She plays a prim English schoolteacher who sets up a school in a poor Welsh mining village. Discerning keen intelligence and aptitude in a young miner she coaches him hard to win a scholarship to Oxford and a better life, in spite of the wiles of a young woman who tries to stop him by waving her baby in his face. Williams had written the play as a tribute to the teacher who had transformed his own life, and apart from the liberal application of what Hollywood perceived to be Welshness—swirling mists, singing miners, flagstoned kitchens, and an air of theatricality that often goes with Broadway successes—the result was satisfying. Newcomer John Dall made the most of the role of the pupil, in lieu of Richard Waring, who had played the part on Broadway but had the misfortune of being drafted.

OPPOSITE Frederic March as America's greatest humorist in *The Adventures of Mark Twain,* 1944. ABOVE Olivia de Havilland, Paul Henreid, Ida Lupino, and Nancy Coleman in *Devotion,* 1946. BELOW Bette Davis and John Dall in *The Corn is Green,* 1945.

SONG CYCLE

Composers' lives made good excuses for musicals. *Rhapsody in Blue* purported to be a biography of George Gershwin, who more than anyone had successfully spanned the gulf between Tin Pan Alley and the classical auditorium by way of a succession of popular songs and Broadway shows, before dying from a brain tumor at only thirty-eight. Irving Rapper's film was made not long after *Yankee Doodle Dandy* and was stockpiled for a couple of years before its 1945 release. In an echo of the earlier film, Joan Leslie was cast as his lost love and Rosemary DeCamp as the mother raising her two sons George (Mr. Music) and Ira (Mr. Words) on the Lower East Side, with Alexis Smith added as a socialite painter who relinquishes her romantic yen for George in the cause of his genius. A newcomer, Robert Alda, who sadly never made it to major stardom, played Gershwin. Inaccuracies and fictions aside, the chief curiosity of the film lies in contemporary performers appearing as themselves, including the orchestra leader Paul Whiteman, pianists Oscar Levant and Hazel Scott, and Al Jolson, who had been off-screen for years, singing "Swanee" in blackface—"I've been away from you a long time…"—then launching into an intense, fast buck-and-wing much as he had in the show *Sinbad* a quarter of a century earlier.

Even more imaginary was *Night and Day,* based on the life of Cole Porter, in Technicolor and directed by Michael Curtiz. It was handicapped by two factors, the first that its subject was still alive and active, with much great work ahead of him (including his biggest hit musical *Kiss Me Kate*), and second that it was impossible under the Production Code to offer any hint of his homosexuality or that his marriage to Linda Lee Thomas (Alexis Smith again) was a front. Cary Grant as Porter imparted a subtle air that made him so attractive to women. He is first seen as a rich Yale student, then serving in France, and after the war playing the playboy and mingling with the *haut monde,* following with his marriage, his musicals, his accident when a horse crippled him, and so on. Jane Wyman, Ginny Simms, and Mary Martin were among those who performed the songs, but the delicate ironies and inferences of the clever Porter lyrics were muffled by heavy-handed production.

ABOVE Jolson sings again in *Rhapsody in Blue,* 1945.
OPPOSITE Belgian poster art for *Night and Day,* 1946.

CRAWFORD COMEBACK

Joan Crawford's stardom faltered in the mid-1940s and from 1943, when her contract with MGM lapsed, until 1945 she languished at Warner Bros. Her fortieth birthday approaching, it seemed her popularity was over. Then Jerry Wald found her the role of her life. *Mildred Pierce* won her an Oscar, took in a box-office fortune, and put her back in the front rank, with a career extending another twenty-five years. Adapted from a melodramatic novel by James M. Cain, and directed by Michael Curtiz, *Mildred Pierce* blends *film noir* and feminine soap. The noir tone is set at the opening, with a mysterious nocturnal

shooting in a Malibu beach house preceding a flashback that eventually returns to events on that ominous night. Crawford plays an indomitable rags-to-riches female powerhouse who, abandoned by her husband, struggles for the sake of two growing daughters—one nice, the other a nasty snob. Her drive and energy bring huge success in the restaurant business and marriage to a double-crossing playboy (Zachary Scott). The loathsome daughter, compellingly played by Ann Blyth, is the catalyst for what follows—her selfish, calculating, duplicitous behavior leads her mother toward a murder charge. The cast also includes the ever-reliable Jack Carson as a stalwart would-be lover, and Eve Arden as her sardonic business partner.

In *Humoresque*, directed with flair by Jean Negulesco, Crawford is a rich woman obsessed by a poor violinist (John Garfield in a particularly compelling performance, even appearing by cunning camerawork to be playing like a master). In *Possessed*, directed by Curtis Bernhardt, she is a tycoon's wife driven to insanity by her unrequited fixation for an architect, played by Van Heflin. In the melodramatic *Flamingo Road*, another Michael Curtiz film, she maneuvers her way from carnival dancer to the top echelon of a southern town, incurring the wrath of the corrupt sheriff, played by Sydney Greenstreet, who has her jailed. Characters played by Crawford invariably endured emotional torment on a Sisyphean scale.

1946

✷ John Garfield plays a violinist in *Humoresque* with Joan Crawford (above)

✷ Humphrey Bogart and Lauren Bacall star in *The Big Sleep*

✷ Fritz Lang makes *Cloak and Dagger* with Gary Cooper

✷ Winston Churchill refers to the "Iron Curtain" in a speech given in Fulton, Missouri

✷ *Devotion*, the story of the Brontë sisters, is released after a three-year delay following the Olivia de Havilland dispute

✷ Cary Grant plays Cole Porter in *Night and Day*

✷ Bette Davis plays twin sisters in *A Stolen Life*

✷ Ingrid Bergman and Gary Cooper appear in *Saratoga Trunk*

✷ Curtis Bernhardt directs Barbara Stanwyck in *My Reputation*

✷ Warner Bros. makes a profit of $20 million

OPPOSITE Joan Crawford making pies in *Mildred Pierce*, 1945.
LEFT Michael Curtiz directs Joan Crawford in *Flamingo Road*, 1949.
ABOVE John Garfield and Joan Crawford in *Humoresque*, 1946.

"THE GERMANS WORE GRAY, YOU WORE BLUE"

Jack Carlson as Wally Fay and Joan Crawford as Mildred Pierce, the role that won her an Oscar and put her back in the front rank, extending her career another twenty-five years.

SECOND THOUGHTS ARE BETTER

The second film that Humphrey Bogart and Lauren Bacall made together was *The Big Sleep.* Directed by Howard Hawks, it was scripted by William Faulkner, Leigh Brackett, and Jules Furthman from Raymond Chandler's Philip Marlowe novel, in which the private eye is hired by the dying General Sternwood to find a missing employee and rescue a wayward daughter (Martha Vickers) from bad company. Playing the older sister, Bacall is cool, assured, and easily a match for Marlowe's repartee. They become romantically enmeshed as he makes his way through a corrupt world of gamblers, kidnappers, pornographers, blackmailers, hitmen, and murderers. The labyrinthine plot never explained away all the bodies and at one point in the shooting the author was contacted by Hawks and asked to reveal who killed the Sternwood chauffeur. Chandler had no idea, so no solution is offered in the film, but its absence went unnoticed given its pace, intricacy, and tension.

Humphrey **BOGART** Lauren **BACALL** in WARNERS'

"THE BIG SLEEP"

COPYRIGHT 1946 WARNER BROS. PICTURES DISTRIBUTING CORPORATION. PERMISSION GRANTED FOR NEWSPAPER AND MAGAZINE REPRODUCTION. MADE IN U.S.A.

PROPERTY OF NATIONAL SCREEN SERVICE CORP. LICENSED FOR DISPLAY ONLY IN CONNECTION WITH THE EXHIBITION OF THIS PICTURE AT YOUR THEATRE. MUST BE RETURNED IMMEDIATELY THEREAFTER.

Prints went out to the armed forces before domestic audiences saw *The Big Sleep,* the delay deliberate as Warner Bros. was trying to get its war-themed product out of the way before the end of hostilities made it seem dated. In the interim *To Have and Have Not* was released. The publicity generated by the Bogart-Bacall pairing, culminating in their marriage in May 1945, prompted Warner Bros. to call *The Big Sleep* back for re-shoots and extra material to beef up their relationship. Another factor giving Jack Warner concern was that Bacall's reviews for *Confidential Agent,* made without Bogart, had been poor.

Hawks came up with a different cut, the one that went on release, and only since 1997 has it been possible to compare both versions. The second is lighter in tone but loses even more in plot logic than the first. It is undeniably the better of

the two, and this version of *The Big Sleep*, thanks to Hawks' evocation of Marlowe's sordid world and Bogart's compelling performance, endures as a classic of its genre.

Bacall's career nearly foundered after her miscasting in *Confidential Agent,* an unsatisfactory interpretation of the Graham Greene novel in which she plays an upper-class English girl who helps Charles Boyer, a Spaniard in London, to buy coal for the republican cause in the Spanish Civil War. In Herman Shumlin's film the nonsense of an American playing an Englishwoman and a Frenchman a Spaniard was compounded by Peter Lorre (Hungarian), Victor Francen (Belgian), and Katina Paxinou (Greek) as other Spanish characters. Twenty years old and at the start of her career, Bacall was totally inexperienced, and Boyer was no substitute for Bogart as a mentor.

OPPOSITE Outside the sound stage during the making of *The Big Sleep*, Bogie lights up Bacall, 1946. ABOVE Lobby card from *The Big Sleep*.

Following the success of *To Have and Have Not* and the marriage of the stars in May 1945, Warner Bros. had Howard Hawks reshoot scenes in *The Big Sleep* and insert new material, creating a classic *noir* thriller.

THE WARNER BROS. STORY

1947

✽ Humphrey Bogart and Bette Davis are Hollywood's best-paid stars (above)

✽ *Life with Father*, starring William Powell and Irene Dunne, is one of the year's biggest hits

✽ *The Beast with Five Fingers* is a rare Warner Bros. horror film

✽ Thor Heyerdahl completes his 4,300-mile voyage across the Pacific on his flimsy raft, the *Kon-Tiki*

✽ India becomes independent of Great Britain and the new nation of Pakistan is hived off

✽ Bogart and Bacall are teamed for a third time in *Dark Passage*

✽ Test pilot Chuck Yeager is the first man to fly faster than sound

✽ Shirley Temple has her first adult part in *That Hagen Girl*

✽ Warner Bros. posts a record profit of $22 million

ABOVE Bette Davis and Humphrey Bogart teamed up in *Marked Woman*, 1937, early in their mutually successful careers at Warner Bros.
RIGHT AND OPPOSITE Gary Cooper in *Cloak and Dagger*, 1946, with Lilli Palmer making her American debut.

NUCLEAR REACTION

In *Cloak and Dagger,* directed by Fritz Lang, Gary Cooper was cast as a nuclear physicist whose unique knowledge qualifies him for a ludicrously dangerous mission on behalf of the Office of Strategic Services (OSS), the forerunner of the CIA, in which he is put ashore in Nazi territory to rescue an atomic scientist who might be forced to betray secrets. In her American debut, Lilli Palmer plays a member of the Italian underground who helps Cooper through a series of arduous and occasionally grisly tussles with the Germans. Lang's original pessimistic ending questioning the ethics of atomic warfare was dropped by the studio. It insisted on a more anodyne payoff that would not excite controversy, reducing what could have been a thought-provoking work to standard espionage entertainment. Even so, touches of the flair that characterized the maker of *Metropolis* and *M* in Europe were occasionally seen, in particular a scene in which a child's ball bouncing down a staircase threatens the revelation of Cooper's hiding place, and a silent, vicious hand-to-hand struggle with a murderous Nazi agent (Marc Lawrence).

THE GOOD OLD DAYS

Clarence Day Jr.'s affectionate *New Yorker* recollections of his youthful upbringing in a prosperous brownstone in the 1880s were published in book form in 1936, a year after his death. Three years later they were the basis of a play by Howard Lindsay and Russel Crouse, which opened on Broadway in November 1939. Warner Bros. bought the film rights, intending to go into production when the run ended. It was a long wait. *Life With Father* was to be the longest-running non-musical in Broadway history, clocking up 3,224 performances before it closed in July 1947.

When finally it reached the screen it had been adapted by Donald Ogden Stewart and directed in Technicolor by Michael Curtiz. The central role of the paterfamilias, the Wall Street broker who tries to be master of his chaotic household, is played to perfection by William Powell, with Irene Dunne also excellently cast as his scatty wife who subtly rules, with James Lydon as the younger Clarence and oldest of a quartet of red-headed brothers, ZaSu Pitts as Cousin Cora, Edmund Gwenn as the minister seeking donations for his church, and a young Elizabeth Taylor whose visit tips the younger Clarence into confused infatuation.

Well-received, the film evoked nostalgic fondness for a gentler, bygone era.

LEFT Michael Curtiz directs a scene from *Life with Father*, 1947, with William Powell and Irene Dunne. Sound man C. A. Riggs is in the foreground.

DEPARTING DIVAS

By 1947 Bette Davis was the highest earning actress in Holly-wood, successfully holding off her rivals at Warner Bros., Joan Crawford and Barbara Stanwyck. The problem was that her films were becoming increasingly less appealing. In the melo-dramatic *Deception,* directed by Irving Rapper and featuring a Korngold cello concerto, Davis incurs the wrath of a com-poser, played by Claude Rains, by marrying a musician (Paul Henreid) believed to have been killed in the war. In the unsat-isfying *Winter Meeting,* directed by Bretaigne Windust, she is a rich poet in love with a bitter war hero (James Davis) who is anxious to become ordained in the Catholic Church, and in *June Bride,* another Windust film, she attempts unsuccessfully a change of pace in a comedy teaming her with Robert Mont-gomery as a pair of magazine journalists taking over an Indiana household to do a wedding story. Eighteen years at Warner Bros. came to an end with her scenery-chewing performance in *Beyond the Forest,* a smalltown murder story which, although directed by King Vidor, is often so melodramatic that audi-ences have been known to laugh at the wrong moments. Once clear of Burbank she freelanced, and soon afterward won the 1950 Oscar for *All About Eve.*

Barbara Stanwyck's later films at Warner Bros. were also not her best. They included *My Reputation,* directed by Curtis Bernhardt, which skirted controversy with her portrayal of a war widow contemplating a new marriage too soon, *The*

Two Mrs. Carrolls, directed by Peter Godfrey, in which she finds herself the second wife of a man who has murdered his first, which was hardly Humphrey Bogart's finest hour, and in the same director's *Cry Wolf,* where she is a suspect widow turning up at an old dark house to disconcert Errol Flynn. She then went to Paramount, scoring a hit in the paranoia thriller *Sorry, Wrong Number.*

The London-born Ida Lupino fared slightly better. She had actually been billed above Humphrey Bogart in the 1941 thriller *High Sierra,* and had her ups and downs with Warner Bros. over dud roles that had been assigned to her. She some-

times described herself as the poor man's Bette Davis, but she was feisty and funny in the now-forgotten late-wartime comedy *Pillow to Post*, directed by Vincent Sherman. She was then brilliant as a nightclub singer with Robert Alda as a mobster in Raoul Walsh's *The Man I Love*, and just about managed to survive the Korngold-scored weepie with Errol Flynn, *Escape Me Never*, a remake of a 1935 British film with Elisabeth Bergner, directed by Peter Godfrey. Finally she was excellent in the atmospheric *Deep Valley*, directed by Jean Negulesco and shot at various locations. Characteristically, she tackled then unfashionable feminist issues. Nevertheless, increasingly dissatisfied with the parts on offer, she left Warner Bros. in 1947, eventually making a breakthrough as a director at a time when the odds were overwhelmingly stacked against women ever taking the canvas chair.

FAR LEFT Bette Davis in a gallery shot for *Dark Victory*, 1939. LEFT One-sheet poster art for *Deception*. ABOVE LEFT Barbara Stanwyck depicted on the Spanish Day Herald for *My Reputation*, 1946. ABOVE Ida Lupino in *Escape Me Never*, 1947, and BELOW with Errol Flynn.

DORIS DAY
A New Day Dawns

She was born in Cincinnati on April 3, 1924, as Doris Kappelhoff. Initially she wanted to be a dancer, but after being injured in a road accident she took up singing instead. By the mid-1940s Doris, now surnamed Day, was singing with Barney Rapp, Bob Crosby, and above all Les Brown (and the Band of Renown).

In 1945 she had an enormous hit, "Sentimental Journey," that perfectly expressed the feelings of homecoming servicemen, and the record eventually sold five million copies. More hits followed, such as "My Dreams are Getting Better All the Time," as well as two failed marriages. In 1948, Jule Styne and Sammy Cahn heard her sing at their Hollywood party and recommended she replace Betty Hutton (who had become pregnant) in the film they were preparing with Michael Curtiz, *Romance on the High Seas*. In spite of occasional Huttonish touches that had not been erased from the script, Day came across as a vibrant new screen personality who could put over a song in an assured bell-like singing voice with an appealing husky edge. Her biggest Cahn-Styne hit, "It's Magic," was so successful it became the new title of the film for its UK release. From her screen debut Day was on her way to be the next big Warner Bros. star.

OPPOSITE Doris Day, a vibrant new screen personality, makes her debut in *Romance on the High Seas*, 1948. ABOVE One-sheet poster art for the film.

GOLD IS WHERE YOU FIND IT

John Huston's third film with Humphrey Bogart pursued, like *The Maltese Falcon*, the theme of greed. Mexico was the setting of *The Treasure of the Sierra Madre*, from a novel by the mysterious B. Traven, with Bogart and Tim Holt as drifting Americans swindled by a contractor and joining forces with a talkative old-timer played by Walter Huston, the director's father. He persuades them to embark with him on a journey to a remote area in the mountains, where he knows for certain that a mass of gold ore is waiting to be extracted.

Their trek is perilous, beset by bandits and inner conflicts, but it is when they find and mine the gold that their troubles really begin.

Max Steiner's score was one of his best, expressing the hardship of every slogging step toward their goal, and Bogart shocked some of his fan following by deviating from his usual tough code and sniveling like a coward. Huston ran over schedule and over budget on location, causing anxiety at the studio, and the production was called back to Burbank. Some key sequences were shot on a sound stage. It is a gripping work, and retains its power.

ABOVE Tim Holt, Humphrey Bogart, and Walter Huston simmer around the campfire in *The Treasure of the Sierra Madre,* 1948. OPPOSITE A photo of Bogart used in the advertising art for the film.

BOGIE STICKS HIS NECK OUT

Humphrey Bogart and Lauren Bacall only starred in four films together, although they were scheduled for a fifth at Warner Bros. in 1957 before his death. *To Have and Have Not* (1944) and *The Big Sleep* (1946) were followed by *Dark Passage* (1947), directed by Delmer Daves. Bogart played a man framed for murder who escapes from San Quentin and is sheltered by Lauren Bacall in her San Francisco apartment. He is unseen initially, the camera taking his subjective viewpoint. He undergoes plastic surgery to render himself unrecognizable, and when the bandages are eventually lifted he has acquired the familiar features of Humphrey Bogart, which he uses as a cover to ambush and unmask the real murderer. Melodramatic and implausible, it is the least successful of the quartet of Bogart-Bacall pairings.

Bogart had been deeply concerned by the actions of the House Committee on Un-American Activities, and he and Bacall—along with other Hollywood figures including John Huston, Danny Kaye, and Gene Kelly—went to Washington to protest. He was shocked to find that some of the so-called "Hollywood Ten" who could have pleaded the First Amendment when they were before HUAC, chose instead to make propaganda speeches on behalf of Communism, wrecking the cases of those who were entirely innocent. Feeling that he had been used, Bogart withdrew and made a statement of regret that to some extent appeased the red-hating Jack Warner.

His last film with Bacall, again directed by John Huston, was *Key Largo* (1948), an adaptation of a stage play by Maxwell Anderson. It is a revisit to *The Petrified Forest* premise, a hotel on a Florida key substituting for the desert. Bogart plays a disillusioned major visiting the widow (Bacall) and father (Lionel Barrymore) of a comrade who died under his command. A fugitive gangster (Edward G. Robinson) arrives and holds everyone hostage as a hurricane blows up. Bogart initially appears to acquiesce to the man of violence, not through cowardice but because the odds are against him. Eventually his moment comes when he puts to sea to take the mobster to Cuba. An effective film, it has an exciting climax and excellent performances, particularly that of Claire Trevor, the gangster's alcoholic moll, which earned her an Oscar.

ABOVE On the set of *Dark Passage,* 1947 Humphrey Bogart with Lauren Bacall.
BELOW The golden couple in *Key Largo,* 1948.
OPPOSITE French poster art for *Key Largo.*

John Huston standing at far right. discusses the scene
from *Key Largo* on the tank stage at Warner Bros., the
Burbank set evoking the Florida Keys. At center, Bacall
and Bogart await the call to "action!"

THE WARNER BROS. STORY

1948

* Jane Wyman wins the best actress Oscar for *Johnny Belinda* (above)

* Doris Day makes her screen debut in *Romance on the High Seas*

* Mahatma Gandhi is assassinated in Delhi

* John Huston wins Oscars for the direction and screenplay of *The Treasure of the Sierra Madre*, Walter Huston wins best supporting actor

* The Russians blockade Berlin and the airlift begins

* Early Hollywood master D.W. Griffith dies

* Claire Trevor wins best supporting actress for *Key Largo*

* The first postwar Olympics are held in London

* Ronald Reagan stars in *The Voice of the Turtle*

* Alfred Hitchcock's *Rope* introduces the "ten-minute take"

* Harry S. Truman beats Thomas Dewey in the presidential poll

ABOVE On March 24, 1949, Ronald Colman presents Jane Wyman with her Best Actress Oscar for her performance in *Johnny Belinda*. RIGHT Ronald Reagan takes up his role as President of the Screen Actors Guild. OPPOSITE Jane Wyman as Belinda in *Johnny Belinda*, 1948.

HANDLED WITH CARE

Although never in the front rank of Warner Bros. stars, Ronald Reagan was a reliable performer. *The Voice of the Turtle* opened in New York at the end of 1947, the year in which he began his first five-year stint as president of the Screen Actors Guild, during which time he faced the turmoil of the HUAC hearings and clashes with more militant unions. Reagan's direct involvement in politics dated from that point. Later, when antitrust legislation had led to the enforced abandonment of vertical integration whereby the major Hollywood companies controlled production, distribution, and exhibition, he achieved an exemption for his agent Lew Wasserman, head of MCA, which would later allow Wasserman to take over Universal, ignoring the obvious conflict of interest.

Irving Rapper directed *The Voice of the Turtle,* adapted from a late-wartime play by John Van Druten, with Reagan playing an army sergeant on leave in New York who through a shortage of hotel beds finds himself staying innocently in Eleanor Parker's apartment. She has been dumped by a Broadway producer, and he has been stood up by her best friend (played by Eve Arden). Left to themselves, the inevitable happens. They fall in love, but in the 1940s such situations were handled carefully in accordance with the Production Code. It is probably the most charming of Reagan's roles, and Eleanor Parker is entrancingly bright-eyed and appealing.

SILENCE IS GOLDEN

Jane Wyman, who from 1940 to 1948 was married to Ronald Reagan, never had a more serious role than that of a deaf-mute in Jean Negulesco's *Johnny Belinda,* and rose to the challenge magnificently. Her character, Belinda McDonald, lives a hard life in a fishing village in Cape Breton, Nova Scotia (actually northern California) and is despised for her handicap by her insensitive father (Charles Bickford). A local bully (Stephen McNally) brutally rapes her but she is unable to tell anyone or name her attacker. A humane doctor (Lew Ayres) protects Belinda when she is found to be pregnant and helps her to learn sign language, but he is suspected of being the father of the child, and tragedy ensues. The story is grim, starkly told, and occasionally melodramatic, but Wyman's performance won her the 1948 Oscar as Best Actress.

UNCUT HITCHCOCK

Alfred Hitchcock's version of the Patrick Hamilton play *Rope*—his first film in Technicolor—attempted a new technique in filming. The action was confined to one set, a New York apartment where two young men (by inference homosexuals, although that could not be openly stated in 1948) strangle a third member of their college class and hide his body in a chest in the apartment where they are about to host a party attended by the boy's father, aunt, and fiancée, and their professor. Hitchcock filmed the action in real time, using the entire stock of film in the camera for a continuous shot, with the roll changes manipulated so that the flow to the next appeared seamless. Not only did it call for strenuous rehearsals and extremely precise blocking of the cast, but also parts of

1949

✱ Danny Kaye plays *The Inspector General*, adapted from Gogol (above)

✱ Bette Davis leaves Warner Bros. after *Beyond the Forest*

✱ Swashbuckler Errol Flynn stars in *Adventures of Don Juan*

✱ Raoul Walsh remakes his 1941 *High Sierra* as a western, *Colorado Territory*

✱ George Orwell's *Nineteen Eighty-Four* is published

✱ Warner Bros. gives up theaters to comply with a Supreme Court decision

✱ Soviet Russia successfully tests its first atomic bomb

✱ James Cagney returns to Warner Bros. for *White Heat*

✱ Gary Cooper stars opposite Patricia Neal in *The Fountainhead*

✱ The Burbank lot is the setting for Doris Day's *It's a Great Feeling*

LEFT Joan Chandler and John Dall pose for a publicity photo for *Rope*, 1948. OPPOSITE Hitch directs James Stewart and cast on the sole set for *Rope*, with a constantly changing diorama of the New York skyline behind.

the set had to be designed for easy maneuverability so that the camera could slide past uninterrupted. A diorama of the New York skyline seen through the apartment's panoramic window was lit to progress from daylight to dusk and then to night.

Modeled to some extent on the infamous Leopold-Loeb case of the 1920s, in which two wealthy undergraduates murdered a fourteen-year-old boy for the thrill of it, *Rope* is something of a dramatic warhorse, the key role being that of the professor who, suspecting what has happened, later returns to confront them. James Stewart delivers a sound performance

calculated to appeal to the box office, and it was the first of his four collaborations with Hitchcock. John Dall was outstanding as the more articulate of the two murderers, with Farley Granger as the weaker, submissive partner. The "ten-minute take," as this idea was known, was not to persist, although Hitchcock modified it slightly in his next film, *Under Capricorn* (1949), which was made in England. The lack of edits and continuous camera flow was only too reminiscent of live television drama, and the knife-edge suspense was not so much with the action but whether such ingenuity could be maintained.

"THE GERMANS WORE GRAY, YOU WORE BLUE"

CAGNEY BACK AT BURBANK

James Cagney had been away from Warner Bros. for seven years before returning to make one of the most successful of all his crime films, *White Heat,* directed with panache by Raoul Walsh. Cagney is Cody Jarrett, a psychopathic gang leader, a mother-fixated epileptic who kills by reflex, or even to make a joke, such as when a victim shut in a car trunk complains of lack of air, the stuffiness is quickly relieved with a few bullet holes. Virginia Mayo is excellent as his neglected, double-crossing wife. A prison scene in which Cagney goes berserk in the mess hall having learned that his mother (Margaret Wycherly in Ma Barker mode) has died has a chilling, devastating impact, not least because the extras playing other inmates had no idea what was coming. A payroll heist goes wrong, leading to the explosive climax, in an enormous Californian chemical plant, and Jarrett, finally cornered at the top of a huge flammable tank, yells his famous epitaph "Made it, ma, top of the world," before disappearing, engulfed in a fiery explosion.

ABOVE James Cagney and Virginia Mayo in *White Heat,* 1949.
BELOW Cagney, as Cody Jarrett, grabs the collar of Edmund O'Brien as Vic Pardo. OPPOSITE One-sheet poster art for the film.

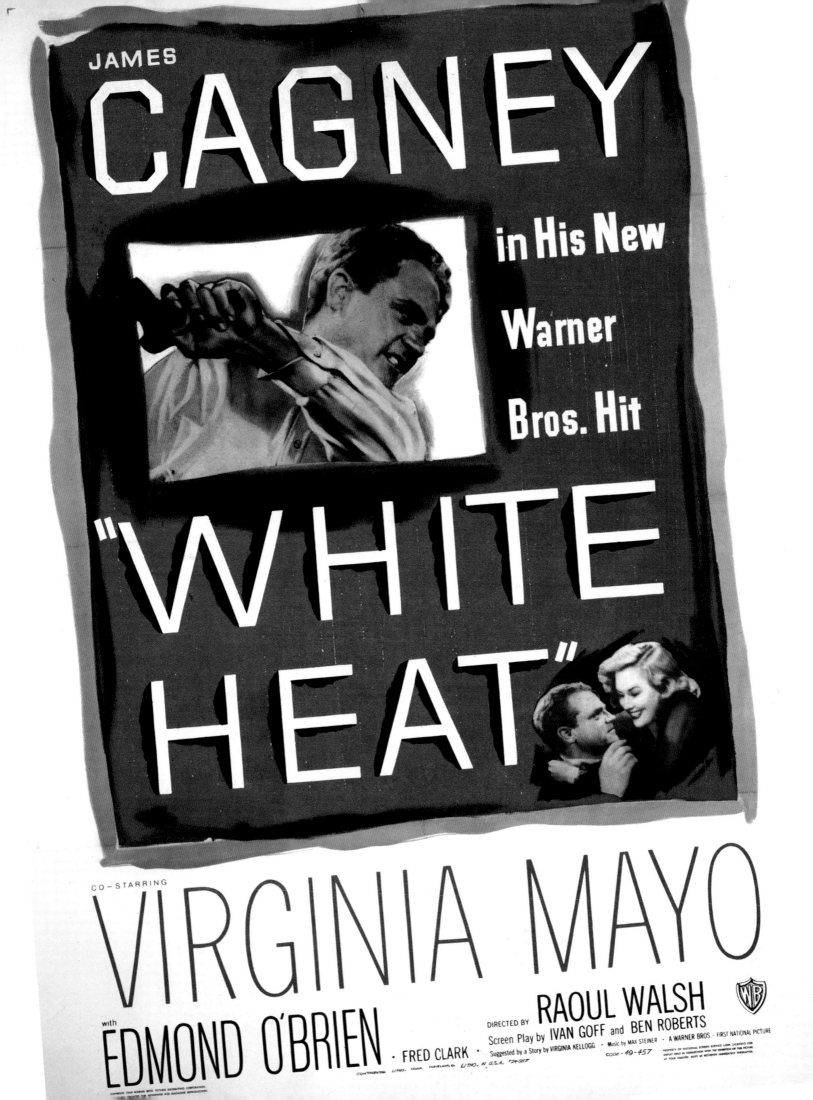

CHAPTER 4

"YOU'RE TEARING ME APART!"

Jim Stark in Rebel Without a Cause

WARNER BROS. STUDIOS
WARDROBE TEST
FOR
'A STREETCAR NAMED DESIRE' 372
OF
M BRANDO
AS
STANLEY

WARDROBE CHANGE # 3
WORN IN { SET Alley
         { SCENE 62-64

WB   8·9·50   WB

STELLLAAA!!!" WAS THAT ANGUISHED CRY OF BAFFLED LUST THE HEART SONG OF THE AMERICAN FIFTIES? WAS THE VOICE OF OUR BRUTAL, BEFUDDLED UNDERCLASS, EXEMPLIFIED BY STANLEY KOWALSKI, POLITICALLY DE-SENTIMENTALIZED IN THE POSTWAR ERA BUT AT THE SAME TIME ANARCHICALLY SEXUALIZED, THE TRUEST, DEEPEST EXPRESSION OF THE UNDERLYING ANXIETY OF THE CHIPPER, SUBURBANIZING SURFACE OF EISENHOWER'S AMERICA?

Or was it an anomaly? What about, "Once I had a secret love…"?

Was the plangent voice of Doris Day—innocent in its way, yet in some subtle way eager for experience—a truer expression of the national mood? Did it perhaps hint at unspoken yearnings, a need for off-the-books excitement, that most middle-class Americans dared not admit, let alone act upon in those days?

In terms of popularity it was no contest. Doris Day was ten times listed by Quigley Publications among the most popular movie stars of the year in the fifties and sixties. Marlon Brando made the list only twice. In terms of passionate regard, the results were a little different. Brando was a generational touchstone; the personification not merely of a new method of acting, but of the inarticulate longings of a restless younger generation for something more anguished and truthful than an essentially bland popular culture was offering.

It was Elia Kazan, who had directed Brando's electrifying stage performance in *A Streetcar Named Desire,* who brought him to Warner Bros. for the screen version of the play, which many believe to be the best movie adaptation of a stage work ever made—the more so since it managed somehow to convey the play's dark subtexts despite the meddlings of the still-potent movie censors. They were, Brando and Kazan, one of the great star-director partnerships. Kazan often said that he did not really have to direct Brando; all he had to do was drop the hint of an idea to the actor then simply step back and watch his instincts take over. What he loved about Brando was the contrasting qualities of his nature. "He was like a child," Kazan later said, full of ambivalence. There was, he said, "a soft, yearning, girlish side to him and a dissatisfaction that is violent and can be dangerous." Unquestionably, in this period Kazan was like a father figure to Brando—or, perhaps more accurately, a sort of older brother, at once instructive and indulgent—and his brilliant replication of his stage performance for the camera remains one of the greatest in the history of American film—brutal, sexy, weirdly funny at times—and utterly unlike anything anyone had up to then accomplished in the movies.

Nothing like that—rather obviously—can be said about Doris Day. Yet there was something more to her than was at the time, or in the years since, fully acknowledged. On the face of it, she seemed to exemplify the blandness of the era. Sure, she was a great singer. But from her first film, *Romance on the High Seas* (1948), she was all pep, bounce, and sunniness. Cast sometimes as a show-biz wannabe looking for her first break, sometimes as a small-town girl looking for romance in all the safe, right places, she was everything Brando and his ilk were not. People did not particularly notice that she sometimes participated in edgier Warner Bros. dramas (*Young Man With A Horn, Storm Warning*) or that there was a gentle feminist subtext to some of her films. She was kind of a can-do sort of gal, eager to pitch a pretty good fast ball or to repair a defunct automobile while her date helplessly watched as engine grease fetchingly dripped upon her adorable nose.

People—especially latter-day feminist critics—noticed these up-and-doing subtexts rather belatedly, though her whip-snapping, buckskin-clad *Calamity Jane* (1953), was a pretty plain statement that there was something more than the merely demure in her screen character, which her later, non-Warner Bros. films like *Love Me or Leave Me* and *The Man Who Knew Too Much* amply proved. In any case, in the late forties and early fifties she was

PREVIOUS PAGE Elia Kazan provides words of advice for Stathis Giallelis in the making of *America America,* 1963. OPPOSITE A wardrobe test for Marlon Brando as Stanley in *A Streetcar Named Desire,* 1951. Kazan said "He was like a child."

the studio's great new star, as big in her way as Cagney, Davis, Flynn, and Bogart had been in earlier times. At a deeply troubled moment in the studio's history, in Hollywood's history, she was, if not a "mortgage-lifter," then the most reliable star at its command.

One does not gain the impression that Warner Bros. had any consistent strategy for confronting the hard times television imposed on the movies during the competing medium's first full decade of existence. Earlier than most studios Warner Bros. embraced the new medium, and it had its successes with series like *Cheyenne* and *77 Sunset Strip.* Jack Warner liked the economics of television—low cost, high volume, and a more or less assured profit margin. It was, at least for a time, a little bit like the old days of studio production—you made a lot of inexpensive little pictures, raked in modest but tidy profits, with enough left over to mount a fair number of major productions.

But not a lot of truly distinguished ones. In part that may be because Jack Warner was smitten by new movie technologies, which offered moviegoers visual experiences that television, with its tiny black and white screens, could not. There was 3-D, for example, which looked so promising to Jack that he announced in 1953 that henceforth every Warner Bros. release would be in that process, which began rather promisingly with Andre De Toth's *House of Wax,* an extremely close remake of Michael Curtiz's *Mystery of the Wax Museum,* made twenty years earlier in 1933.

It has come to be regarded as the best of all 3-D productions (a dubious distinction and one that might be challenged by the studio's very solid John Wayne western, *Hondo*). In part the horror film worked because of De Toth's clever staging, with objects closer to the camera swinging suddenly, shockingly, into view. Even Alfred Hitchcock, then under contract at Warner Bros., was induced to make a 3-D picture (*Dial M for Murder*), which is among his lesser and more uninterestingly claustrophobic works. Still, once the novelty wore off, the public drifted away from 3-D.

CinemaScope, and its many widescreen offshoots proved to be a much more durable novelty. Indeed, the widescreen aspect ratio of the anamorphic lens quite quickly became the standard of the industry, and it must be said that one of its CinemaScope offerings was one of the most interesting Warner Bros. films of the decade—although you would not think that from listening to Paul Newman, whose debut film *The Silver Chalice* was. For the rest of his life he has gone on grousing that the picture nearly wrecked his career before it got started, and from an actor's point of view he is right. It is a truly awful story, about a slave-sculptor in biblical times, who has trouble imagining an image for Christ that he is supposed to engrave on the eponymous urn. That, however, reckons without the unprecedented and still unduplicated use of the wide screen by the journeyman producer-director, Victor Saville, whose last film as a director this was. Visually speaking, this was one of the most stylized films ever made in Hollywood. Saville's basic device was to block off huge portions of the wide screen—sometimes as much as ninety percent of it—with massive yet entirely unrealistic architectural structures, confining the action to a narrow staircase or alleyway. In one memorable shot, a gigantic aqueduct fills most of the screen with some tiny horsemen racing along the top of it and close to invisible to the watching eye. The picture was a gigantic flop, but if those directors, like Fritz Lang, who insisted Scope was good only for photographing snakes and funerals, had attended more closely to it, CinemaScope might have had a much more interesting aesthetic impact on the movies.

On the whole, particularly in the early part of the decade, and leaving aside Doris Day's musicals, Warner Bros. did better with low-budget, largely black and white genre pictures—pictures that harkened back to the kind of films the studio had more or less routinely made in the 1930s—than it did with its more spectacular offerings. There were many modest, energetic movies from the studio—De Toth's *Crime Wave,* about a young couple

OPPOSITE Doris Day, a "whip-snapping, buckskin-clad *Calamity Jane,*" 1953.

recruited against their will for a bank robbery and pursued by Sterling Hayden, doing an excellent Inspector Javert imitation. Or *Them!*, about giant mutant ants (their nest was too close to an atomic test explosion), threatening American civilization, or *The Beast from 20,000 Fathoms* about a dinosaur, awakened from the sleep of the ages beneath the polar ice cap by another atomic bomb test (Ray Bradbury conceived the idea, he said, during a walk along the Pacific shore one night, when he heard the mournful cry of a fog horn, which he said sounded to him like the mating call of some prehistoric monster). These were good, quick, well-made little pictures that have worn rather better than some of Hollywood's more pretentious efforts of the time.

Even Alfred Hitchcock got in on this action. His *Strangers on a Train* (1951) is, I think, one of his best films—certainly at the very top of his second tier. In it a psychopathic Robert Walker encounters a tennis player (Farley Granger) in a parlor car heading from New York to Washington and proposes a perfect crime. No one knows they know each other, so why doesn't each of them commit a murder that will benefit the other? Granger thinks he's kidding. Walker knows he isn't and proceeds with his crime. It's a wonderfully witty conceit, with Walker spookily determined and Granger never better as a weak-willed man almost undone by his own fecklessness. Hitchcock would later say that the tennis-match sequence—in which Granger must polish off a determined opponent in time to catch a train—was the most difficult he ever shot. He couldn't storyboard the real-life Forest Hills match he used in the sequence, and ended up with thousands of feet of film, which he had to intercut with his close-ups of Granger playing tennis at a different time. It went totally against his usual meticulously planned manner of shooting.

On the whole, the Master's work for Warner Bros. was much more realistic than his norm. Only the unsuccessful *Rope* (1948), about a cocktail party in which two killers hide the body of their victim in a chest in the room where their friends banter merrily, and the aforementioned *Dial M for Murder* are stylized, largely studio-bound films typical of the manner Hitchcock perhaps most often employed. He did, however, do more location shooting than we sometimes remember, and that was true during his Warner Bros. years. For *Stage Fright* (1950) he shot on location in London. For *I Confess* (1953) he was in Quebec, but it was in his masterly *The Wrong Man* (1956) that he seemed to outdo himself, in what may be the most atypical of all Hitchcock movies. He worked very extensively in New York City as he told the true story of a modest musician—Manny Balestrero (Henry Fonda), who played the bass in the Stork Club orchestra—wrongly accused (that great Hitchcock theme) of robbing a loan company. Coming late in Hitchcock's Warner Bros. career, the film is about plain, ordinary folks, not the wealthy and often glamorous people Hitch generally portrayed. These are people without the wit and material resources that often help see his more typical protagonists through their difficulties. Their life is grimly lower middle class and under the pressure of events, Manny's wife (Vera Miles) endures a mental crack-up before the real criminal is apprehended. The movie is richer in Catholic iconography than Hitch's movies generally are, and precisely because of their lack of means the Balestreros' situation seems more hopeless and desperate than is typical of a Hitchcock film, imparting to the audience an emotional involvement with their fates that is richer, edgier, than we are used to in most of his work. It is, I think, a great (and greatly under-appreciated) film and it has about it a classic Warner Bros. feel—an on-the-streets grittiness that, without loss of Hitchcockian elegance in its *noir*ish design, harkens back to the classic Warner Bros. style of earlier times.

Indeed, as one looks at the studio's output in the fifties and even later, one cannot escape the feeling that its films carried the imprint of DNA that continued to condition the style and content of Warner Bros.' releases. Yes,

OPPOSITE Farley Granger as Guy Haines bumps into a double bass
and Alfred Hitchcock boarding the train in *Strangers on a Train,* 1951.
Hitch's cameo was filmed at the Danbury, Connecticut, station.

color and wide screen changed the look of the company's major films. And yes, there was a shift in generic and thematic emphasis—more westerns and sci-fi/horror, for example, a more psychologically probing, less overtly sociological approach, than had formerly been so. But still, Doris Day aside, there was a seriousness of intent that contrasted with, say, the often leaden pseudo-seriousness of the films Dore Schary was producing at MGM or the glitz and gloss of the women's pictures Douglas Sirk was doing at Universal. There was, on the whole, a coiled tension in the Warner Bros. films that was missing elsewhere in Hollywood.

Some of that derived from Elia Kazan and his discovery, James Dean. The director was at the time a close friend of and collaborator with John Steinbeck, and had acquired the rights to the novelist's epic family saga,

ABOVE Julie Harris as Abra and James Dean as Cal Trask in *East of Eden*, 1955.
OPPOSITE Half-sheet poster art for *East of Eden*.

East of Eden. He decided to make a film about the one-third of the book that most interested him—the story of Cal Trask and his epic struggle for autonomy with his moralistic and misunderstanding father, Adam (Raymond Massey). It was a theme that echoed Kazan's similar struggle with his own father, and it was one that he had explored in the past and would revert to in his later work as well. He wanted Brando for the young man's role, despite the fact that he was too old for the part, and when the actor turned him down he went looking for a substitute. It was Paul Osborn, who wrote the *Eden* screenplay, who sent him to see James Dean as an Arab street kid in a short-lived adaptation of Andre Gide's *The Immoralist* on Broadway. He didn't entirely like what he saw, but thought it worthwhile to interview the kid, whom he found sprawling sullenly, uncommunicatively, in his office. Dean finally mumbled an invitation to share a ride with him on his motorcycle, which turned out to be not much fun for Kazan. But in its course and in later encounters, he began to sense that the kid had issues with his own father that were not unlike those of Cal Trask.

James Dean and Jo Van Fleet wait for a shot to be lined up. Kazan in white T-shirt is on the camera dolly. Some regard *East of Eden* as his best film.

211

He called Steinbeck, saying, "I found a guy who may not be much of an actor, but he is *it*." He sent him to the writer who agreed with Kazan on two counts. He didn't much like Dean either, but he also sensed that he was, well, *it*. So Kazan took him west to the studio for tests, with Dean carrying his spare clothes in a paper bag on his first-ever airplane ride. He beat out Paul Newman, among others, for the part. And entered formidably into the history of American celebrity.

The *East of Eden* shoot was not an easy one, in particular because Dean and Massey loathed one another. Massey was a stuffy, independently wealthy, McCarthyite Republican—the opposite in every way of Dean, who had a tendency to improvise his lines and generally mess with the older actor's head. When Massey complained, Kazan would promise to discipline Dean, though in fact he encouraged him in waywardness. "Do you think I

would do anything to stop that antagonism?" Kazan said later. "No, I increased it. I let it go … because it was the central thing I photographed… The absolute hatred that Ray Massey felt for Jimmy Dean and the hatred Jimmy Dean felt for Ray Massey. That's precious man. You can't get that. I mean, you can pretend that you have it, but you don't."

It worked. Their mutual loathing is manifest on the screen; it's the motor that keeps driving the film forward. And Kazan's respect for Dean kept growing. The kid had an authentic gift for self-exposure. What he did not have was what Kazan called "technique." He would instinctively do something marvelous, but he could not replicate those moments in the shots the director needed to cover the action from different angles. This, Kazan noted, was the opposite of Brando, who in those days could strike off those arresting moments and then repeat them as often as Kazan needed him to.

But the picture worked—at least for some people. There are critics who think *East of Eden* is Kazan's best film, though there are those of us who regard it as his most problematical, a sort of soap opera masquerading as an epic. But no matter. This was a period when "juvenile delinquency" was much on the nation's mind, and James Dean quickly came to symbolize the inarticulate rebelliousness of troubled youth, those worms in the shiny apple of American prosperity. Somehow, Kazan's instinct for interesting and distinctive performers had—as it had with Brando—brought him to the right man-child for the right moment, though it was not this film that announced the fact.

For while *Eden* was in post-production, Warner Bros. cast Dean in *Rebel Without a Cause,* in which he played a contemporary youth whose parents (a mean-spirited Mom and a weakling father) want him to be a nice respectable boy while he wants to race hot rods and make out with Natalie Wood. Directed by Nicholas Ray, it was a bang-on exploration of everything that was troubling adult America about the developing "youth culture" (Elvis was already waiting in the wings) and everything about adult America that was driving its children crazy. "You're tearing me apart," Dean screams at his parents—and all over the country his contemporaries mouthed agreement with him.

212

THE WARNER BROS. STORY

OPPOSITE Raymond Massey as Adam Trask with Julie Harris as Abra and James Dean as Cal Trask on the front porch. "Dean and Massey loathed one another." ABOVE Nicholas Ray directs James Dean in *Rebel Without a Cause*, 1955, "a bang on exploration of everything that was troubling adult America about the developing 'youth culture.'"

If anything, Dean's performance here is more annoying than it is in *Eden*—he's mewling, almost feminine in his anguish, but he struck something like a universal chord. He was on his way toward becoming the permanent symbol of youthful disaffection, a position he has posthumously retained for over a half-century. That dubious distinction aside, the studio historian cannot help but think that this picture represents a continuation of Warner Bros. "ripped from the headlines" tradition—a seriously intended, melodramatically arresting examination of a social problem that was currently on everyone's mind.

In any event, the studio had discovered a new star—someone with the potential to rank with such previous icons as Cagney and Bogart as a central figure in the endless psychodrama that constitutes the mass audience's relationship with the dominant movie stars of the moment. George Stevens' *Giant* had more on its mind than teen idolatry. Indeed, Dean's Jett Rink would eventually be obliged to age (unconvincingly) out of rebellious youth into middle age, in which he becomes an oil-rich, gray-haired Texas plutocrat. Basically, this is the story of a cattleman (Rock Hudson) and his high-spirited wife (Elizabeth Taylor), big-time cattle ranchers whose land contains oil and who are obliged to come to terms with the vulgar riches (and vulgar behavior) their newfound wealth imposes on them and on Texas itself, as the story slowly unwinds.

The picture is as big as the state it anatomizes (it runs for well over three hours), yet quite beautiful in its way. It is, as the film critic Kenneth Turan notes, rather an old-fashioned film, tending to look backward, stylistically and emotionally, to faux epics like *Jezebel* and *Gone With the Wind,* but heated by the presence of two other stars, Elizabeth Taylor and Rock Hudson, who were as interesting to the public as Dean was. And it has a certain good nature to it, as his liberal-minded Southern wife slowly civilizes her reactionary mate. Stevens' directorial manner was slow, painstaking, and, frankly, sometimes draggy. He loved multiple takes and many angles, preferring to shape his films more in the editing room than on the set, so much so that, according to his son George, Jr., the studio briefly considered replacing him with Gordon Douglas, a quick-footed B-picture director who knew how to keep to a schedule. That didn't happen, but still, the son notes that he worked on the picture in pre-production, served two years in the Air Force, then returned to the film in time to work on it in post-production.

Dean was, as usual, erratic during the endless shoot, but he seems to have found in Stevens, as he had in Kazan and Ray, the kind of father figure he required, though things got a little scratchier when the company returned from location in Marfa, Texas, and entered upon studio work on the Warner Bros. lot. One of the things that worried Stevens was Dean's love of fast cars and his careless driving habits. George, Jr. recalled his father asking his star if he planned to ship his car on ahead of him to the sports-car rally he was attending in northern California on his final, fatal weekend. The actor assured him that he did not intend to drive it there himself. But, of course, he did, with shocking results that turned him into a legend. Stevens was in a screening room when news of Dean's death reached him. He simply left it and wandered the lot, alone with his devastating thoughts.

There was still much work to be done on the picture. Stevens and Dean had worked alone, at night, on the actor's big scene—the rambling, incoherent, drunken speech he gives at a banquet after the opening of a hotel he has built. There was much mumbling in his performance and he would have been required to loop many of his lines. Nick Adams, a young actor who was also a friend of Dean's, was brought in to do that work, which he did secretly, never claiming any credit for helping to save the picture. Which despite the tragedy, and despite going so radically over budget and over schedule, turned out to be the biggest-grossing Warner Bros. picture until *Superman* supplanted it in the record books.

The loss of Dean was unquestionably a blow to the studio. Yet one cannot help but think that, however briefly it had claimed his services, it had been very lucky to have him—an authentic phenomenon, a source of avid public interest and critical debate in a time when such figures were rare, especially in the faltering, panic-ridden movie industry. When Carroll Baker was hired for her first movie job, her strong supporting role in *Giant,* she was taken in to meet Jack Warner, who did a strange little soft shoe shuffle as he rose from his desk to greet her. You had to wonder: was he aging and losing his grip? Or were the pressures he was then laboring under getting to him? Or was he simply, as Baker later put it, "A very weird man?"

And, by most accounts, a duplicitous one. It was at this point that Warner Bros. was coming into play in the financial markets. The brothers were aging: Abe was eager to retire and to realize the small fortune a sellout

OPPOSITE Director George Stevens positions James Dean
as Jett Rink in *Giant,* 1956, on location in Marfa, Texas. The
house, Reata, was constructed for the film.

215

"YOU'RE TEARING ME APART!"

would bring him (he was convinced that the studio would soon be valueless). Harry was increasingly unwell and Jack, too, was beginning to sing retirement songs—insincerely as it turned out. It was he who recommended a sale to a group headed by a financier named Serge Semenenko. The price was around $22 million for approximately ninety percent of the brothers' stock, with Jack agreeing to stay on as interim head of production until a permanent replacement could be found.

Or so he said. The general thought is that Jack had made a secret agreement to buy back most of his shares and to become, at long last, president of the company, a title that had always belonged to Harry, a fact that had rankled Jack for decades. Indeed, the brothers had hated each other almost from the moment Jack was born. The sources of their enmity have never been clear, but in later years it manifested itself in Harry's disapproval of Jack's raffish conduct of his private life and doubtless in business disagreements. Every history of the studio mentions an incident in which the portly and dignified Harry was observed chasing Jack around the lot, brandishing an iron pipe, seriously intending to maim his brother. The date of that attempted assault is never mentioned, but it seems to have occurred in the late forties or early fifties. There can be no doubt that Jack's betrayal of his brother contained a huge element of revenge for a lifetime of patronization and contempt. "I've got the old bastard by the balls," Neal Gabler reports Jack saying to another studio executive in *An Empire of Their Own*. "He can't do a goddam thing."

His "betrayal" caused an irreparable breach in the family. To this day their descendents rarely speak to one another. Harry suffered an incapacitating stroke upon reading in the trade press of Jack's coup and died two years later. Jack was at his home in the south of France, where he was now spending more and more time, largely indulging his gambling habit. He refused to return to Los Angeles for the funeral, despite the urgings of friends like Darryl Zanuck, also spending much time on the Riviera in those days. But then, returning from a night in the casinos, Jack was involved in a terrible car accident. He was literally more dead than alive when the police arrived on the scene. Somehow, however, he recovered, and when Zanuck arrived at his hospital room after he regained consciousness, he found, according to his son Richard, a bereft and sobbing Jack L. Warner. The accident, he insisted, was God's punishment for not attending his brother's last rites.

I am not entirely certain that Jack was completely a blackguard in this matter. Yes, of course, he had struck like a thief in the night—and in a way that was all-too-typical of this essentially cowardly man, famous for avoiding direct confrontations about everything (a typical example was having intermediaries fire his own son around this same time). On the other hand, however, Harry must bear a certain amount of responsibility for his own sad fate. He was a man of good principals in many respects, but he was also a stiff and rectitudinous man. He was now aging and unwell, which exacerbated his bad long-term relationship with his much younger brother. Harry, so far as one can tell, never made the slightest attempt at reconciliation with his brother. It must also be said that he received his full payout from the Semenenko deal and that his health at the time was such that he could not have continued in an active role at the studio. All that he had really lost was his title and such dwindling influence as a sick man might have exercised in a studio that, at that moment, was pretty much a shadow of its former self.

On her first day at the studio Carroll Baker was given a tour of the lot, and she remembers people apologizing for its under-population. Only about a third of its twenty-some sound stages housed shooting companies and people kept talking wistfully of recent, better days, when every stage was up and running and the studio streets were crowded with workers. The success of Dean's pictures briefly alleviated some of the pressure on Warner. But still, attendance and box-office receipts were less than half what they had been, industry-wide, and even before *Giant* went into release, Warner's management sold off its pre-1950 library (it eventually ended up at United Artists, though it has since returned to Warner Bros.) for far less than it was worth because the studio needed a cash infusion.

One fringe benefit of that sale, however, was the sudden prominence of the studio's great cartoon unit. These seven-minute shorts, featuring the likes of Bugs Bunny and the brilliant Daffy Duck, had always been the best in the business, wildly inventive and hilarious. Now television made them ubiquitous. But the fifties were already a high point for *Looney Tunes* and *Merrie Melodies*. Chuck Jones, in particular, entered upon an especially fecund phase of his career. In *Duck Amuck* (1953), an unseen hand kept erasing the little film's backgrounds and eventually Daffy himself in an act of self-referential filmmaking. Later in the decade Jones created what is, by common consent, the greatest short cartoon of all time—*What's Opera, Doc?,* which finds Bugs and Elmer Fudd involved in a parody of Wagnerian opera. It is a tragic tale, in which the cross-dressed rabbit and his bumbling pursuer eventually play out a love-death theme. Despite its brevity, I think it is one of the greatest films ever made at the studio, so-

phisticated in its operatic parody and hilarious about their curiously ambiguous relationship, particularly on Elmer's part. He entertains thoughts both murderous and amorous about the Wabbit, but it's best not to overthink this matter. Much better just to sit back and shake with laughter.

Making at least a third fewer films in these years Warner Bros. remained profitable, though much less so than previously, but still, on average doing as well as, or even slightly better than, its competitors. It did well with *Mister Roberts* (1955), despite John Ford's breakdown on the set (the film was finished by Mervyn Leroy), the Judy Garland remake of *A Star is Born* (1954), Brando in *Sayonara* (1957) among them. And it had its critical successes, too. Many people, for example, regard Ford's *The Searchers* (1956) as his finest film, which in certain respects—its breathtaking pictorialism and John Wayne's tower- ing performance as Ethan Edwards, the frontiersman seeking to find his niece, abducted by marauding Indians—it is. But the film is marred by graceless com- ic and romantic interludes and certain crucial psychological carelessnesses.

I prefer Wayne's other great west- ern of the fifties, Howard Hawks' *Rio Bravo* (1959). The director always said he made it as a response to *High Noon,* in which, as he saw it, Gary Cooper "ran around like a chicken with his

ABOVE German poster art for *Rio Bravo*, 1959.

head chopped off" looking for people to aid him in his fight against bandits pursuing a purely personal vendetta against him. In *Rio Bravo,* Wayne has to fight a much larger force, in the employ of the local cattle baron, aided only by a dubiously recovering alcoholic, a lame old man, and an untried kid (in order, Dean Martin, Walter Brennan, and Ricky Nelson). It's a sometimes comic film and a testily romantic one (the divine Angie Dickinson is the object of Wayne's flinty attentions), and one that suspensefully makes a good, simple moral point, namely that real men do what they gotta do as best they can, with what the fates hand out to them in the way of resources.

Meanwhile, Kazan continued to be a significant factor at the studio. Warner Bros. was now financing his independent productions, which were very much in its traditional vein—small in scale, mostly shot in black and white, and on the whole taking up (or raising) serious issues. In Kazan's view, his 1956 adaptation of Tennessee Williams' *Baby Doll* was a "cute" little story about three love-addled southerners (Baker, Karl Malden, and Eli Wallach), far more funny than it was sexy. This was not the view of Francis Cardinal Spellman, the arch-conservative leader of the New York Archdiocese, who mounted the pulpit at St. Patrick's Cathedral to denounce the movie. Particular reference was made to Baker, wearing what came to be known as a "Baby Doll" nightie, curled up in a crib, sucking her thumb while Malden, as her sexually denied husband watched her through a hole he had drilled in the wall. Kazan appeared to be unaware, until it was pointed out to him later, of the *Lolita*-like aspects of

ABOVE Carroll Baker in *Baby Doll,* 1956. This image scandalized the Catholic Church. OPPOSITE *Splendor in the Grass,* 1961. Natalie Wood as Wilma Dean Loomis next to Warren Beatty as Bud Stamper. Directed by Kazan, it had "an agenda more psychological than sociological."

the film, but they were present if you had the evil eye to see them. The result was one of those one-week press sensations, which hurt the film because theaters in the more conservative parts of the country refused to book it.

A Face in the Crowd (1957) is an excoriating study of how television, controlled and manipulated by corporate America, could grant fascist-like power to an innocent-seeming entertainer (brilliantly played by Andy Griffith). Written by Budd Schulberg and based on one of his short stories (and on what he thought was the truth about the beloved Will Rogers), the picture evoked the old socially conscious Warner Bros. tradition better than any of its releases in this period. Like *Baby Doll,* it didn't do much business, but over the years it has come to be recognized as a pioneering study of media manipulation—and as a film of particular verve (and, one must say, of great energy, sexual and otherwise).

Kazan's *Splendor in the Grass* (1961) had an agenda more psychological than sociological. It was Kazan's most vicious assault on bourgeois pieties as well as another of father-son wrangles, though its chief victim turned out to be the young woman the lad loved. Its chief beneficiary was Warren Beatty, making his star movie debut—less angry and sullen, gentler and more quietly muddled than James Dean had ever been. Again Kazan, working from a William Inge script, had tapped into the now more fully formed youth culture and the result was his last hit movie—and the beginnings of Beatty's career, which a few years later would greatly benefit the studio.

Kazan's last Warner film, *America America,* had quite a different impact. Warner Bros. had intervened in that production when funding from another source suddenly dried up and his company was virtually stranded in Turkey, without money to begin the picture. It was a highly personal story, about how Kazan's uncle had come to America, to which, eventually, he brought the rest of the family. It is epic in length, but not in style. The black and white film is very rough hewn and loosely structured, never a crowd pleaser. Kazan called it "not my best film, but my favorite film"—a sort of love letter to the immigrant yearning for a better place, a better world, than they had known in the old country. It was a feeling that Kazan, born in Anatolia, shared for his entire life.

America America was released in 1963, by which time it was becoming impossible to characterize the studio's output conveniently. For inexplicable reasons, Jack Warner had fallen in love with musical comedy, and beginning with *The Pajama Game* (1957) and including *Gypsy* (1962), *The Music Man* (1962), *My Fair Lady* (1964), and ultimately *Camelot* (1967), these films represented the studio's major efforts as the fifties turned into the sixties. They were not hugely innovative, as the Berkeley musicals—all originals, not based on Broadway successes—had been in the thirties or the Minnelli and Donen musicals at MGM had been in the forties and early fifties. But they were cheerful, well-made and profitable.

Fred Zinnemann contributed *The Nun's Story* and *The Sundowners,* both earnest, placid, and typical of his mature manner. There was also *PT-109,* an account of John F. Kennedy's wartime adventures—a movie ripped from distinctly yellowing headlines. Unfortunately, the story was more of an incident than a fully, fledged drama. Maybe it would have been sexier if the studio had acceded to JFK's casting advice, which was to have Warren Beatty play him as his younger self. And there was 1960's *Ocean's Eleven,* with Sinatra and the rest of the Rat Pack cracking insider jokes in a caper movie. The old try-anything quickness of the studio was subsumed in caution.

Until, in 1966, it took a shot at another sort of Broadway hit, the adaptation of Edward Albee's *Who's Afraid of Virginia Woolf?* As a play it was a milestone in pop cultural postmodernism—full of bad language and unexplained enigmas. There would have been no point in bringing it to the screen cleaned up and tidied up, and producer-screenwriter Ernest Lehman thought it could be done pretty much as Albee had written it. The Motion Picture Production Code, that antiquated list of "don'ts" and "be carefuls" which had for decades kept movie characters from talking and behaving as adults did in the real world, had for a time been under gnawing assault. Pictures were now occasionally being released without the Motion Picture Producers Association's seal of approval and succeeding commercially. Its informal enforcement arm, the Catholic

OPPOSITE Audrey Hepburn as Eliza Doolittle, in Cecil Beaton's black and white Ascot Gavotte costume for *My Fair Lady,* 1964.

Director Mike Nichols and, with pipe, Haskell Wexler, rehearse a shot with Elizabeth Taylor as Martha and Richard Burton as George in *Who's Afraid of Virginia Woolf?*, 1966.

Legion of Decency, whose "condemned" rating was thought to destroy a film's box-office prospects, increasingly seemed a paper tiger. And films from abroad were playing successfully in the U.S., no matter how nude their actresses were, no matter how compromising the situations they explored. The new head of the MPPA, Jack Valenti, was toying seriously with replacing the code with a rating system, which focused on protecting children from material that might be damaging to them while (ostensibly) permitting adults to see what they felt like.

In light of this new situation, Warner Bros. was prepared to endure a certain amount of controversy in order to produce what was manifestly a hot property. They engaged Broadway's latest star director, Mike Nichols, to make his film debut with *Virginia Woolf* and hired the hottest star team of the moment, Elizabeth Taylor and Richard Burton, for the leading roles. Nichols' decision to shoot the film in black and white—now beginning to disappear from the movies—promised and delivered a sort of artistic austerity to the enterprise; no one could accuse this movie of being exploitative. And Nichols did a wonderful job with the film. He had the good stage director's gift for imparting subtle movement to a film that is all talk and no action, and a promising film director's skill at "opening up" the play while retaining its essentially claustrophobic spirit. Prior to release the studio reached an agreement with the Motion Picture Producers Association in which the latter agreed to pass the film intact if the studio advertised it as an "Adults Only" attraction, and if it made a real effort to prevent children from gaining admission to the theaters where it played. This was a good compromise and the picture achieved considerable success at the box office without undue controversy. The critics and the general conversation about the film focused not so much on its slightly woozy dramaturgy, but on the question of how it would do commercially, given the challenge it posed to the standards of faith and morals that had for so many years pertained in Hollywood. The answer was, "Just fine." The movie was a hit and received a number of Oscar nominations, though it won in only two categories—Sandy Dennis for best supporting actress and Haskell Wexler for best black and white cinematography. It's impossible to determine if this success emboldened Warner Bros. But it was surely clear to everyone everywhere in the industry that there was an appetite in the audience, which was increasingly a youthful one, for something new. Conventional filmmaking could sometimes still reassemble the old mass audience for staid, traditional movies—but only perhaps a half dozen times a year. The year after *Virginia Woolf* the average weekly audience for movies, which had been hovering around thirty-six million, took another sickening downward lurch, to seventeen million. Something had to be done.

And Warren Beatty knew what it was. He had heard about a script called *Bonnie and Clyde,* the work of an editor and an art director at *Esquire* magazine, David Newman and Robert Benton. The latter had grown up in Texas on the legend of the doomed, populist bandits of the 1930s, and the pair thought that something fresh—and frankly New Wave in manner—might be done with their story, something at once romantic and rather rollicking. They worked on their script for years and, true to their impulse, pursued François Truffaut and Jean Luc Godard to direct it. Both of them eventually wafted away, but people kept talking about the script and one Sunday morning Beatty called Benton out of the blue, dropped over for brunch, and came away with the script. His good friend, screenwriter Robert Towne, liked it and supplied a polishing hand to the manuscript after Benton and Newman burned out on it. Beatty interested two or three studios in it, but he had the best relationship with, of all people, Jack Warner. He had made his debut there with *Splendor in the Grass.* After the Kazan film he had enjoyed a modest box-office success (*The Roman Spring of Mrs. Stone*) and a modest flop (*Kaleidoscope*) at Warner Bros., and was definitely a rising star.

The old mogul, estranged from his own son, and the young actor (he was still under thirty, young to be a producer as well as a star in Hollywood at that time) somehow bonded—even though Warner never quite got what the project was driving at. He thought it was pretty much an old-fashioned Warner gangster picture.

OPPOSITE Warren Beatty as Clyde Barrow and Faye Dunaway as Bonnie Parker, in *Bonnie and Clyde,* 1967.

Beatty's efforts to persuade Warner to risk maybe $3 million on his dream have passed into legend. He has denied dropping to his knees to beg Warner for his backing. But he does admit responding to Jack Warner's gesturing to the studio water tower, on which Warners' trademark shield was emblazoned, observing that his name was still on it. "Yeah," Beatty said, "but whose initials are on it?" referring to the big WB that the shield enclosed. Jack couldn't help but like the kid's cheek and eventually green-lit the picture.

Because the budget was so low, Beatty cast less expensive New York stage actors (Faye Dunaway, Estelle Parsons, Gene Hackman, Gene Wilder) in the film, and persuaded Arthur Penn, most of whose hits had been on Broadway, not in the movies, to direct. They had worked together on *Mickey One,* which had been very New Wavish—arguing their way through it in ways that were more stimulating than acrimonious to both men. Penn was not easily persuaded; he was coming off a horrible experience on *The Chase* and was seriously thinking of never doing another movie. He has always credited Beatty's relentless encouragement with changing his mind.

It was, by all accounts, a tough shoot, many scenes of which were shot in locales that the real Bonnie and Clyde had raced through during their short run to dubious glory. It had its New Wave style all right, but it had something more as well: a modern-day resonance. The war in Vietnam was producing images of bloodshed and futility almost every night on television, and Penn in particular wanted to draw the analogy between America's past and America's present. That was especially so in the film's climactic sequence. From the moment he first read the script, Penn has said, he knew how he wanted to shoot that sequence; it was completely realized in his mind's eye and when he came to do it he flew on disciplined instinct and was, in his own word, "sublime." He had four cameras, all running at different speeds, to record the carnage as the ambushing Texas Rangers pumped hundreds of bullets into the pair (which, incidentally, was historically true).

Returning to the studio for post-production, Penn found himself the recipient of lonely phone calls from Jack Warner. Nothing besides *Camelot* was shooting on the lot and the old man kept requesting Penn's company for lunch in the commissary. Yet the studio didn't know how to handle the picture—as a work of art or as a genre picture. Finally it took it to the Toronto Film Festival, where Bosley Crowther, the hopelessly square *New York Times* critic, took out against it. Eventually he wrote three articles decrying the movie's violence and historical accuracy (as if biopics had ever been models of truthfulness and as if this was, indeed, a biopic instead of the free-form American legend that it was). Other critics saw that it was, perhaps, the most radical departure from long-held American studio conventions since the beginnings of sound. This controversy eventually became one of the central aesthetic debates of the sixties. Everyone had to have an opinion about it, though at first the buzz did little for the film. But Joe Morgenstern, the *Newsweek* critic, publicly reversed his stand on it, replacing his initial negative review with a positive one a week later. Pauline Kael weighed in with a long essay defending *Bonnie and Clyde* in *The New Yorker,* a piece that secured her a job as the magazine's film critic. And, by the end of the year, the *Times* fired Crowther, largely for his failures of hipness.

Meanwhile, Beatty was everywhere, promoting the film to anyone who would interview him and, more important, campaigning for the studio to re-release it. It did, and the film became a very substantial hit, as well as a multiple Oscar nominee. Official Hollywood, typically, was hesitant to award it many golden statuettes. And in truth the *Bonnie and Clyde* style was rarely imitated in Hollywood thereafter. It was its attitude that became more and more operative. Movies in the seventies, at Warner Bros. and elsewhere, became bolder in their choice of subject matter. And they became somewhat sexier, a lot more violent, and a lot less wedded to longstanding narrative conventions. A convenient example was the 1969 Warner Bros. release, *The Wild Bunch.* It was in the vein of a new variant on the western genre—a sort of end-of-the-west western, in which all the forces of modernism, ranging from motor cars to a more flexible morality, threatened the simple values the western had always upheld. The eponymous "bunch," aging exemplars of macho tradition, ride into Mexico to trade guns for money that will, perhaps, permit them to retire from outlawry. In the end they accept death rather than dishonoring their traditional masculine code and are killed in a famously bloody sequence. Director Sam Peckinpah nearly always saw his protagonists as fated and doomed. And so it was here. His technique—lots of blood squibs bursting, blooming like poisonous flowers—owed something to Penn, but the scale of his bloodletting was far grander than anything that had previously appeared. Old timers like Howard Hawks were contemptuous. He thought that death in the movies ought to be played as it is in life—quickly, almost noncommittally. "I could get a half dozen actors down and off to the morgue in the time it takes him to kill one guy," he sniffed.

The studio had trouble with the picture—it snipped some twenty minutes out of its first release prints and Peckinpah, who rarely made a movie without falling into a fight with its financiers, began to become the paradigm of the artist-auteur, the rebel-genius who was always being thwarted or fired by his backers. There was more to his story than that—he had a huge self-destructive streak, not alleviated by his alcoholism—but this film may be his masterpiece. At the very least it set off a new round of controversy about violence in film, and, as much as *Bonnie and Clyde,* it predicted the issues that would roil American movie history in the 1970s.

Jack Warner, however, was not around to participate in those discussions. In 1967 the studio was acquired by Seven Arts (a Toronto-based company that began in television distribution and had become a producer of films) with Kenneth Hyman, the scion of its principle owner, Eliot, taking over from Jack as head of production for a brief period, until the studio was sold again in 1969. Jack L. Warner, the last of the brothers, lived on until 1978, producing a couple of unsuccessful movies and dabbling in the Broadway musical theater. He did not participate in the great revival of the studio's fortunes that began a year later—a revival that owed a great deal to the spirit of the studio in the glory years over which this unlikely man had presided. He was, at last, something he had never dreamed of being—a ghost presiding over a newly laid banquet, an irrelevancy.

RICHARD SCHICKEL

ABOVE Six-sheet poster art for *The Wild Bunch,* 1969, directed by Sam Peckinpah, who nearly always saw his protagonists as fated and doomed.

1950

* Jane Wyman stars in Alfred Hitchcock's *Stage Fright*, made in England (above)

* In *Kiss Tomorrow Goodbye*, James Cagney is a hood; in the musical *The West Point Story* a Broadway producer

* The Korean War begins

* Michael Curtiz directs John Garfield in Hemingway's *The Breaking Point*

* Al Jolson dies at the age of sixty-four

* In *Young Man with a Horn*, Doris Day plays her first dramatic part

* Errol Flynn makes his last western, *Rocky Mountain*

* *Peanuts* comic strip is launched

ABOVE Jane Wyman in *Stage Fright*. RIGHT Elia Kazan runs over a scene with Marlon Brando on the set of *A Streetcar Named Desire*, 1951. OPPOSITE The classic T-shirt shot that helped established Brando as a movie icon.

MARLON BRANDO
Transformed Greatness

Serious American theater in the postwar years needed a severe jolt out of its torpor, and got it in 1947 when Marlon Brando (1924–2004) appeared on Broadway as Stanley Kowalski in Tennessee Williams' *A Streetcar Named Desire*. It was almost as if the art of acting had been reinvented. The earthy intensity, conviction, and soul-baring that Brando brought to the role made the conventional performances of other notable stage actors seem like histrionic posturing. Yet Brando, with American theater his to command, turned his back on the stage, and took off for Hollywood, making his auspicious film debut as a paraplegic veteran in *The Men,* directed by Fred Zinnnemann in 1950. He then went to Warner Bros., recreating his Stanley Kowalski for Elia Kazan's *Streetcar*. He would go on to make many more films in a long, sometimes glorious, often disordered career, and although he never returned to theater Brando's influence both on stage and screen ran deep and is still felt.

ELIA KAZAN
A Life

Elias Kazanjoglou was born in Constantinople, Turkey, in 1909, and was four years old when his parents left for America. Elia Kazan studied drama at Yale and was an actor with the Group Theatre in New York in the 1930s, a radical ensemble company that pioneered the Stanislavski approach to acting in America. He appeared in the notable Clifford Odets plays *Waiting for Lefty* and *Golden Boy,* and later in two Warner Bros. films directed by Anatole Litvak, *City for Conquest* and *Blues in the Night.*

In the 1940s Kazan developed a career as a Broadway director, and in 1947 was a co-founder of the Actors Studio.

His early films at 20th Century Fox were realistic and socially conscious in accord with Darryl F. Zanuck's policy. In New York he achieved massive success in staging *A Streetcar Named Desire* and the film version showed that he had the instincts to turn great theater into great cinema.

In the Group Theatre days he had been associated with the Communist Party and so was called before the HUAC. When faced with the choice of naming others who had been in the party or losing his career, he cooperated with the committee, first ensuring that he would only mention those whose names were already on record. But had Kazan refused to testify his films *East of Eden, On the Waterfront, Baby Doll,* and *A Face in the Crowd* would not have been made.

KINDNESS OF STRANGERS

Even though the steamy temperature of the film version of *A Streetcar Named Desire* was lowered to comply with the Production Code and the Catholic Legion of Decency, it still exerted a visceral power. In recent years it has been possible on DVD to see how the film might have been without the censor's nibblings, but in the moral climate of 1951 the raw shock of Tennessee Williams' play was considered too much for the audience at large. Elia Kazan transplanted almost the entire Broadway cast to Burbank, with the exception of Jessica Tandy who was replaced as Blanche DuBois. Vivien Leigh had played the part in London, and it was Blanche rather than Scarlett O'Hara that was the defining role of Leigh's career.

Although she was top-billed above Brando, it was he who energized the film with a performance that instantly elevated him to the topmost heights of film acting. Inexplicably his performance failed to win him the Academy Award, which went that year to Humphrey Bogart for *The African Queen,* although Leigh, Malden, and Hunter were all honored with Oscars. As Stanley Kowalski, a brutal, uncouth yet vulnerable bully in a grubby, torn T-shirt, Brando is disquieting in his inability to comprehend the faded southern belle Blanche who, lost in a sexually charged world of her own, has come to stay with his wife Stella, her younger sister. Kazan's direction adheres to the shabby New Orleans apartment to emphasize the claustrophobia and emotional heat, and Alex North's score with its jazzy harmonics, novel in their day, influenced film music thereafter.

1951

✳ *A Streetcar Named Desire* receives twelve Oscar nominations and wins four, including Best Actress for Vivien Leigh

✳ The United Nations opens its new headquarters in New York

✳ *Strangers on a Train* is a triumph for Alfred Hitchcock

✳ President Truman relieves General Douglas MacArthur of his Far East commands

✳ Death of Robert Walker, star of *Strangers on a Train*

✳ In his last film for Warner Bros., Humphrey Bogart stars as a crusading district attorney in *The Enforcer*

✳ Warner Bros. profit for the year is $9.5 million

OPPOSITE On the set of *East of Eden,* 1955, Marlon Brando visits with Elia Kazan at left, Julie Harris, and James Dean. ABOVE LEFT Lobby card art from *A Streetcar Named Desire.* ABOVE Vivien Leigh as Blanche du Bois, the defining role of her career, in a dramatic moment with Marlon Brando as Stanley Kowalski.

"YOU'RE TEARING ME APART!"

BURT
LANCASTER AND VIRGINIA
MAYO

performing actual feats of daring unmatched by any star

ALL THE ADVENTURE A MAN CAN LIVE HE LIVES...
ALL THE STIRRING EXCITEMENT SCREEN DRAMA CAN GIVE
WILL BE GIVEN YOU WHEN **WARNER BROS.** PRESENT

The
**FLAME
AND THE
ARROW**

COLOR BY
TECHNICOLOR

Distributed by
WARNER BROS.

Directed by
JACQUES TOURNEUR · A **NORMA-F.R.** Production · **WARNER BROS.**
Written by WALDO SALT

ABOVE One-sheet poster art for *The Flame and the Arrow*, 1950, in which Burt Lancaster's circus skills were appropriately applied.
OPPOSITE Two shots of Lancaster on the set of *The Crimson Pirate*, 1952, directed by Robert Siodmak. The huge three-strip Techni-color camera in the picture below was soon to be obsolete.

SWING TIME

Among the young actors who emerged in the latter 1940s Burt Lancaster exerted a special appeal, particularly in several tense thrillers that he made for other studios. Tall, athletic, firm-jawed, with steely blue eyes and a clipped manner of speaking, he had the intensity of a spring that could pop the moment control was relaxed. His agility was a product of his early adult-hood as a circus acrobat, and he liked to stay limber on a set of parallel bars close by when he was filming. When he came to Warner Bros. in 1950 he was seizing a chance to utilize his circus skills properly in a twelfth-century action adventure set in Lombardy, *The Flame and the Arrow,* directed by Jacques Tourneur, a Robin Hood-William Tell variant with much rooftop leaping and deployment of archery weapons. After playing the Native American Olympic athlete in *Jim Thorpe—All American* (1951) under Michael Curtiz's direction he was to excel in *The Crimson Pirate* (1952), a delicious, colorful romp recalling the days of Douglas Fairbanks, Sr., directed by Robert Siodmak on location in Italy and at Teddington, Warner Bros.' London stu-dio. The acrobatic stunts are far more effectively integrated with the plot than in *The Flame and the Arrow,* as Lancaster, the pirate, outwitting the Spanish in the Caribbean, dazzles with his swordplay, gallantry, and zest. Nick Cravat, his small but powerful circus partner of old, is his mute sidekick. In both *The Flame and the Arrow* and *The Crimson Pirate* he played speechless, as his native Brooklyn accent was beyond redemption.

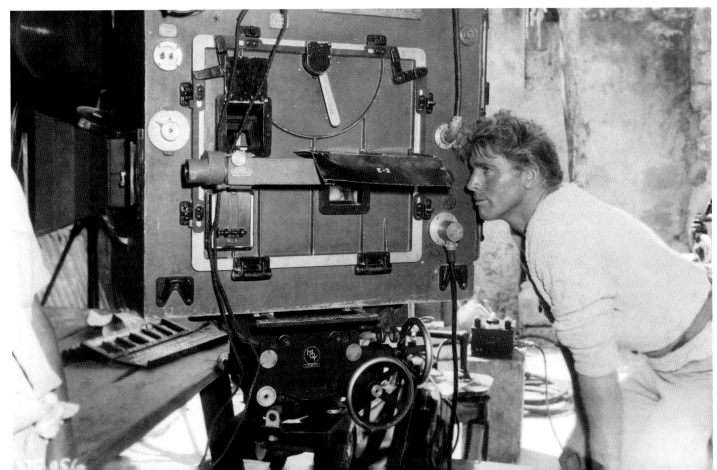

FAREWELL BOGIE

Humphrey Bogart's last film at Warner Bros., *The Enforcer* (1951), was in many respects a throwback to earlier days, not least in that most of the direction was undertaken by an uncredited Raoul Walsh, who had moved in when Bretaigne Windust was taken seriously ill. Bogart plays an assistant district attorney charged with nailing the boss of a crime syndicate, played by Everett Sloane, but on the eve of the hearing a key witness dies, necessitating the reconstruction of the prosecution case in a matter of hours. The style is stark and noirish, with deep, nocturnal shadows, and an overwhelming sense of imminent violence.

In *Come Fill the Cup* (1951), directed by Gordon Douglas, James Cagney plays an alcoholic newspaperman, helped back by James Gleason, a reformed alcoholic, and later prevailed on by his boss, Raymond Massey, to get his playboy nephew, Gig Young, back on the wagon. Only once the sound of "angel feathers" is heard, a euphemism for impending death, can that be achieved, says Cagney. The performances are strong, but the intrusion of a gangster theme blunts the narrative.

ABOVE James Cagney and Gig Young in *Come Fill the Cup*, 1951.
OPPOSITE Humphrey Bogart in his last film at Warner Bros., *The Enforcer*, 1951.

FROZEN DOLLARS

In the late 1940s the United Kingdom faced a serious balance-of-payments crisis and imposed a high tax on American film imports. In response Hollywood boycotted the British market, and for several months new American films were embargoed in Britain. When eventually the situation was resolved it was agreed that dollar funds would be frozen and set against production in the UK. Among the early fruits of a partnership with Associated British was Vincent Sherman's film from a Broadway play by John Patrick, *The Hasty Heart* (1949), set in a military hospital in Burma in 1945. Richard Todd portrays a spiky young Scottish corporal, unaware that he has only a short time to live. He rebuffs attempts to befriend him, but Ronald Reagan's plain-speaking American with malaria and an ancestral animus against Scots rallies the others to treat him decently. A brazen tearjerker, it transcends its contrivances on the strength of performance.

In Hitchcock's *Stage Fright* (1950), Todd is suspected of the murder of his mistress's husband. Marlene Dietrich, as the mistress, decorates the film with stylish *hauteur*. Jane Wyman, a Royal Academy of Dramatic Art student, performs a Nancy Drew act to prove his innocence. Michael Wilding plays an implausibly posh Scotland Yard man and an assortment of British character actors including Alastair Sim, Joyce Grenfell, Miles Malleson, and Sybil Thorndike entertainingly populate the cast list. Some critics have complained that Hitchcock cheated by misleading the audience, but then things not being what they seem to be is a constant throughout his films.

C. S. Forester's gallant naval hero of the Napoleonic wars against the French and Spanish fleets came to the screen in the person of Gregory Peck in *Captain Horatio Hornblower*, directed by Raoul Walsh on the soundstages of Teddington. An early intention had to been to cast Errol Flynn, but after *Adventures of Don Juan* it was thought that the star of *The Sea Hawk* had lost his ability to command. Exciting battle sequences enliven the action.

OPPOSITE Marlene Dietrich and Richard Todd in *Stage Fright,* 1950.
ABOVE Ronald Reagan and Patricia Neal near Tower Bridge, London. They were filming *The Hasty Heart* at Elstree Studios in 1949.
RIGHT One-sheet poster art for *Captain Horatio Hornblower,* 1951, in which Raoul Walsh directed Gregory Peck.

CRISS-CROSS MURDER

After making *Under Capricorn* and *Stage Fright* in his native London, Alfred Hitchcock returned to California for *Strangers on a Train* (1951), adapted from Patricia Highsmith's thriller by Whitfield Cook, with a screenplay by Czenzi Ormond and Raymond Chandler. After a row of disappointing films suddenly Hitchcock was back at the top of his game with this story of Guy Haines, a tennis player (Farley Granger) unwillingly befriended by a smug, self-confident fellow train passenger Bruno Anthony (Robert Walker), who knows how Guy's relationship with a senator's daughter is blighted by a wife

who refuses a divorce. Bruno suggests that he murder her and Guy in return should dispatch his tyrannical father, making both homicides motiveless. To Guy's horror Bruno carries out his side of the deal, trapping him into reciprocation. Having placed his hero in a nightmare, Hitchcock sends him on an unspeakable ordeal of extrication, with a terrifying climax on a carnival carousel.

His following film, *I Confess* (1953), was set in the walled French-Canadian city of Quebec, with Montgomery Clift as a priest who hears a murderer's confession, then finds he is suspected of the same killing but bound by his vows to remain silent. The concept is ingenious and some of the detailing, laden

1952

✱ Dwight D. Eisenhower is elected 34th U.S. President (above)

✱ Burt Lancaster has an acrobatic success in *The Crimson Pirate*

✱ *Retreat, Hell!*, directed by Joseph H. Lewis, is a tribute to the U.S. Marines in the Korean War

✱ Cary Grant and his wife, Betsy Drake, star in *Room for One More*

✱ Alan Ladd makes his Warner Bros. debut in *The Iron Mistress* as the inventor of the Bowie knife

✱ Charles Chaplin is denied re-entry into the U.S.

✱ Actor John Garfield dies at the age of thirty-nine

✱ Kirk Douglas stars in the Californian redwood adventure *The Big Trees*

✱ Comedians Bud Abbott and Lou Costello appear in *Jack and the Beanstalk*

with Catholic imagery, is characteristic of Hitchcock's psyche, but the film is heavy and sober, and was less successful.

He returned to Warner Bros. in 1956 to make *The Wrong Man,* based on a true-life case in which a New York nightclub musician was wrongly identified as a hold-up man and thrown in jail. His wife (Vera Miles), mentally broken, is institutionalized. With Henry Fonda as the musician, living a harassed existence in Queens, it epitomized Hitchcock's paranoid horror of the plight of an innocent wrongly accused and treated as a criminal. Shot in grainy black-and-white like a documentary drama, it is effective, and one of his most disturbing films.

OPPOSITE Robert Walker strangles Laura Elliott in *Strangers on a Train,* 1951. RIGHT In *The Wrong Man,* 1956, Henry Fonda with Vera Miles, wrongly identified as a hold-up man and thrown in jail. BELOW Hitchcock managed to make an appearance on this color lobby card but not in the film itself, except to introduce it at the beginning.

Warner Bros. Presents HENRY FONDA and VERA MILES in ALFRED HITCHCOCK'S *The Wrong Man*

"YOU'RE TEARING ME APART!"

1953

* Warner Bros.' *House of Wax* with Vincent Price is a 3-D hit

* *The Jazz Singer* is remade with Danny Thomas in the Jolson role

* Joseph Stalin, dictator of the Soviet Union, dies

* Doris Day's song "Secret Love" from *Calamity Jane* wins an Oscar

* Queen Elizabeth II is crowned in London

* The summit of Mount Everest is reached for the first time

* *The Desert Song* is filmed for the third time, with Gordon MacRae and Kathryn Grayson

* A Ray Harryhausen dinosaur terrorizes New York in *The Beast from 20,000 Fathoms*

ABOVE Ad art composition of Vincent Price from *House of Wax*. RIGHT Ad art for *House of Wax*. OPPOSITE Hitch in an unsubtle publicity shot for his 3-D thriller *Dial M for Murder*, 1954.

NEW DIMENSIONS

By the 1950s the rapid growth of broadcast television had started to have a serious effect on box-office figures, and the whole economy of the film industry began to look perilous. Although domestic receivers displayed small, flickering black-and-white pictures, the signals plucked from the ether by large, unsightly roof antennas, people often preferred to stay at home clustered around the TV than visit the neighborhood picture house. Attempts were made to find ways to lure them back by offering an experience beyond prevailing television technology. More color, for a start, as multi-hued regular TV programming was still a decade away. Changing the shape of the screen, by making it broader or even panoramic, was another option. An indifferent film called *Bwana Devil* was premiered in November 1952. It was filmed in a process called Natural Vision, to be viewed stereoscopically through Polaroid glasses, and it was in color. Its audiences were attracted by the novelty, and it sparked off a craze for 3-D films

from most of the studios, many of them made hastily with poor plots and shaky production values. The craze would last only a little over a year before the novelty faded, and many films that had been made in 3-D and not released immediately went out in normal "flat" versions.

The most effective film during the short-lived 3-D craze was *House of Wax,* directed by Andre De Toth. Ostensibly a remake of *The Mystery of the Wax Museum* from 1933 it has Vincent Price in the Lionel Atwill part of the sculptor who uses real-life models to create his wax effigies, and he plays the role with such relish that he was to become renowned as a master of horror. Also in the cast was Charles Bronson as his assistant Igor (an echo of *Frankenstein*) but listed as Charles Buchinsky. Many 3-D effects were employed that are bewildering when a flat version is viewed, for instance a huckster with a paddle ball which he repeatedly hits into the camera lens. Andre De Toth had only one eye, and wore a black patch. When asked how he had managed to make such an effective 3-D film he pointed out that to look through a camera viewfinder it was necessary to close one eye anyway.

Among Warner Bros.' 3-D films were the westerns *The Charge at Feather River* (1953), directed by Gordon Douglas with Guy Madison and Vera Miles, and Roy Rowland's *The Moonlighter* (1953), with Fred MacMurray and Barbara Stanwyck. Better was *Hondo* (1953), directed by John Farrow with John Wayne as a cavalry scout and Geraldine Page in her film debut as a widow whose farmstead is about to be attacked by the Apache. Fresh from New York theater and used to "the Method," Page was nevertheless disconcerted on her first day of shooting to find herself playing a scene in which Wayne delivers his lines while expertly shoeing a horse. Even Hitchcock made a 3-D film (mostly released flat), *Dial M for Murder* (1954), a stagey thriller in which a philandering husband (Ray Milland) sends a hit man to kill his wife (Grace Kelly) in their London apartment. Unexpectedly she finishes him with a pair of scissors in his back. Some strangely angled shots and the odd placing of lamps and other items to give the impression of depth are the clues to its original 3-D.

MONSTER TIME

In the quest for spectacular film material not easily replicated by television a cycle of horror fantasy, with mutants, monsters and humongous insects emerged. For Warner Bros., *The Beast from 20,000 Fathoms* (1953), directed by Eugene Lourie from a story by Ray Bradbury, provided the then-original notion of a dinosaur being roused from its frozen slumbers by a nuclear bomb test in the Arctic, and somehow making its way to New York to lay waste the better part of Manhattan. The effects are by Ray Harryhausen. In *Them!* (1954), directed by Gordon Douglas, another set of atomic tests in New Mexico mutates ordinary ants into creatures hundreds of times their natural size, and sends them on their way to wreak havoc in Los Angeles. Neither film is all that remarkable but originated the clichés of dormant dinosaurs and colossal insects.

ABOVE *The Beast from 20,000 Fathoms*, 1953, a classic creature by Ray Harryhausen. OPPOSITE Poster art for *Them!*, 1954.

ALL ABOARD THE DEADWOOD STAGE

In the early 1950s, Doris Day projected exactly the right qualities of cheerful optimism and wholesomeness that appealed to a Middle America made paranoid by the Cold War, Communists within, and the threat of nuclear annihilation. Solace was found in materialism, chrome-heavy automobiles, lustrous refrigerators, mammoth washing machines, suburban "elegant" living with candlelit dining and two-car garages, and the cheerfully anodyne musicals of Doris Day, such as *Tea for Two, On Moonlight Bay, April in Paris, Lullaby of Broadway, By the Light of the Silvery Moon,* and others. Occasionally she was given a dramatic role, in *Young Man With a Horn* as the sweet girlfriend of the musician Kirk Douglas, and *Storm Warning,* the wife of a Klan member in a southern state, and was perfectly credible.

Doris Day excelled in her most successful musical, *Calamity Jane,* a comedy western directed by David Butler with Howard Keel as a fine-voiced Wild Bill Hickock. In a nightmare agenda for feminists, her tough whip-crack-away, buckskin-and-leather outfit is replaced by demure gingham, making him realize that she is his kind of woman. Sammy Fain and Paul Francis Webster's "Secret Love" became one of Day's most famous numbers, and won the Best Song Academy Award.

OPPOSITE Doris Day's most successful musical, *Calamity Jane,* 1953. ABOVE In *On Moonlight Bay,* 1951, she played a classic tomboy who has to learn how to behave like a proper young lady, here pictured with Leon Ames, Rosemary DeCamp, and Billy Gray with his dog.

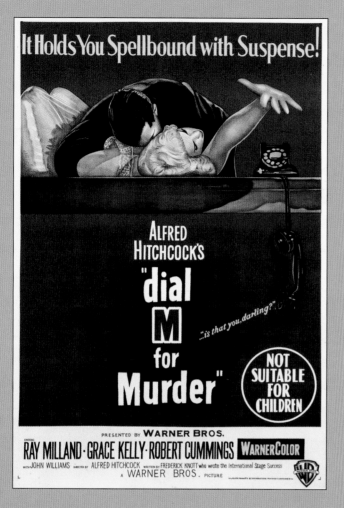

1954

✳ Alfred Hitchcock makes *Dial M for Murder* in 3-D

✳ Judy Garland is outstanding in *A Star is Born*

✳ Sydney Greenstreet dies at the age of seventy-four

✳ Warner Bros.' first film in CinemaScope is *The Command*

✳ In William Wellman's *The High and the Mighty*, John Wayne pilots a stricken airliner in CinemaScope

✳ *Lucky Me* with Doris Day is the studio's first CinemaScope musical

✳ Giant killer ants go on the rampage in *Them!*

✳ Elvis Presley's first broadcast record is aired by WHBQ Memphis

✳ Paul Newman makes his screen debut in *The Silver Chalice*

✳ The Dow Jones index regains level prior to the 1929 crash

ABOVE Australian poster art for the non-3-D version of *Dial M for Murder*. RIGHT Phyllis Kirk and Gene Nelson in the film noir *Crime Wave*, 1954. OPPOSITE Lobby card for *Lucky Me*, 1954.

NOIR NIGHTS

Andre De Toth followed *House of Wax* with a tough *film-noir* thriller set in Los Angeles. *Crime Wave* (1954) had actually been shot before but delayed. Sterling Hayden is a hard-nosed homicide detective who swoops down on an ex-convict played by Gene Nelson (until then largely seen in musicals), believing him to be harboring escaped San Quentin prisoners who have held up a gas station and killed a policeman. Nelson is innocent but is pushed against his will into a bank heist. The cop, who has contempt for all transgressors, is using him as a means to nail the gang. At the time of release it was a "programmer," occupying the lesser half of a double bill. In retrospect it can be seen as a distillation of many of the elements that comprise *film noir*, and is one of its better examples. Particularly impressive is the way the director used real city locations rather than sets, giving an immediacy and realism so often lacking in the studio age, as well as providing an invaluable glimpse of how Los Angeles looked in the mid-twentieth century.

WIDER HORIZONS

In the effort to find new methods to attract audiences, the shape of the screen itself changed. Under Darryl F. Zanuck 20th Century Fox turned heavily to a system called CinemaScope that used anamorphic lenses in the camera to squeeze an image on to 35mm film and similar lenses on projectors to open it out to two and a half times the width of a normal picture. It was not a new idea. Various widescreen processes had been tried in the 1920s, and the anamorphic system had been invented by Henri Chrétien in France in the late twenties. Having bought the rights in 1952, Zanuck ordered all Fox films to be in CinemaScope. Meanwhile Paramount was pressing ahead with a system called VistaVision, in which the exposed image was placed on the camera negative vertically rather than horizontally, the larger area of emulsion enhancing its clarity. Other studios had to decide which horse to back, and eventually it was CinemaScope that was the victor, although not all theaters were suitable for conversion. Exhibitors faced the costs of new screens with adjustable masking, and new projection equipment.

Warner Bros. decided to make films in CinemaScope, actually the inferior WarnerScope, which did not use Bausch & Lomb lenses. WarnerScope was not a success so the studio licensed CinemaScope from Fox. Their first CinemaScope film, *The Command,* a western directed by David Butler, was also shot simultaneously in 3-D but never released in that form. Butler also made a historical film, *King Richard and the Crusaders,* with George Sanders as the monarch and Rex Harrison as Saladin. Doris Day starred in a musical *Lucky Me,* John Wayne impressively skippered a planeload of terrified passengers in a stricken airliner in William Wellman's *The High and the Mighty,* Raoul Walsh's *Battle Cry* was a lengthy homage to the Marine Corps in World War II, and perhaps best forgotten, a youthful Paul Newman made his debut in *The Silver Chalice,* directed by Victor Saville.

COPYRIGHT 1954 WARNER BROS. PICTURES DISTRIBUTING CORPORATION.
PERMISSION GRANTED FOR NEWSPAPER AND MAGAZINE REPRODUCTION.
MADE IN U.S.A.

Property of National Screen Service Corp. Licensed for display only in connection with the exhibition of this picture at your theatre. Must be returned immediately thereafter.

EXPLOSIVE ENTRANCE

A middle-aged woman walks past a boy sitting on a dusty curb. He rises and tails her, occasionally darting out of sight as she makes her way to a house on the edge of a small coastal town. So James Dean made his debut in Elia Kazan's film based on John Steinbeck's *East of Eden*, the first of his three leading roles and the only one released in his lifetime. In a Cain and Abel story set in 1917 in the lettuce fields of California's Salinas Valley, Dean is Cal Trask, the wayward, loner son of an upright farmer Adam (Raymond Massey), who discovers that his long-departed mother (Jo Van Fleet, followed by him in the opening scene) runs a Monterey brothel. He deduces it to be the reason for the rot in his soul, and for his father's despair of him in favor of his righteous brother Aron (Richard Davalos). When his father loses a fortune trying to ship lettuce in an ice-packed train that runs into long delays, Cal secretly works hard to recoup the money, growing beans on a loan from his mother and selling the crop at a handsome profit to the war procurement authorities for shipping to Europe. In a memorable scene Adam spurns Cal's cash as tainted money,

and so rejects his love. Kazan had deliberately provoked conflict between Dean and Massey—the one cocky and fresh from New York and "the Method," the other a respected stalwart of the old school—to ignite their tension on screen. Dean immediately became a sensation, the hottest new young star since Brando, his idol with whom he was constantly compared.

JAMES DEAN
Fast Life, Early Death

James Dean (1931–1955) was born in Marion, Indiana, and when he was six his parents migrated to Santa Monica, California. His mother died when he was nine, and his father sent him back to Indiana to be raised by an uncle and aunt on a farm near Fairmount. Jimmy grew up in a Quaker community, and after graduation from high school, where he had been a keen basketball player and actor, he returned to California and his father. Rather than study law he shifted to drama against his father's wishes; he made it into UCLA, where his Hoosier accent was mocked. He dropped out and found occasional work in television. Encouraged by the actor James Whitmore, whose classes he attended, and by television executive Rogers Brackett he went to New York and for a time was the youngest member of the Actors Studio. He eventually played a couple of parts on Broadway. After the second, Elia Kazan, without particularly liking him, cast him as Cal Trask in *East of Eden* (1955).

Dean had only eighteen months left, during which time he made *Rebel Without a Cause* (1955) for Nicholas Ray and *Giant* (1956) for George Stevens. Other than acting, his great passion was for automobiles, and he had visions of becoming a professional racing driver. He competed in the little spare time he had, and shortly after his role in *Giant* was over had entered in a race at Salinas, deciding to drive there in his new Porsche Spider. At Cholame, near Paso Robles, he was descending a hill toward a right-hand junction. A car coming the other way turned across his path. Dean died. The Porsche mechanic traveling with him was seriously injured and the other driver was unscathed physically although undoubtedly would forever bear the mental scars.

The release of *Rebel Without a Cause* was a month away. Warner Bros. rapidly changed the advertising campaign. The film was an enormous hit, with Dean—a cult figure worldwide—representing a generation of the young who now had found their idol.

LEFT James Dean in *East of Eden,* 1955. OPPOSITE Dean in his trailer during *Rebel Without a Cause,* 1955, "the hottest new young star since Brando."

DEAN AND HIS LEGACY

A few days after production of *Rebel Without a Cause* began under Nicholas Ray's direction it was halted. A decision had been taken to switch from black and white to color to utilize the CinemaScope format to the full and in color, Jim Stark, played by James Dean, wears a zipped scarlet windbreaker that would become iconic. Ray's film, scripted by Stewart

Stern, broke new ground by indicating that teenage dysfunction was not confined to urban slums but spread as easily across the affluent middle classes, as a product of emotional deprivation and parental alienation. The deeply troubled Jim is at odds with his bickering parents, and his unstable history has meant a move to yet another California neighborhood and a new school. He meets a girl (Natalie Wood), desperate for her father to love her, and a boy with a rich but absent father (Sal Mineo), who latches on to Jim as a new hero. Jim is challenged to a knife fight with the leader of the school pack (Corey Allen) followed by a nocturnal "chickie run" in which his rival dies, unable to leap from his speeding car before it goes over the cliff. By dawn there will be another tragedy. The densely compressed drama takes place over little more than twenty-four hours.

Dean's death inevitably raised its box-office profile. Jim's cool yet vulnerable image seemed to apply as much

1955

✳ James Dean is killed in an automobile accident at the age of twenty-four

✳ John Ford is replaced on *Mister Roberts* by Mervyn LeRoy

✳ Singer Peggy Lee is impressive in *Pete Kelly's Blues*

✳ The introduction of the Salk vaccine conquers polio

✳ James Dean makes an electrifying debut in *East of Eden*

✳ Gary Cooper plays the lead in *The Court-Martial of Billy Mitchell*, directed by Otto Preminger

✳ Dean's *Rebel Without a Cause* is released to wild acclaim a month after his death

✳ Disney's first theme park, Disneyland, opens in Anaheim, CA

✳ Warner Bros. begins television production

ABOVE Grieving four visit James Dean's grave in Fairmount, Indiana.
RIGHT James Dean plays Jim Stark in *Rebel Without a Cause*, in a scene shot at the Griffith Observatory, Los Angeles, when it was still a black and white movie.

to Dean himself as his screen persona, elevating him as a figurehead for young people everywhere uncertain of their place in an adult world. Dean's dramatic technique would exert an influence on other actors for decades to come.

His last film, *Giant,* directed by George Stevens, was an epic work based on Edna Ferber's novel about a Texas ranching dynasty in possession of 600,000 acres, with Dean—third-billed after Elizabeth Taylor and Rock Hudson—as a hired hand who strikes oil and becomes a mega-tycoon, eclipsing their wealth. Dean was required to age during the 201-minute movie, its action encompassing more than thirty years, and the latter part of the film offers an intriguing glimpse of how he might have been had his life not ended in 1955 at only twenty-four.

RIGHT preparing for *Giant,* 1956, Dean learned lasso techniques from Bob Hinkle, a Texan. OVERLEAF James Dean on location in Texas for *Giant.*

DEAN'S **DEATH** INEVITABLY RAISED ITS BOX-OFFICE PROFILE. JIM'S COOL YET VULNERABLE IMAGE SEEMED TO APPLY AS MUCH TO DEAN HIMSELF AS HIS SCREEN PERSONA, ELEVATING HIM AS A SYMBOLIC **FIGUREHEAD** FOR YOUNG PEOPLE EVERYWHERE UNCERTAIN OF THEIR PLACE IN AN ADULT WORLD. DEAN'S DRAMATIC TECHNIQUE WOULD EXERT AN INFLUENCE ON OTHER ACTORS FOR DECADES TO COME.

STAR STRUCK

The story of an ingénue who becomes the protégée and the love of a fading, doomed star had first appeared on film as *What Price Hollywood,* directed by George Cukor in 1932, and was then reworked as *A Star is Born* in 1937 with William Wellman directing. It received its most ambitious treatment in the 1954 film of the same title, with George Cukor again as director. In CinemaScope and Technicolor, it was intended to showcase the massive talent of Judy Garland, whose long career at MGM had ended ignominiously when she was fired after making *Summer Stock* in 1950. It was to be the triumph of her bumpy career.

The role of the star in decline was to be played by Cary Grant, but he backed out, some think in the false belief that the public might feel that he was really washed up. James Mason took over as Norman Maine, in one of his finest performances.

Garland performed memorable numbers by Harold Arlen and Ira Gershwin, including "The Man That Got Away," "You Gotta Have Me Go with You," and "Someone at Last," plus a *tour de force,* the eighteen-minute "Born in a Trunk," a show-business life story related through a medley of songs. Sequences were later removed from the film after its initial release to reduce it from over three hours to what was considered a manageable length. In 1983 a reconstructed version was released restoring the excised material (with five minutes where footage had been irretrievably lost presented as a montage of stills), demonstrating the ambitious vision of Cukor. Although nominated, both Garland and Mason failed to achieve deserved Academy Awards.

ALL AT SEA

Although John Ford was initially happy that Henry Fonda had been signed to play the title role of *Mister Roberts* after its lengthy run on Broadway, rather than the preferred choice, William Holden, serious artistic differences occurred fairly early in the production. The star and the director, at odds, came to blows. Ford was replaced by Mervyn LeRoy and harmony of sorts was restored. The film was memorable for another reason. It was the last Warner Bros. film in which James Cagney appeared, as the petty tyrant of a captain of a naval cargo ship in the Pacific during World War II. Fonda's lieutenant, who really wants to be in combat against the Japanese, attempts to be a bulwark between him and the crew, while William Powell, in his last screen role, wryly observes the tensions as ship's doctor, and Jack Lemmon (who won an Academy Award) is notable as Ensign Pulver.

OPPOSITE Judy Garland in a publicity shot for *A Star is Born*, 1954.
ABOVE Doris Day visits Judy Garland filming the "Born in a Trunk" sequence.
ABOVE RIGHT In *Mister Roberts*, 1955, James Cagney as the captain, yells at Henry Fonda as Lieutenant Doug A. Roberts. RIGHT James Dean lassos Elizabeth Taylor while she talks with co-star Rock Hudson on *Giant*.

1956

✳ Elizabeth Taylor and Rock Hudson star in *Giant*, James Dean's last film (above)

✳ Elia Kazan's *Baby Doll* upsets the Catholic Legion of Decency and scores at the box office

✳ John Huston films *Moby Dick* in England and Ireland with Gregory Peck as Captain Ahab

✳ John Ford's *The Searchers* is one of John Wayne's best

✳ Grace Kelly marries Prince Rainier of Monaco

✳ Hitchcock stars Henry Fonda in a true account of mistaken identity, *The Wrong Man*

✳ Egypt nationalizes the Suez Canal

✳ The Soviet Union quells the Hungarian uprising by force

✳ Warner Bros. sells its library of pre-1950 films, ownership eventually going to United Artists Television

THE OBSESSED

Herman Melville's *Moby Dick* formed the basis of two earlier films made by Warner Bros.— *The Sea Beast,* the silent version, in 1926 and a talkie in 1930, both starring John Barrymore as the obsessed Captain Ahab, scouring the seas to find and kill the great white whale that cost him a leg years earlier. John Huston's excellent water-soaked 1956 version is the most faithful to Melville's book, and he co-wrote the screenplay with Ray Bradbury. Gregory Peck as Ahab has more solidity and less passion than Barrymore, and in ranting mode he seems at the limit of his skills, but it is a bold work, with creditable support from the crew of the Pequod, which includes Richard Basehart, Leo Genn, Bernard Miles, and Harry Andrews. Orson Welles sets the mood at the start as Father Mapple, delivering a stirring pulpit sermon on the perils of the sea. Much of the filming took place at studios in London, following serious difficulties with full-size fake whales at sea, and the opening scenes intended to represent nineteenth-century New Bedford were filmed at Youghal in Ireland. The cinematographer Oswald Morris evolved a method of desaturating the Technicolor image to give the appearance of steel engravings of the period.

In a vintage Warner Bros. year *The Searchers* was released, arguably John Wayne and John Ford's best western, with a screenplay by Frank Nugent from an Alan LeMay novel. In the elegiac narrative Wayne stars as an obstinate Civil War veteran, Ethan Edwards, who embarks on a quest with his "nephew" (Jeffrey Hunter), an orphan rescued years earlier, to find his niece (Natalie Wood) who was seized as a child in a Comanche raid. Like Ahab, his search—which lasts for years—becomes an obsession, and his hatred of Indians is such that it is his intention to kill her when she is found, as she will have ceased in his eyes to be a white person. Although the mission is supposed to encompass vast areas of the West and Southwest, Ford shot most of the film in his beloved Monument Valley, Utah, where the thrilling landscapes of red mesas and tall buttes rising over rocky desert provided the finest of backdrops to this raw account of lonely fixation.

Elia Kazan returned to Tennessee Williams with *Baby Doll,* with Carroll Baker, briefly seen in *Giant,* playing the slatternly virgin wife of Karl Malden, a befuddled cotton gin owner who has promised her dying father he will not consummate the marriage until she is twenty. At nineteen she lies sucking her thumb and half-naked in a real crib in their crumbling Mississippi plantation house while her husband spies on her through a peephole. Eli Wallach, a rival gin owner, in his screen debut, seduces her for revenge after her husband burns his mill down. A black farce, adapted from two of Williams' one-act plays, it attracted condemnation from the Catholic Legion of Decency, the surest way to achieve a healthy box office, and launched the careers of Wallach, Baker, and shortie pajamas.

1957

✳ Humphrey Bogart dies from cancer at fifty-six (above)

✳ James Stewart plays Lindbergh in *The Spirit of St. Louis*

✳ President Eisenhower begins his second term

✳ Marlon Brando plays an American major in love with a Japanese woman in *Sayonara*

✳ Governor Faubus of Arkansas calls out the National Guard to stop black students enrolling at Little Rock high school

✳ Elia Kazan's *A Face in the Crowd* portrays a media demagogue

✳ Mamie Van Doren goes wild on rock 'n' roll in *Untamed Youth*

✳ The composer Erich Wolfgang Korngold dies at sixty

✳ Doris Day stars with much of the Broadway cast in *The Pajama Game*

✳ The Boeing 707 jetliner makes its maiden flight

✳ The U.S.S.R. launches its Sputnik satellite

OPPOSITE TOP Gregory Peck as Captain Ahab in *Moby Dick*, 1956. OPPOSITE BELOW John Wayne as Ethan Edwards in the classic end shot from *The Searchers*, 1956, directed by John Ford. LEFT Half-sheet poster from *Baby Doll*, 1956. ABOVE Bogart in an iconic pose.

...this is baby doll

She's nineteen. She makes her husband keep away --she won't let the stranger go.

KARL MALDEN · CARROLL BAKER · ELI WALLACH STORY AND SCREEN PLAY BY TENNESSEE WILLIAMS DIRECTED BY ELIA KAZAN A NEWTOWN PRODUCTION PRESENTED BY **WARNER BROS.**

WEST MEETS EAST

A James Michener novel formed the basis of *Sayonara* under Joshua Logan's direction, examining interracial tensions and fraternization between occupying American military personnel and Japanese locals. Marlon Brando (who carefully adopted a southern accent to play the role) is a pilot from the Korean War posted to Japan, where in spite of the veto on relationships and his own inbuilt prejudice, he falls in love with a dancer (Miiko Taka) in an updating of the *Madame Butterfly* theme. The production earned several Oscar nominations and awards for supporting roles by Red Buttons and Miyoshi Umeki as another couple breaking the official taboo.

In Billy Wilder's *The Spirit of St. Louis* (1957), James Stewart faced the arduous job of carrying the major part of a long, painstaking CinemaScope account of Charles A. Lindbergh's epic solo flight across the Atlantic in 1927 by himself (apart from a stowaway fly in the cockpit.) Wilder also co-wrote the screenplay with Wendell Mayes and weaves a certain amount of Lindbergh's earlier flying experience into the narrative. Stewart, although much too old (forty-seven) to play the twenty-five-year-old Lindy, was accomplished enough to carry off what is essentially an extended internal monolog. Unpopular at the time of its release, it has gained its reputation since as a laudable tribute to Lindbergh's extraordinary feat of endurance and airmanship.

ABOVE Miiko Taka and Marlon Brando in *Sayonara*, 1957, directed by Joshua Logan. OPPOSITE German poster art for "My Flight Over the Ocean," aka *The Spirit of St. Louis*, 1957, Billy Wilder's painstaking, CinemaScope account of Lindbergh's solo flight across the Atlantic.

JAMES STEWART

LINDBERGH

Mein Flug über den Ozean
(THE SPIRIT OF ST. LOUIS)

Ein FARBFILM in
CinemaScope
und
WARNERCOLOR

Nach dem mit dem Pulitzer-Preis ausgezeichneten Buch „THE SPIRIT OF ST. LOUIS" von

CHARLES A. LINDBERGH
Erschienen in der Fischer-Bücherei, Frankfurt

BILLY WILDER und WENDELL MAYES
Drehbuch: BILLY WILDER
Musik: FRANZ WAXMANN
Produktion: LELAND HAYWARD · Regie: BILLY WILDER

WARNER BROS.

UNELECTED POWER

The rise and fall of a media demagogue is sharply etched in Elia Kazan's *A Face in the Crowd* (1957), from a satirical, razor-edged screenplay by Budd Schulberg. An eager radio producer (Patricia Neal) finds a homespun pontificator and guitar strummer (Andy Griffiths in an outstanding debut) in a southern jailhouse and promotes him on her station. Soon his man-of-the-people act resonates with listeners. He rapidly progresses to national television, where his natural charisma conquers the ratings and delivers power sufficient to make politicians quake. At a relatively early stage in the development of television Schulberg and Kazan had realized its capacity to persuade and influence, and what might happen to a gullible audience in the hands of an unprincipled megalomaniac with an undemocratic agenda. The method of destroying the beast is amazingly simple, his microphone is left live when he thought he had gone off air. In spite of a fine cast that also included Lee Remick (another debut), Anthony Franciosa, and Walter Matthau, the film was ahead of its time.

ABOVE Lee Remick's striking debut in *A Face in the Crowd*, 1957. OPPOSITE TOP Cliff Robertson and Raymond Massey in *The Naked and the Dead*, 1958. OPPOSITE BELOW Departure of the first Atlantic jet. RIGHT One-sheet poster art for *The Left-Handed Gun*, 1958.

The novelist Norman Mailer never surpassed his epic of World War II *The Naked and the Dead* (1958), but Raoul Walsh's film version disappointingly turned out to be a standard action film in which a beleaguered platoon fights desperately to hold out on a Pacific island. In his book Mailer caught the flavor of soldiers' speech, so much so that its accurate repetitions of obscenities inflamed the morality groups. All that had to go, removing authenticity and believability. Aldo Ray plays the tough sergeant, Raymond Massey the heartless general who regards men as cannon fodder, Cliff Robertson the officer who detests his methods.

Another fumbled interpretation was Arthur Penn's film from a Gore Vidal television play, which attempted a revisionist look at a familiar story. *The Left-Handed Gun* (1958) features Paul Newman as the western outlaw Billy the Kid, with Hurd Hatfield as a pulp novelist who wants to elevate him to hero status, and John Dehner as his friend Pat Garrett. The title perpetuated a myth stemming from a famous tintype reversed image.

1958

✳ Jet air travel across the Atlantic is inaugurated by B.O.A.C.

✳ The Treaty of Rome comes into force, establishing the European Economic Community

✳ Cary Grant co-stars with Ingrid Bergman in *Indiscreet*

✳ Stanley Donen and George Abbott follow *The Pajama Game* with *Damn Yankees*, both choreographed by Bob Fosse

✳ Spencer Tracy stars in the John Sturges film of Hemingway's *The Old Man and the Sea*

✳ Elvis Presley is drafted into the U.S. Army

✳ Rosalind Russell repeats her Broadway role on screen in *Auntie Mame*

✳ Mervyn LeRoy directs *No Time for Sergeants* with Andy Griffith

✳ Raoul Walsh's version of Norman Mailer's seminal *The Naked and the Dead* has its expletives deleted

THAT'S ALL, FOLKS

Warner Bros.' interest in cartoons began in the 1930s, when the former Disney animators Hugh Harman and Rudolf Ising were hired to make *Looney Tunes* and *Merrie Melodies,* in which songs from the vast Warner music library were featured in cartoons, in direct competition with Walt Disney's *Silly Symphonies. Merrie Melodies* were produced first in two-color Technicolor, and then in the new three-color process, with *Looney Tunes* following. Tex Avery, Friz Freleng, Bob Clampett, Frank Tashlin, and Chuck Jones arrived as animators and Carl Stalling came to write the music. They worked in an enclave on the Warner Sunset lot known as "Termite Terrace." Among the animation stars they developed were Porky Pig, Daffy Duck, Elmer Fudd, Bugs Bunny, Tweety Pie, Sylvester

the Cat, Wile E. Coyote and Road Runner, and Speedy Gonzales. During World War II they worked on *Private Snafu* cartoons for the Army Air Corps to train troops on how to stay alive.

Warner Bros. Cartoons continued into the 1950s, when it was briefly closed down amid fears that the vogue for 3-D would spell the end for animation subjects. It started up again and relocated to the Burbank lot. In 1960 *The Bugs Bunny Show* premiered on ABC in prime time and became an immediate hit. Theatrical cartoons sputtered along until 1969, when the plug was pulled and Warner Bros. Cartoons closed. In later years, Warner Bros.' talent for breakthrough animation would continue in television with programs such as *Steven Spielberg Presents Tiny Toon Adventures, Pinky and the Brain,* and *Batman Beyond.*

OPPOSITE Mel Blanc, the voice of Bugs Bunny, in the Cartoon Department at Warner Bros. ABOVE The stars of animation from left: Sylvester, Yosemite Sam, Elmer Fudd, Tweety, Porky Pig, Speedy Gonzales, Daffy Duck, Bugs Bunny, Pepe le Pew, Road Runner, Wile E. Coyote, Foghorn Leghorn.

1959

* Fidel Castro ousts the Batista government and becomes premier of Cuba (above)

* Buddy Holly, Richie Valens, and the Big Bopper die in a plane crash

* Audrey Hepburn is Oscar-nominated for her role in *The Nun's Story*

* John Wayne stars in the Howard Hawks western *Rio Bravo*

* Mervyn LeRoy's lengthy *The F.B.I. Story* stars James Stewart

* Alaska becomes the 49th state, Hawaii the 50th

* Delmer Daves directs Troy Donahue and Sandra Dee in *A Summer Place*

* *The Young Philadelphian*s features Paul Newman and Barbara Rush

* Errol Flynn dies at fifty

BREAKING THE VOW

Audrey Hepburn starred in Fred Zinnemann's long, carefully rendered screen version of *The Nun's Story*, Kathryn C. Hulme's novel adapted by Robert Anderson about a young woman who embarks on a long path to taking her vows, working in the Belgian Congo in a field hospital, struggling with her vocation and eventually renouncing the order. It is a *tour de force* for Hepburn, a performance of beauty, dignity, and compassion, with Edith Evans as her Mother Superior, Peggy Ashcroft, Colleen Dewhurst, and Mildred Natwick as nuns, and Peter Finch as a doctor in the Congo to whom she finds herself attracted. Franz Waxman's score fades as the film ends and the end titles unfurl in total silence—a calculated decision.

ABOVE Audrey Hepburn in *The Nun's Story*, 1959—"a performance of beauty, dignity, and compassion." OPPOSITE TOP Robert Mitchum on location for *The Sundowners*, 1960. OPPOSITE BELOW The stars and crew of *Rio Bravo*, 1959, in front row from left, Dean Martin, Howard Hawks, John Wayne; behind left and right, Walter Brennan and Ricky Nelson.

Zinnemann's version of Jon Cleary's outback novel *The Sundowners*, adapted by Isabel Lennart, was shot in Australia, with Robert Mitchum as an itinerant sheep drover in the 1920s and Deborah Kerr as his affectionate but long-suffering wife who wants to settle in one place. Glynis Johns and Peter Ustinov are among the characters who amble into this leisurely work, wondrously photographed on location by Jack Hildyard.

Howard Hawks' western *Rio Bravo,* scripted by Jules Furthman and Leigh Brackett, is also lengthy, but one of John Wayne's finest. Both Hawks and Wayne were angered by the thesis of *High Noon*—that a marshal in trouble would be abandoned by the citizenry and made to face it all by himself. In their view this was not the American way. As a small-town sheriff charged with holding a killer against the attempts of badmen who come to force his release, Wayne enlists the aid of a sobering-up drunk (Dean Martin), a gung-ho fast shot with little experience (Ricky Nelson), and a crabby old man with a limp (Walter Brennan), with Angie Dickinson as a shapely saloon girl called Feathers. It is great fun, its length allowing time for every familiar moment to be properly savored.

THE CHIPS ARE DOWN

A bunch of wartime comrades reunite in *Ocean's Eleven* (1960), directed by Lewis Milestone, to carry out a monumental heist of five Las Vegas casinos on New Year's Eve, with every move mapped out like a military operation. Elaborate capers, dependent on precise timing and technology, have become commonplace, but not so in 1960, and the premise is an intriguing one. Given that Danny Ocean, the heistmaster, is played by Frank Sinatra and the gang includes Dean Martin, Sammy Davis Jr., Peter Lawford, and Joey Bishop—the so-called "Rat Pack" of super-cool Hollywood celebrities, renowned for hanging out together—the acting has a lazy, self-regarding air, with everybody appearing to have a great time.

Elia Kazan's *Splendor in the Grass* (1961), with an original screenplay by William Inge, is an overheated yarn about the sexual repression of young lovers in rural Kansas in the late 1920s, just before the Wall Street crash. Natalie Wood is a poor girl in love with an equally besotted rich boy (Warren Beatty), but parents on both sides hinder their relationship and with the best intentions ruin their children's lives. The boy's father (Pat Hingle) wants him to head for Yale, urging him to sow his oats with a worthless high-school tramp, while good girl Wood undergoes a breakdown and is institutionalized. Both Wood and Beatty, in his first film, respond to Kazan's masterly direction and give exemplary performances.

Beatty also made *The Roman Spring of Mrs. Stone* (1961) as an Italian gigolo, pimped by Lotte Lenya for a faded actress—a harshly photographed Vivien Leigh. Gavin Lambert's screenplay made much of the Tennessee Williams novel that was its source, but the direction of Jose Quintero is less incisive. Leigh had by then separated from Laurence Olivier but her performance was spot on. Unfortunately there was only one more film to come before her death in 1967.

1960

✳ Frank Sinatra and "the Rat Pack" appear in *Ocean's Eleven*

✳ John Ford examines racial prejudice in *Sergeant Rutledge*

✳ William Inge's *The Dark at the Top of the Stairs* is filmed by Delbert Mann

✳ Clark Gable dies aged fifty-nine

✳ Richard Burton is a New England doctor in *The Bramble Bush*

✳ Jane Fonda makes her debut in *Tall Story*

✳ John F. Kennedy defeats Richard M. Nixon in the U.S. presidential election

OPPOSITE Ten of *Ocean's Eleven,* left to right: Akim Tamiroff, Clem Harvey, Norman Fell, Buddy Lester, Dean Martin, Henry Silva, Joey Bishop, Sammy Davis Jr., Peter Lawford, and Frank Sinatra. TOP Vivien Leigh and Warren Beatty in *The Roman Spring of Mrs. Stone,* 1961. ABOVE Warren Beatty and Natalie Wood in *Splendor in the Grass,* 1961. ABOVE RIGHT Peter Lawford greets President John F. Kennedy. RIGHT The air was electric in Las Vegas.

SHOW TIME

Broadway in the 1960s supplied superb musical entertainment to be translated into film. Robert Preston had played the central part of *The Music Man* (1962) on stage. Jack Warner only saw him as a second-rank film actor and wanted Frank Sinatra to play the conman who comes to River City, Iowa, seeking funds to set up a boys' marching band with the intention of skipping town with the money. Meredith Willson—whose show it was—insisted on Preston, and as Morton DaCosta, who was both producer and director, was in full agreement, he had his way. As Professor Harold Hill, Preston repeated his charismatic turn, and through the prevailing sweetness of Shirley Jones, the town's winsome librarian, the band with its uniforms, plumes, and seventy-six trombones actually materializes in one of the greatest screen finales ever.

Natalie Wood played the title role in *Gypsy* (1962), directed by Mervyn LeRoy and based on the early show-business life of the wholesome striptease artist Gypsy Rose Lee, with music by Jule Styne and lyrics by Stephen Sondheim. In the role of Rose—one of the most formidable stage mothers of all time—was Rosalind Russell, who had been cast in preference to Ethel Merman, the creator of the role on stage, deemed too much of a powerhouse for the screen portrayal. Russell performs admirably, although most of her singing, including her big number, "Rose's Turn," was dubbed by Lisa Kirk. Natalie Wood impressively metamorphoses from a gawky, timid thirteen-year-old into a beautiful, sophisticated woman, a feat requiring acting ability rather than prosthetics.

Warner Bros. paid a record $5.5 million for the rights of *My Fair Lady* (1964), the Lerner and Loewe musical based on Shaw's *Pygmalion,* almost a third of the entire budget. In place of Julie Andrews, the Eliza of the Broadway production, Audrey Hepburn was assigned to the role, with most of her singing dubbed by Marni Nixon, but Rex Harrison was retained as Professor Henry Higgins, the speech mentor who transforms her from cockney flower girl to society beauty. George Cukor's direction, Cecil Beaton's elegant costumes,

1961

✳ The Russian cosmonaut Yuri Gagarin is the first man in space (above)

✳ Joshua Logan directs *Fanny* with Charles Boyer, Leslie Caron, and Maurice Chevalier

✳ Connie Stevens is an unwed mother in *Susan Slade*

✳ Fidel Castro condemns the U.S. for the failed Bay of Pigs attack

✳ Gary Cooper dies at sixty

✳ Claudette Colbert's last theatrical film is *Parrish*

✳ William Inge's screenplay for *Splendor in the Grass* wins an Academy Award

✳ Ernest Hemingway commits suicide in Sun Valley, Idaho

and the magnificent score ensured success for an expensive, ambitious, and literate musical.

Lerner and Loewe's *Camelot* (1967), based on T.H. White's Arthurian tale *The Once and Future King,* cost almost as much to film as *My Fair Lady* but achieved little of the impact. Under Joshua Logan's direction Vanessa Redgrave played Guinevere, Richard Harris the king, and Franco Nero the gallant Sir Lancelot. The largest stage on the Burbank lot (Stage 16) was filled with the Great Hall and Throne Room, and the Alcazar at Segovia in Spain supplied the exteriors of King Arthur's castle.

LEFT Shirley Jones and Robert Preston lead "76 Trombones" in *The Music Man,* 1962. ABOVE Natalie Wood takes it off in *Gypsy,* 1962. TOP Audrey Hepburn as Eliza Doolittle in *My Fair Lady,* 1964. RIGHT Joan Crawford listens to Bette Davis in *Whatever Happened to Baby Jane?,* 1962.

1962

✱ *Whatever Happened to Baby Jane?* evokes old Hollywood with Joan Crawford and Bette Davis

✱ Robert Preston repeats his Broadway triumph in *The Music Man*

✱ Marilyn Monroe is found dead at her home in Brentwood, aged thirty-six

✱ Rosalind Russell and Natalie Wood are mother and daughter in *Gypsy*

✱ Rosalind Russell and Alec Guinness co-star in *A Majority of One*

✱ Jeff Chandler's last film is Sam Fuller's *Merrill's Marauders*

✱ The Hungarian-born director Michael Curtiz dies aged seventy-five

✱ The nine-day Cuban missile crisis brings the threat of world war

✱ *Gay Purr-ee* is an animated film about a cat finding love in Paris

"YOU'RE TEARING ME APART!"

LEFT Camera rehearsal on the Covent Garden set with Audrey Hepburn for "Wouldn't it be Loverly" in *My Fair Lady*. TOP Richard Harris and Vanessa Redgrave in *Camelot*, 1967. ABOVE Jack L. Warner and his dog Camelot on the set of the movie of that name, 1967.

1963

* President Kennedy is assassinated in Dallas

* In *Days of Wine and Roses* Jack Lemmon plays an alcoholic advertising executive

* Dick Powell (fifty-eight) and Jack Carson (fifty-two) die within days of each other

* Elia Kazan's *America America* is a personal account of his uncle's struggles to reach the New World

* Bob Hope plays a drama critic in *Critic's Choice* with Lucille Ball

* Frank Sinatra and Dean Martin co-star in *4 for Texas*

* *Spencer's Mountain* with Henry Fonda, based on Earl Hamner's novel, presages *The Waltons*

* Lee Harvey Oswald, in custody as Kennedy's killer, is shot dead by Jack Ruby

ABOVE Dallas, November 22, 1963. RIGHT Stathis Giallelis (right) in the lead role in *America America*, 1963, directed by Elia Kazan.

AMERICAN DREAM

Elia Kazan wrote and directed *America Americ,* (1963), which was based on his novel, an account of the struggle his uncle underwent to escape to the United States from under the harsh thumb of Turkish-occupied Anatolia at the end of the nineteenth century. A story very personal to the Constantinople-born Kazan and his family, it is lengthy and impassioned, with a Greek actor, Stathis Giallelis, in the lead, and a music score by Manos Hatzidakis abets Haskell Wexler's rich black-and-white cinematography. Although somewhat forgotten, few better tributes to the "huddled masses" exist on film.

In *Days of Wine and Roses* (1962), originally a teleplay by J. P. Miller, and soberly directed by Blake Edwards, Jack Lemmon is a San Francisco PR man whose tippling in the course of his work extends too far, tragically enveloping his non-drinking wife in an alcoholic embrace even more acute than his. The Henry Mancini-Johnny Mercer theme song to this sharply observed view of the dangers of alcoholism won an Oscar.

ABOVE Half-sheet poster art for *Days of Wine and Roses*, 1962.

"YOU'RE TEARING ME APART!"

EPIC JOURNEYS

Like most filmmakers of his generation if they made westerns, John Ford at one time or another unsympathetically portrayed Native Americans, often casting them as savage predators hindering the white man's desire to bring civilization and progress to the Old West. Raoul Walsh was still doing it in *A Distant Trumpet* with Troy Donahue as a young lieutenant obliged to rein back his sympathies to maintain military order. Ford's sprawling *Cheyenne Autumn* (1964) is his last western and his belated atonement, looking from their point of view at the disillusionment of the Cheyenne, depleted in numbers, forced on to a reservation in Oklahoma many hundreds of miles from the Yellowstone River, and betrayed by false promises. They embark on the long trek back to their homelands with Sal Mineo, Gilbert Roland, and Dolores del Rio in their ranks, Richard Widmark as a cavalry officer, Carroll Baker a Quaker schoolteacher accompanying. James Stewart as Wyatt Earp and Arthur Kennedy as Doc Holliday appear as light relief in a Dodge City interlude that was cut after initial screenings.

Blake Edwards made a comedy epic, *The Great Race* (1965), a tribute to the custard-pie era of the Keystone Kops and to Laurel and Hardy. A huge cast—led by Natalie Wood as an early "new woman," Tony Curtis as the hero in immaculate white and glinting teeth, a villainous Jack Lemmon, mustachioed and always garbed in black and Peter Falk as his maltreated assistant—embark on an automobile race from New York to Paris. The gags are incessant and set-pieces include a parody of *The Prisoner of Zenda* and the biggest pie fight ever staged for a film.

1964

✳ John Ford's *Cheyenne Autumn* examines the harsh treatment and neglect of displaced Native Americans

✳ The film of the year is *My Fair Lady*, winning eight Oscars including Best Picture

✳ The war escalates between North and South Vietnam

✳ Bette Davis plays twin sisters for second time in *Dead Ringer*

✳ Natalie Wood, Tony Curtis, Henry Fonda, and Lauren Bacall star in *Sex and the Single Girl*

✳ *Kisses for My President* anticipates the first woman to occupy the Oval Office

✳ Frank Sinatra and Bing Crosby appear in *Robin and the 7 Hoods*, set in 1920s Chicago

✳ President Lyndon Johnson beats Senator Barry Goldwater in the presidential election

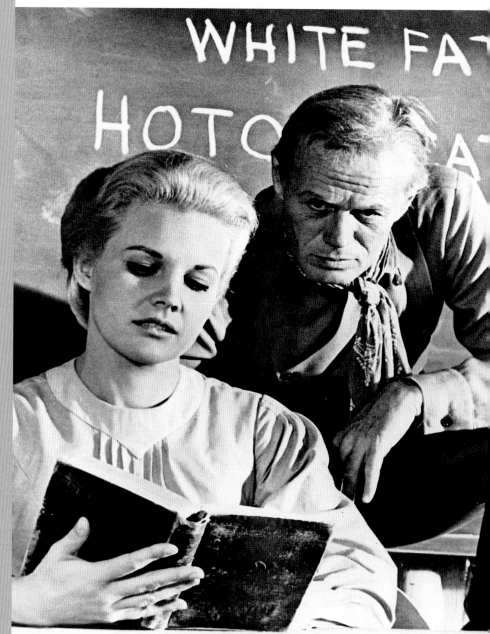

FAR LEFT The cavalry in Monument Valley for *Cheyenne Autumn*, 1964.
LEFT Carroll Baker and Richard Widmark in *Cheyenne Autumn*, directed
by John Ford. ABOVE On location in Paris, Tony Curtis, Jack Lemmon,
and Natalie Wood in *The Great Race*, 1965. ABOVE RIGHT One-sheet
poster art for the film.

1965

✱ *The Great Race* is an epic comedy by Blake Edwards with
the biggest custard-pie battle in screen history

✱ Frank Sinatra directs *None But the Brave*, in which U.S.
Marines engage a Japanese Pacific garrison

✱ U.S. combat forces land in Vietnam

✱ Winston Churchill dies at ninety

✱ Black Muslim leader Malcolm X is assassinated

✱ Maureen O'Hara and Rossano Brazzi co-star in
The Battle of the Villa Fiorita

✱ The 1945 Ardennes breakthrough is the basis of
Battle of the Bulge

✱ Glenn Ford and Geraldine Page star in Delbert Mann's
Dear Heart

✱ George Peppard has amnesia in Jack Smight's *The
Third Day*

1966

* Ronald Reagan becomes governor of California

* Natalie Wood stars in *Inside Daisy Clover*, directed by Robert Mulligan

* Paul Newman plays a cynical private eye in *Harper*

* *Who's Afraid of Virginia Woolf?* wins five Oscars

* Henry Fonda is the lead in Fielder Cook's western *A Big Hand for a Little Lady*

* Jane Fonda stars in the screen version of *Any Wednesday*

* Sean Connery goes insane in *A Fine Madness*

* Warren Beatty and Susannah York co-star in *Kaleidoscope*

STRESSED OUT

Edward Albee's scathing stage portrait of a marriage in full-destruct mode was skillfully adapted for the screen by Ernest Lehman and directed by Mike Nichols. *Who's Afraid of Virginia Woolf?* (1966)) starred Richard Burton and Elizabeth Taylor as a New England history professor and his wife, with George Segal and Sandy Dennis as their guests who become involved in the alcohol-fueled orgy of ranting character assassination. Elizabeth Taylor had never displayed such emotional release before, and the dialogue broke new ground in its use of words and phrases not previously heard on screen.

In Jack Smight's *Harper* (1966), Paul Newman plays Ross MacDonald's jaded private eye Lew Archer (the name change was for Newman's benefit, as he had a good track record with titles beginning with "H"—*Hud, The Hustler, Hombre,* etc.) who lives in his office, makes coffee from yesterday's used grounds, and drives a battered car with mismatched panels. Lauren Bacall is the rich woman hiring him to locate her missing husband. Pauses on his journey include encounters with a muscle-builder, a junkie singer, a time-expired actress and a weird Californian sect. Newman's sardonic tone hits the note perfectly.

Paul Newman is 'Harper'

and Harper is just not to be believed!!!

Girls think Harper is kicky.
But sometimes he makes
them feel funny.
See Harper make girls feel funny.
See Harper.

A GERSHWIN-KASTNER Production

LAUREN **BACALL** · JULIE **HARRIS** · ARTHUR **HILL** · JANET **LEIGH** · PAMELA **TIFFIN** · ROBERT **WAGNER** · SHELLEY **WINTERS**

TECHNICOLOR· PANAVISION· FROM WARNER BROS.

FAR LEFT Ronald Reagan in Sacramento. LEFT Richard Burton and Elizabeth Taylor, with George Segal in the background, in *Who's Afraid of Virginia Woolf?*, 1966. ABOVE Poster art for *Harper*, 1966, another movie beginning with the letter H for Paul Newman.

1967

* Faye Dunaway and Warren Beatty are bank robbers who kill in Arthur Penn's *Bonnie and Clyde*

* Spencer Tracy (sixty-seven) and Paul Muni (seventy-one) die

* Sandy Dennis is the lead in Robert Mulligan's *Up the Down Staircase*

* Warner Bros. is acquired by Seven Arts

* In Sidney J. Furie's *The Naked Runner*, Frank Sinatra is hijacked into an espionage intrigue

* Israel wins the Six-Day War against Egypt, Jordan, and Syria

* Richard Harris and Vanessa Redgrave are King Arthur and Guinevere in *Camelot*

* Paul Newman is acclaimed for his role in *Cool Hand Luke*

* Audrey Hepburn is a threatened blind woman in *Wait Until Dark*

* Marlon Brando and Elizabeth Taylor co-star in *John Huston's Reflections in a Golden Eye*

ABOVE Spanish poster art for *Bonnie and Clyde*. RIGHT Faye Dunaway as Bonnie Parker. OPPOSITE Warren Beatty on the set of what was to be one of 1967's biggest hits.

WE ROB BANKS

Initially Warner Bros. did not expect too much from *Bonnie and Clyde,* and its release was muted. Unexpected audience reactions caused a re-think and a re-launch, and it turned out to be one of 1967's biggest hits. Bonnie Parker and Clyde Barrow were itinerant bank robbers across the Depression-ravaged Southwest in the 1930s. Warren Beatty and Faye Dunaway were far more glamorous than their real-life counterparts, and Arthur Penn's film elevates them to Robin Hood status as they wage war on the banks foreclosing on bankrupted farmers. Their eventual end—writhing balletically in a barrage of gunfire—almost elevates them to martyrdom. The supporting cast with Gene Hackman, Michael J. Pollard, Estelle Parsons, and Gene Wilder in his debut role, is excellent and the use of Earl Scruggs and Lester Flatt's "Foggy Mountain Breakdown" enlivens the pace of their bank getaways.

In Stuart Rosenberg's *Cool Hand Luke*, Paul Newman is sentenced to two years on a prison farm for vandalizing parking meters. All the hell of *I Am a Fugitive From a Chain Gang* is there in glowing color, and Luke becomes a hero and figurehead for other prisoners on account of his refusal to ever give up, even when beaten to pulp. George Kennedy delivers his best performance as the bully who eventually reveres Luke.

WARREN BEATTY

Elia Kazan had made stars of Marlon Brando and James Dean. Completing the triad was Warren Beatty, directed by Kazan in his feature debut in William Inge's *Splendor in the Grass* in 1961. Beatty brought to the role of the rich high-schooler who takes up with a girl from the wrong side of the tracks a quality immediately perceived as exciting and auspicious. It brought out the best in his young, yet firmly established co-star Natalie Wood, and their inner chemistry ignited the screen. Here was a new actor who was physically fit, intelligent, and good-looking.

He went on to play an Italian gigolo in *The Roman Spring of Mrs. Stone* and a handsome, selfish drifter in *All Fall Down* (1962), a charming porn filmmaker in *Promise Her Anything* (1965), and an engaging upscale cardsharp in *Kaleidoscope* (1966).

His apotheosis came with *Bonnie and Clyde,* directed by Arthur Penn with Beatty producing. He reshaped the image of the bank robber Clyde Barrow to suit his own persona and, with an accurate eye for what would woo the public, made him into a compelling antihero.

Beatty was born in 1937 in Richmond, Virginia, his father a psychology professor, his mother a drama teacher who encouraged him to act. Another spur was his sister, Shirley MacLaine, three years older and well ahead of him in the game. After a spell studying drama at Northwestern University, he dropped out to join Stella Adler's acting classes in New York, where he appeared in many off-Broadway productions, and one Broadway play, Inge's *A Loss of Roses.* He moved to television, becoming known for his performance as the rich-boy antagonist of the amorous hero in *The Many Loves of Dobie Gillis* (1959).

In Hollywood he was excellent as the antihero of the Robert Altman western *McCabe and Mrs. Miller* (1971) opposite Julie Christie, with whom he made *Shampoo* (1975). His directing debut came with *Heaven Can Wait* (1978) in tandem with Buck Henry, and he showed ambition and courage, and won the Best Director Oscar for *Reds* (1981), a biographical account of John Reed and the Russian Revolution.

Dick Tracy (1990) was photographed in the vibrant rich colors of a comic strip and was received well at the box office. He played another real-life gangster who kicked off the postwar boom in Las Vegas and was rubbed out for his pains in *Bugsy* (1991), directed by Barry Levinson.

THE WARNER BROS. STORY

Paul Newman relaxes between takes as Lucas "Cool Hand" Jackson, in *Cool Hand Luke*, 1967.

DRIVE TIME

In *Bullitt* (1968), a British director, Peter Yates, first exploited the phenomenon in which cars driven at excessive speed down the vertiginous streets of San Francisco would on exiting the level plateaus at intersections soar into the air like ski jumpers. The chase—Steve McQueen in his Ford Mustang and the villains in a Dodge Charger—was a turning point in the depiction of motorized pursuit, and took three difficult weeks to film. McQueen is a determined police lieutenant beset by the Mafia and a slimy politician (Robert Vaughn), who refuses to give up when a key witness under protection is killed. Yates uses his San Francisco locations with imagination, and his police thriller is prototypical of many to follow.

Richard Lester's *Petulia* (1968), photographed with immense style by Nicolas Roeg, is a very different San Francisco film, with George C. Scott as a divorced surgeon having an affair with a kooky, unpredictable girl (Julie Christie) married to a violent husband (Richard Chamberlain). The film is nihilistic, implying that life in 1960s America has become pointless, and Lester uses modish jump cuts to fracture the continuity, as if to reinforce the thesis.

1968

✳ Julie Christie appears with George C. Scott and Richard Chamberlain in *Petulia* (above)

✳ Paul Newman makes his directorial debut with *Rachel, Rachel*

✳ John Wayne, with Ray Kellogg, directs and stars in Vietnam heroics, *The Green Berets*

✳ Martin Luther King, Jr. is assassinated

✳ Steve McQueen guns a Ford Mustang through San Francisco in *Bullitt*

✳ Russians send tanks in to quell the "Prague Spring" of reforms

✳ Fred Astaire appears in Francis Ford Coppola's musical *Finian's Rainbow*

✳ Robert F. Kennedy is shot and killed in Los Angeles

✳ Richard M. Nixon is elected 37th president of the United States

RIGHT Steve McQueen, off-camera in *Bullitt*, 1968 on a favorite British motorbike, projecting the definitive and iconic cool look.
OPPOSITE One-sheet poster art for *Bullitt*.

STEVE McQUEEN AS 'BULLITT'

A SOLAR PRODUCTION

The word 'cop' isn't written all over him—something more puzzling is.

ROBERT VAUGHN

Co-Starring
JACQUELINE BISSET·DON GORDON·ROBERT DUVALL·SIMON OAKLAND·NORMAN FELL   Executive Producer ROBERT E.RELYEA
Music by Lalo Schifrin · Screenplay by ALAN R. TRUSTMAN and HARRY KLEINER · Based on the novel "Mute Witness" by Robert L. Pike · Produced by PHILIP D'ANTONI · Directed by PETER YATES   TECHNICOLOR® FROM WARNER BROS.-SEVEN ARTS

1969

* Neil Armstrong and Buzz Aldrin are the first men on the moon (above)

* Rod Steiger plays Ray Bradbury's *The Illustrated Man*, directed by Jack Smight

* Elia Kazan adapts and directs his own novel, *The Arrangement*

* *The Wild Bunch*, directed by Sam Peckinpah, is a watershed in screen violence

* The Manson Family murders Sharon Tate and others

* The Boeing 747 takes to the skies

* Gordon Parks directs *The Learning Tree*, a semiautobiographical account of growing up black in 1920s rural Kansas

* Francis Ford Coppola's *The Rain People* stars Shirley Knight and James Caan

* Kinney National purchases Warner Bros.–Seven Arts

RIGHT William Holden in *The Wild Bunch*, 1969. OPPOSITE Holden with, from left, Ben Johnson, Warren Oates, and Ernest Borgnine on their long walk to destiny.

BLOOD AND DUST

For some, Sam Peckinpah's film *The Wild Bunch* was the most violent film made to that date, the first in which effects simulated the realistic impact of bullets tearing into flesh. For others it was a valedictory western, set in 1913 when the automobile age was beginning to bite. John Wayne considered that Peckinpah's film had succeeded in destroying the Old West, ignoring the fact that within its context the march of progress had already achieved that purpose. The past can still be savored across the border in Mexico. Half a dozen outlaws, their leader (William Holden), weighted by advanced middle age, Ernest Borgnine, Ben Johnson, Warren Oates, Jaime Sanchez, and Edmond O'Brien, having failed to rob a bank, attempt their last job—the robbery of a train laden with arms. A former gang member, Robert Ryan, leads merciless bounty hunters after them. The bloodbath is horrific. Cut on initial release, restoration to its full 144 minutes reveals the background to the conflict between Holden and Ryan, and gives it substance.

GEORGE PERRY

"YOU'RE TEARING ME APART!"

CHAPTER 5

"WHO'S GOING TO SEE THIS MOVIE?"

TED ASHLEY TO JOHN CALLEY, DISCUSSING *DELIVERANCE*

PREVIOUS PAGE Poster art from *Dirty Harry*, 1971.
ABOVE A look at *Woodstock*, 1970, Michael Wadleigh's mammoth documentary, covering the peace and love rockfest of August 1969.

THE WARNER BROS. STORY

As of 1969, just eighteen months after Seven Arts had acquired it, Warner Bros was once again in play, with the leading player being Kinney Services Corp, a ragtag but profitable conglomerate the holdings of which included a car rental business, an office cleaning company, and even a string of funeral homes. It had been put together by Steven J. Ross, an utterly charming, completely good-natured man who had an astonishing talent for number-crunching and deal-making. His eye had fastened on Warner Bros. not so much for its nearly moribund movie business, which he was quite prepared to spin off (if he could find a buyer), but for its music business.

In those days, especially in the record business, it was a license to print money. It had a huge audience, especially among adolescents, and—unlike the movies—it cost next to nothing to produce and market a disc. Its margins were, to put it simply, fantastic and Warner Bros. had one of the hottest of labels, Reprise, which was partially owned by Frank Sinatra. Kinney also had an excellent entrée to show business in the person of Ted Ashley, who had built his talent agency, Ashley Famous, into Hollywood's second largest representative of actors, directors, and writers. He was bored with serving these monumental egos and believed he should preside over either a movie studio or a television network. When he sold his company to Ross there was a synergy of ambitions; so when Ross acquired Warner Bros. Ashley was made studio chairman, with steady, reliable Frank Wells as head of business affairs, and bright, funny John Calley as head of production.

Calley had been producing films and television shows, and thought that gave him an edge over his production chief rivals at other studios: "They were ex-agents or people who had somehow levitated up from marginal jobs," but really didn't know what to do in a crisis. "They'd get in a limo and drive to the set and have lunch at craft services and talk to the director and leave," but with their problems essentially unsolved. "I thought what you do is work with the filmmakers—the guys who look through the camera. It's their judgment, it's their taste, it's their vision" that he felt he had to bank on. Putting it simply, he judged that this was a business that had to rely not on focus groups or surveys, but on gut instinct, which this very confident man felt he could supply.

All he needed was a little luck, which he got, largely in the form of *Woodstock* (1970), a split-screen, hard-rocking documentary about the famous peace and love rock concert that riveted the world's attention in the summer of 1969. Director Michael Wadleigh and his youthful associates thought they could make some sort of concert film about it, but less than a week before it was scheduled he lacked money to rent cameras and buy film. He needed $15,000, and hearing about that, Calley advanced the sum as a down payment on all rights to whatever film resulted. At the time he had no idea what an astonishing event it would turn out to be. But he figured, if nothing else, that he could recoup his investment by licensing the stock footage from Wadleigh and his team of cameramen (which included Martin Scorsese, who would also work on the editing until he was fired). The shoot—foodless days, sleepless nights, stopped-up toilets—remains one of his most vivid movie-making experiences. The footage a huge post-production team began cutting (on specially designed equipment) was astonishing, but not so much so as the results. The studio cleared over $13 million on initial domestic release, with millions flowing in through the ancillary markets over the many years to come—on a movie that, by feature-film standards, had cost almost nothing.

Suddenly, Steve Ross was very interested in the movie business. He and Ashley gave free range to Calley's eclectic gut. On the one hand he would rescue Donald Cammell and Nick Roeg's deeply perverse *Performance* (1970), which starred Mick Jagger, from the shelf to which the previous management had relegated it, and enjoy a *succès de scandale;* on the other he would make a series of undistinguished but profitable John Wayne westerns, beginning with *Chisum* in 1970. A year later there would be *Klute,* with tough-talking, dangerously threatened

Vice. And Versa.

Mick Jagger.   And Mick Jagger.

James Fox.   And James Fox.

See them all in a film about fantasy. And reality. Vice. And versa.

performance.

Hear **Mick Jagger** sing his own song "Memo From Turner."

James Fox / Mick Jagger / Anita Pallenberg / Michele Breton

Written by Donald Cammell / Directed by Donald Cammell & Nicolas Roeg / Produced by Sanford Lieberson in Technicolor.
A Goodtimes Enterprises Production from Warner Bros. THIS FILM IS RATED (X) NO ONE UNDER 17 ADMITTED
Hear Mick Jagger sing "Memo From Turner" in the original sound track album on Warner Bros. Records and tapes.

70/66

COPYRIGHT © 1970 WARNER BROS. INC.

Jane Fonda as a prostitute helping an out-of-town detective solve a missing persons case, *Summer of '42,* a sentimental, highly popular romance and, most powerfully, *A Clockwork Orange,* beginning Stanley Kubrick's long relationship with the studio. It was a futuristic study in violence—most notably a daringly erotic rape sequence set to the music of Gene Kelly singing "Singin' in the Rain"—that was hated (for Kubrick's characteristic existential coldness), admired (for its bravura filmmaking), and hugely profitable.

In the long run, probably the most important film Warner Bros. produced in Calley's second year was *Dirty Harry,* which initiated the studio's longest-running relationship—thirty-seven years and still counting—with a star-director Clint Eastwood. Clint had been tracking the script, by the writing team of Harry Julian Fink and his wife Rita, for some years. But it drifted away from Universal, where he was under contract and where he first heard about *Harry,* wandered around town a bit and finally landed up at Warner Bros. The studio had written down some $60 million of the previous regime's projects, was desperate for product, and detective stories were hot. Frank Wells, who had been Eastwood's attorney and remained a close friend, called to inquire if he was still interested in the project. He was, but was directing his first film (*Play Misty for Me*) and had to pass. Frank Sinatra, who had been a major stockholder in Reprise Records, enjoyed a close relationship with the studio, and had had a success at Fox with *The Detective,* and he was now attached. But, typical of him, he wanted to make the picture within commuting distance of his Palm Springs home—if not in Palm Springs itself. That wouldn't do, so the studio put out a cover story about his withdrawal from the project—something about a hand injury—and rang Eastwood again. Soon Wells sent over "a whole mess" of scripts as Eastwood put it—rewrites of rewrites that had been done to accommodate various actors and directors as the years had passed. The actor was interested only in one of them—the Finks' original. He brought in Dean Reisner, a writer who had worked with him before, and with director Don Siegel, a frequent collaborator, set about creating *Dirty Harry*'s final draft.

OPPOSITE One-sheet poster art for the highly controversial *Performance,*
1970. ABOVE Malcolm McDowell as Alex in *A Clockwork Orange,* 1971:
"a futuristic study in violence."

Eastwood was the *de facto,* uncredited producer of the film—Calley has said of him that he was a great producer and someone who would have been "one of the best heads of production ever" if he had chosen that line of work. In any case, the picture was shot with his and Siegel's typical efficiency. And it became a great hit upon release. Before *Dirty Harry* Eastwood had clearly been a rising star; after it, he became a superstar. There was something in Harry that spoke to something in Eastwood's soul. He found in the newly widowed cop a sadness, a loneliness, that gave him a resonance that was not typical of such figures. Also there was a kind of anger with bureaucratic dithering and temporizing that spoke to Eastwood's own impatience with the way the movie business was run.

Despite its success, however, the picture became "controversial," largely on the strength of a review by Pauline Kael, the influential *New Yorker* reviewer, who called it an example of "fascist medievalism." She insisted that the motivelessly malign Scorpio, the serial killer Harry pursues, ought to have been given more explicable, sociological motives for his depredations, as the classic criminals of the Warner Bros. 1930s had been—not perhaps noticing that that sort of thing had gone out with *White Heat* in 1949. She also found that his crimes had been "sexualized" (which they rather obviously had not been) in order to "suck up" to the "thugs" in the audience. She also believed the film was an assault on the recent Miranda Decision, which insisted that criminals be read their rights before they were arrested. This it was—in part—but with mitigating circumstances, based on Harry's character and situation.

Looking back on the controversy now, one senses something weirdly personal in Kael's attack, a misunderstanding of Eastwood as a right-winger of the order of John Wayne, when politics was on his mind. But David Thompson is much closer to the mark when he observes that Eastwood had sensed a national mood shift driven "by the intractable growth of disorder and liberal bureaucracy" that was troubling to a lot of people that were far from the right wing. That, coupled with the sheer narrative drive of the filmmaking, drove the picture to a success that swept many a liberal along in its wake.

Eastwood continued to make movies at Universal until 1975 and that year moved his offices and his loyalties to Warner Bros., where he had made *Magnum Force,* first of the *Dirty Harry* sequels. His only question, as he recalls, was whether there were any tour buses on the lot; he had hated the way the Universal Studio tour trams had always paused at his office, at his very self, hoping to give the gawkers a look at him. Reassured on that point, in 1975 he moved into the little bungalow on the lot, where once Harry Warner had reigned, and has remained there ever since, growing steadily toward iconic status. Increasingly he seems to me a living link to the old Warner Bros. tradition—a genre filmmaker always striving to make carefully budgeted and scheduled movies, which press their genre boundaries, and as often as not redefine them, whether we are talking about *The Outlaw Josey Wales* or *Unforgiven, Tightrope* or *Bird, Mystic River* or *Million Dollar Baby.*

No one—not even John Calley or Eastwood himself—could in the early 1970s have seen that coming. But still, as far as one can tell, Eastwood from this point onward was denied nothing he wanted to do by the studio. His instincts, his track record, were simply undeniable. He would return the favor, making movies—including a couple of *Dirty Harry* sequels he was a little bit dubious about—out of loyalty and, especially in the seventies and eighties, out of his relentless need to keep busy. What was true of him was true of other filmmakers as well.

That atmosphere stemmed from the top. Steve Ross was, in a sense, the anti-mogul. He rarely intervened in the choice of movies; indeed, he often complained that when he suggested something to his operating executives his ideas were invariably dismissed with a laugh. That was OK with him. He was star struck; he loved the company of his stars and directors, and couldn't do enough for them. The studio had a small air force of private jets that were ever at their disposal. It had a villa in Mexico and it was almost always available to them for mini-vacations. In the entire history of Hollywood there was never a more beloved boss than Steven J. Ross. He was all carrot, no stick.

OPPOSITE Clint Eastwood in *Dirty Harry*, "which initiated the studio's longest running relationship with a star director."

Calley remembers only two movies about which his judgment was questioned. The first was *Deliverance,* in which a group of vacationing city folk are set upon by violent and primitive inhabitants of Georgia's deepest backwoods. Ashley thought the script, based on the bestselling novel by the poet James Dickey, was disgusting. "What appeals to you about this movie?" he asked Calley. "I mean, you have a feeble-minded boy playing a banjo. You've got a toothless guy schtupping one of the leads in the ass. Who's going to see this movie?"

To which Calley replied: "What you ought to do before you decide about this, is get a gorgeous blonde—flashy, big tits—and drive out to Mohave and go into a trucker's bar and you'll have a sense of what this movie's about—small Jewish person in a double knit suit with this big blonde… You leave the Beverly Hills Hotel and go out there and you're in trouble." Or as he slightly more fancily put it to Ashley: "It's about the thickness or thinness of society's veneer. I mean you don't know what you're gonna be dealing with. And its getting worse." Ashley sighed and relented, and the new Warner Bros. had another hit.

A year later, in 1973, *Mean Streets* was not a huge hit. It was something better, the annunciation of what is perhaps the most significant American directorial career of the last decades of the twentieth century. Martin Scorsese had made movies before—the radically independent, and still-underrated *Who's That Knocking at My Door,* and a Roger Corman exploitation picture, *Boxcar Bertha.* Now he returned to the streets of New York's Little Italy, as he had in *Knocking,* and to the kind of violent, feckless, priest-ridden youths he had grown up with. The film starred Harvey Keitel as a kid caught up in a doomed romance and resisting being caught up in the life of a smalltime mobster, and Robert De Niro as a totally irresponsible—better make that marginally insane—figure, whose doom is written all over his curiously lovable face.

In movie historical terms, *Mean Streets* might be looked upon as a new variant on the genre most closely associated with Warner Bros., the gangster drama, but without the rise to power that was traditionally prec-

edent to the protagonist's demise. Scorsese remembers being thrilled when Calley picked up his picture precisely because of that historic resonance.

Calley, of course, loved Scorsese's manic intensity. He also saw something else in him, a desire to be, of all things, an old-fashioned studio director, a jack of all the generic trades, an ambition to which Scorsese had cheerfully admitted. By this time it was impossible to be that kind of director—auteurism demanded obsessive focus on one or two passionate themes. Anything else smacked of opportunism, even hackery. It was Calley who briefly enabled Scorsese's dream, bringing him *Alice Doesn't Live Here Any More,* the romantic comedy of a widowed woman and her wise-guy son, living hand to mouth in the American Southwest as she pursues a none-too-promising career as a lounge singer. Ellen Burstyn won the 1974 Best Actress Oscar for her portrayal of Alice, and Scorsese had the time of his life working in the wide open spaces. For the first time, the director, of whom there are little boy pictures duded out as a cowboy, got to ride a horse.

That's the way it went at Warner Bros. in the 1970s. It was no longer balancing its schedule as studios traditionally had—so many westerns, so many musicals, so many crime pictures. The mood was permissive if the person "looking through the camera" had a passion for the project. Consider just the following run of movies between 1973 and 1978.

Blazing Saddles: Andrew Bergman was one of the writers on Mel Brooks' satirical western. Before that he had written a smart little book on Warner Bros. in the Depression years and he remembers having tears in his eyes as he drove on to the lot for the first time, so rich was it in associations to his movie-going past. It was Brooks' first big opportunity and he and his colleagues pretty much took an everything-but-the-kitchen-sink approach to the film. It was irreverent to a sacred movie form. It was often tasteless and sometimes unfunny. But those are the prices we pay for joyous anarchy. Still, it was the kind of picture that can drive a studio boss crazy—especially if his wife thinks the result, especially the flatulence gags, is simply disgusting. It was an opinion she expressed at the Westwood sneak, devastating Brooks and alarming Ted Ashley. Maybe this was a bet he should have resisted. Brooks felt that the studio didn't fully appreciate him or back his picture to the full. And despite Calley's entreaties he became the first and only major talent to depart Warner Bros. in this era never to return, even though his film was a big hit, and for some of us—who love lowbrow laughs, even think that just maybe "good taste" is the enemy not just of comedy, but of life itself—a beloved memory.

The Exorcist: The novel had been a huge bestseller. But it only described, it did not actually show in Technicolor all the horrific things that happen when the devil takes possession of an innocent child. The possibility of a massive turn-off haunted the studio and the film's director, William Friedkin, as the picture moved through production. On the night it opened in Westwood, Calley and Ashley decided to spin past the theater to see if anyone was trickling in. What greeted them was the ambulance hired, largely as a publicity stunt, to treat those who had fainted at, say, the sight of Regan's head turning around 360 degrees, and a line of eager customers entirely circling the block. This success was deserved. The picture's premise was nonsensical, but it unleashes authentic emotions—in Ellen Burstyn's anguished struggle for her daughter's soul, in one's admiration for the self-sacrificing courage of Max von Sydow's priest in his lonely, climactic confrontation with Satan. This may have been popular entertainment, pitched to the less elevated edge of the mass market, but it was also good, gripping entertainment.

Dog Day Afternoon: A nut job, determined to buy his male partner a sex-change operation, decides to fund it by robbing a New York branch bank on a hot summer's day. The robbery fails, a standoff with the police develops, and Al Pacino, playing the half-cracked mastermind (who can ever forget him yelling "Attica, Attica?"—a reference to the recent prison riot), heats up the sympathies of the sweltering and volatile mob gathered to watch the

OPPOSITE Martin Scorsese directing *Mean Streets,* 1973: "A new variant on the genre most closely associated with Warner Bros."

drama. Brilliantly directed by Sidney Lumet and scorchingly written by Frank Pierson, it is an utterly original crime drama that, among its other virtues, evokes the dark side of 1960s America without entirely trashing it. Call it Woodstock on a bad trip.

Barry Lyndon: Implicitly Stanley Kubrick seemed to be promising the studio a rollicking eighteenth-century romp, something along the lines of *Tom Jones*—sensual, sensuous, and essentially mindless. Mindless? From Kubrick? Not likely. What he delivered was an existential tragedy, in which the eponymous protagonist seeks fame, fortune, heroic status, and achieves some of his dreams before falling into hopeless despair. The film is astonishingly beautiful—Kubrick, for example, used special lenses developed by NASA so he could light some of his scenes only with candles, and actually drove his art director into a mild nervous breakdown. The man wanted to build his antique settings on sound stages. Kubrick insisted on authenticity—a corner of a castle for one part of a scene, the corner of a country house forty miles down the road for another angle on the same scene. The picture is slow, not rich in dialogue, and what there is of it is wit-free and full of irony. Most significantly, it is relentless in its insistence on the stupidity and venality of the human race; there is not a single likeable character in it. In short, it applies a bleak, modern sensibility to a distant historical era. Everyone hated it when it came out—except, of course, the French who, as so often happens in these matters, turned out to be annoyingly correct. The film's reputation has grown steadily over the years. And though there are people who will never "like" Kubrick, there are yet those of us who regard him as one of film's great masters, and consider *Barry Lyndon* to be one of his masterpieces. Oh, and incidentally, it eventually turned a profit for the studio.

All The President's Men: Robert Redford wanted to do it. The year was 1975. The Woodward-Bernstein book about the Watergate burglary had appeared and it was a bestseller. Moreover, the actor was at the height of his career. He had made *The Candidate* (1972), about a cute young politician desperate for office but without a clue about what he wants to achieve therein, and *Jeremiah Johnson* (1972), a unique western about a Mountain Man learning to live at peace in the wilderness, among vengeful savages whose sacred lands he had despoiled. They were both Warner Bros. films and there had been others, elsewhere, which had secured his power in Hollywood. The decision to make this movie should have been a slam-dunk. But it worried Ted Ashley. Warner Bros. was part of a growing conglomerate whose businesses were subject to government regulation. And, as of this moment, Nixon's successor, Gerald Ford, was in office and just maybe a Republican government might take revenge. Ashley and Calley got on the phone with Steve Ross to get his opinion on the project. He asked Calley if he really loved the material and if he truly believed it could be shaped into a good film. He did. "Then have a good time with it," came the reply. The result was a superb political picture, dark, slightly spooky, yet also very witty, with Redford playing the square WASP to Dustin Hoffman's more impassioned and erratic Jew—a curiously appealing odd couple.

Every Which Way But Loose: Is he kidding? He wants to play a slightly dimwitted trucker and bare-knuckle boxer whose best buddy is an orangutan named Clyde? Just about everybody at the studio—and among his closest advisers—thought Clint Eastwood had lost his marbles. But shrewd judge of his own career that he is, he wanted to take the chance. There comes a time in every great star career when he or she is obliged to throw the fans a curveball. It's not just a matter of "stretching." It's a matter of subverting an image at the point it threatens to become oppressive. In Eastwood's case, the film was a chance to demonstrate his chops as a producer. So it was done. And it had enough action to satisfy his more hairy-chested fans, enough low humor to engage people who were not yet his close followers. An iconic moment: Clyde has stolen some Oreos from Ma Boggs, Clint's best human pal's mother, who has read him the riot act. Clint chances upon Clyde, who throws up his arms. Clint shapes his hand into a gun, says "Bang" and the ape flops down, playing dead. OK maybe you had to have been there. And maybe you had to set aside certain high cultural ambitions. Eastwood remembers a screening for

OPPOSITE *Barry Lyndon,* 1975, an existential tragedy, here with Dominic Savage as young Bullingdon and Marisa Berenson as Lady Lyndon.

the studio brass, at which someone judged it unreleasable. But from the back of the room came Calley's voice: "Someone's gonna make a lot of money on this one." And so it came to pass—*Every Which Way But Loose* became Eastwood's biggest-grossing movie to date and the year's second biggest box-office success...

After *Superman* (1978), that is. It, too, was a Warner Bros. picture—and it was a symbolic entrance into a radically changing movie world. For years, movies had been released in a standard fashion. A picture would open in a downtown theater in one of the several major markets, then make its way slowly toward the second- and third-run houses, then into the small towns and foreign markets, then finally to its television release. It was a time-tested way of doing business, and an economical one. You probably didn't have to make more than a hundred prints to satisfy this pattern. But then in 1975 came *Jaws*. Based on a bestselling book, it had a well-publicized over-schedule shoot that threatened Steven Spielberg's career almost before it started. There was a lot of curiosity about the movie and Universal decided to release it in something over five hundred theaters on its opening weekend. It was a strategy that had been tried before and it usually signified panic of the get-the-money-and-run sort. But that rogue shark was not just attacking audiences out of the depths of the ocean, it was rising up out of the depths of their unconscious, that place where our primal fears lurk. In short, the picture was a sensa-

ABOVE Clint Eastwood and Clyde, the orangutan, in *Every Which Way But Loose*, 1978, which became Eastwood's biggest-grossing movie to that date.
OVERLEAF Christopher Reeve and the Metropolis skyline in *Superman*, 1978.

tion for Universal. And a year later, when *Star Wars* followed a similar pattern to an even larger success, the old way of doing business was transformed—except for independent and foreign releases. Now the American studios would stake everything on the first weekend grosses. There would be no more nursing films along, waiting for word-of-mouth to build for them. Newspapers began printing the results of the weekend's grosses and, generally speaking, if you didn't make the top ten the life of your picture would be nasty, brutish, and short.

Superman was Warner Bros.' first test of this market, which was essentially designed to appeal to adolescent males who generally determined which movie they would take their Saturday night dates to see. It was a boldly stated, tongue-in-cheek story about the time-tested comic book hero—fast moving, improbably plotted, brightly-hued, with a nice, square-cut but wised-up performance by Christopher Reeve in the title role, a seductive one from Margot Kidder as his reluctant love interest Lois Lane (there's a lovely romantic sequence when Superman takes Lois for a soaring ride through the skies), and the over-the-top wickedness of Gene Hackman as the villain. With the comic book source and the simplicity and straight-forward direction by Dick Donner, it was almost as if the film were satirizing the superhero blockbuster form that had not yet been fully realized—but soon would be, at Warner Bros. and elsewhere, and the obvious sequel possibilities predicted the future of movies.

As our brief listing of a few of its more memorable films indicates, the 1970s had been good for Warner Bros—transformative. These films have very little in common thematically. They are in every imaginable genre and in every case they refresh those genres, even sometimes reinvent them, give them a new life. Naturally, the studio made many other films in this decade, not all of them by any means successful or regenerative. But, taken as a whole, this decade represents for the studio a rare triumph of instinct over market-driven calculation. They fulfilled Calley's initial idea about how to run a studio, which was also an acting out of screenwriter William Goldman's now famous adage that when it comes to moviemaking, "Nobody knows anything."

It is a statement that is no less true for being, by now, a cliché. And that being the case, it follows that you will do no less well if you fly by the seat of your pants. David Picker, another production chief who was successful in this era, put it this way: he would have done about as well if, instead of following the dictates of market research, he had simply posted the titles of potential projects on his office wall and tossed darts at them, producing the films his missiles happened to land on.

This is a lesson most people in the business have still not taken fully to heart. But Calley and Ashley—instinctively, of course—thought they had proved its validity to their own satisfaction. When their contracts came up for renewal, Steve Ross was in a mood to be generous. Calley re-upped. Then began having second thoughts. He hauled out a legal pad, made a list of his assets in one column, his liabilities on the other. He decided he had enough to live on quite comfortably and decided to resign. He didn't know quite what he wanted to do next but told Ross that he was not entertaining any offers from rivals. He would, he said, never work in the movies for anyone but Ross. While Ross pondered the bad news, Calley showed his calculations to Ashley, who hauled out a foolscap of his own, saw results that were even happier than Calley's, and decided to follow him into premature retirement. Ross reluctantly said all right—and then told Calley he was going to continue payments on his new contract. He had earned the money, he said.

So the 1970s ended as they had begun, with a couple of top executives following their bliss (as people used to say) and their boss being his usual cheerfully generous self. As it happened, no harm was done. The managers chosen to lead the studio through the eighties and early nineties were very different types—but they embraced the principles of the old regime, and backed by Ross's hands-off style, achieved results that fully matched those of the decade now ended.

RICHARD SCHICKEL

THE WARNER BROS. STORY

1970–74

✳ *Woodstock* wins Best Documentary Oscar, 1970

✳ Jimi Hendrix and Janis Joplin die from drug overdoses, 1970

✳ National Guardsmen kill four students at Kent State University, Ohio, 1970

✳ Stanley Kubrick's *A Clockwork Orange* ignites controversy, 1971

✳ Columbia joins Warner Bros. at Burbank Studios, 1972

✳ Eleven Israelis are massacred at the Munich Olympics, 1972

✳ Five White House officials are arrested for the Watergate break-in, 1972

✳ *The Exorcist* grosses more than any other Warner Bros. film to date, 1973

✳ *The Towering Inferno* wins three Oscars, 1974

✳ 37th President Richard M. Nixon resigns over the Watergate scandal, 1974

ABOVE Richard Nixon departs the White House, 1974.
RIGHT Jason Robards in *The Ballad of Cable Hogue*, 1970.
OPPOSITE John Wayne in *Chisum*, 1970.

WEST WORLD

 Sam Peckinpah's *The Ballad of Cable Hogue* (1970) was not a hit, yet it is one of his best films—a delightful comment on the passing of the Old West and the capacity of the loner in the wild to turn misfortune to advantage. Jason Robards plays a prospector left to die in the desert by unsavory partners. By chance he finds a waterhole that saves his life, and turns it into a prosperous stagecoach stop. With the support of a heart-of-gold hooker, the magnificently rounded Stella Stevens, he finds a sort of contentment, although the advent of the automobile will push the stagecoach into oblivion. David Warner plays a crazy bogus preacher who becomes his best friend: "Since I cannot rouse heaven I intend to raise hell." Usually expected of Peckinpah is violence and bloodshed, but it is lacking here, except for an opening moment when a basking gila monster is blasted to bits, which may have accounted for its lukewarm box-office appeal.

More conventional, and financially more successful is *Chisum* (1970), with John Wayne as a New Mexico landowner at odds with a corrupt incoming land-grabber played by Forrest Tucker. Andrew V. McLaglen's film has a better sense of history than many westerns, and depicts real-life events, with Pat Garrett and Billy the Kid floating naturally into the action. Set-piece shootouts and stampedes add to the elements that attracted audiences.

"WHO'S GOING TO SEE THIS MOVIE?"

SHOCK TREATMENT

In *Performance* (1970), a ruthless hitman (James Fox) hides out in the London house of a rock star (Mick Jagger) who has shunned the limelight to live in a drug haze with two girls (Michelle Breton and Anita Pallenberg). In a succession of bizarre mind games that follow the ingestion of magic mushrooms, identities are swapped and the characters blend into each other in a hallucinogenic orgy of sadomasochism. Donald Cammell wrote the screenplay, Nicolas Roeg shot the film, and both of them directed it. Its release was held for two years, but Jagger's fans were prepared to wait.

The British director Ken Russell's unrestrained style reached its apogee with the adaptation of Aldous Huxley's book *The Devils of Loudun* and John Whiting's play *The Devils* (1971), about the persecution of the witches of Loudun in the seventeenth century by Cardinal Richelieu. His filming of unbridled orgies with enthusiastic naked extras at London's Pinewood Studios attracted newspaper headlines. Oliver Reed plays the sexually charged priest who inflames a nunnery, leading to his denunciation for consorting with the Devil and graphically depicted martyrdom at the stake. He and Vanessa Redgrave, who plays a demented nun, so upset the Catholic Church in Italy that both were threatened with jail if they set foot in the country.

Outrageous in both content and treatment was *Portnoy's Complaint* (1972), adapted from Philip Roth's novel, and directed by Ernest Lehman, the screenwriter of *North by Northwest* and *The Sound of Music*. This was essentially the story of a nice Jewish boy, played by Richard Benjamin, his mother (Lee Grant), and his masturbatory fantasies. Noteworthy is the performance of Karen Black as "the Monkey." Lehman, one of the most successful screenwriters of all time, did not direct again.

ABOVE Ken Russell watches Oliver Reed and Vanessa Redgrave in *The Devils*, 1971.
OPPOSITE Mick Jagger trading his identity for a gangster in *Performance*, 1970.

SPIRIT OF THE AGE

By the 1970s, the appealing innocence of adolescent boys on their extended family vacation on Nantucket Island in *Summer of '42* (1971) would have seemed remote and anachronistic. Robert Mulligan's film is from a reminiscence by the screenwriter Herman Raucher, on how in the first summer after Pearl Harbor, when he was fourteen, he lost his virginity to a new war widow called Dorothy, and never saw her again. Gary Grimes plays young Hermie and Jennifer O'Neill the twenty-two-year-old woman, alone because her husband is at war, and the object of the boy's intense crush. Great care was taken to establish an accurate period atmosphere, and a Michel Legrand score added to the poignant nostalgia, resulting in a gigantic box-office hit.

The *zeitgeist* of the late 1960s was captured in Michael Wadleigh's lengthy documentary *Woodstock* (1970), a visual account of a three-day event in August 1969 when nearly half a million young people converged on a farm at Bethel in upstate New York and listened to the music of their time—Hendrix, Baez, Joplin, Richie Havens, Joe Cocker, the Who, Jefferson Airplane, and many others—in spite of gridlock, downpours, food shortages, overwhelmed toilets, and the threats of Governor Rockefeller to send in the National Guard. There was pot-smoking, skinny-dipping, open lovemaking, anti-Vietnam protests, but no rioting. Editing 120 miles of footage from a dozen cameras was a team that included Martin Scorsese and Thelma Schoonmaker. A director's cut decades later resulted in a final running time of three hours forty-five minutes.

ABOVE Jennifer O'Neill, with Gary Grimes in the background, in *Summer of '42*, 1971. OPPOSITE Roger Daltry in *Woodstock*, 1970.

MAKING HIS DAY

Clint Eastwood's San Francisco police detective Harry
Callahan is a maverick cop who doesn't play by the rules, but
always in the public interest. The first of five films in which he
appears is *Dirty Harry*, directed by Don Siegel. (The others:
Magnum Force, 1973, Ted Post; *The Enforcer*, 1976, James Fargo; *Sudden Impact*, 1983, Clint Eastwood; *The Dead Pool*, 1988,
Buddy Van Horn.) Harry's stance on the rights of criminals is
totally negative, and he has no time for woolly liberalism that
lets malefactors go free. Stalking the streets with his unofficial,
dreaded Magnum .44 at the ready, he achieves results, and
nails a serial killer no matter what it takes. Eastwood's appeal
ensured the success of the film, which in the hands of Siegel is
exceptionally well made, but unquestionably some of its audience enjoyed it for other reasons, seeing it as the assertion of
a right-wing approach to justice aligned with an evocation of
the vigilante spirit of the frontier era.

OPPOSITE BELOW Don Siegel directs Clint Eastwood in
Dirty Harry, 1971 OPPOSITE TOP AND ABOVE Clint Eastwood as Harry Callahan in *The Enforcer,* 1976, with
identifying symbols, his police I.D. and the Magnum
.44; San Francisco's Grant Avenue in the background.

"WHO'S GOING TO SEE THIS MOVIE?"

CLINT EASTWOOD
Taking No Prisoners

Clinton Eastwood Jr. was born in San Francisco in 1930. As a child of the Depression his early life was spent in various West Coast locations where his father, a steel worker, could find jobs. Clint graduated from Oakland Tech in 1949, was a gas-station attendant and a logger. On release from the Army he settled in Los Angeles and his tall physique and good looks secured him a few small roles and a good part in a B-western, *Ambush at Cimarron Pass*. Television made him famous, as Rowdy Yates in the *Rawhide* series, which ran for eight seasons until the mid-1960s.

He became a movie star playing the mysterious "Man With No Name" in three notable spaghetti westerns, *A Fistful of Dollars* (1964), *For a Few Dollars More* (1965), and *The Good, the Bad, and the Ugly* (1966)—all released in the

U.S. in 1967—shot on the dusty plains of Spain by the Italian Sergio Leone. Back in Hollywood he was the lead in a few action films directed by Don Siegel. The most important was as the take-no-prisoners police detective *Dirty Harry* (1971), which became the first of a celebrated series. He also made his directorial debut and starred in the paranoid thriller *Play Misty for Me* (1971), which was set on his beloved Monterey Peninsula in California. Later, in the 1980s, he was to become mayor of Carmel, the picturesque coastal city there. In 1975 he located his production company Malpaso at Burbank, making it a Warner Bros. fixture.

His output as an actor and director has been prolific. In the 1970s his westerns *High Plains Drifter* (1973) and *The Outlaw Josey Wales* (1976) were well regarded, and he eventually won an Academy Award for his direction and Best Picture with *Unforgiven* (1992). He has not confined himself to one genre, attempting slapstick comedy with *Every Which Way But Loose* (1978), jazzman hagiography with *Bird* (1978), and even a musical, *Paint Your Wagon* (1969). His versatility extended to mountain climbing (*The Eiger Sanction*, 1975), country singing (*Honkytonk Man*, 1982) and composing background music (*Space Cowboys*, 2000, and others).

In his eighth decade his output has not abated, but has reached new heights of maturity with *Mystic River* (2003), *Million Dollar Baby* (2004, another Best Picture Oscar), *Flags of Our Fathers*, and *Letters from Iwo Jima* (both 2006). He cuts a heroic figure, respected throughout the world. As Stephen Fry, the British host of the annual Britannia Awards, observed in 2006 when Eastwood and Sidney Poitier were honored: "I feel I am at filmland's Mount Rushmore."

LEFT Clint Eastwood as Philo Beddoe in *Every Which Way But Loose*, 1978. ABOVE Clint directs. OPPOSITE TOP As Wes Block in *Tightrope*, 1984. RIGHT Having a look through the camera on location for *Dirty Harry*.

LOSERS AND WINNERS

Being what they are, politics are hard to satirize because so often reality outstrips imagined possibilities. Robert Redford, looking every inch the popular image of a Democratic contender for the Senate seat against a Republican incumbent, is gulled into running, but not expected to win. In *The Candidate* (1972), in Michael Ritchie's cynical but somehow prescient view, when he is a loser he can say what he wants with an engaging freshness and an idealistic glint in his eye, but when his situation changes he is sucked into the machinery and mouths the platitudes of all the others. Peter Boyle and Allen Garfield play campaign supervisors and Melvyn Douglas the candidate's father.

DARK JOURNEYS

Four friends in Atlanta take time out to go on a weekend canoe trip in the backwoods. Burt Reynolds is the macho one, envied by Jon Voight, and the others are Ned Beatty and Ronny Cox. Their jaunt becomes a nightmare in which they are confronted by murderous hillbillies and the inexorable forces of nature. John Boorman's *Deliverance* (1972), from James Dickey's stark novel, is memorable and terrifying, making a powerful case for staying at home. A sequence in which Cox engages in frenetic fingerplay in "Dueling Banjos" with a wild-looking mountain boy is a strange respite from the horror to come.

In *Klute* (1971), Jane Fonda won an Oscar for her portrayal of a New York prostitute who assists an out-of-town detective (Donald Sutherland) hunting a missing friend. A relationship develops in which her professional control recedes into dependency when she realizes that she is the object of a sadistic killer. Alan J. Pakula's thriller, laden with psychological overtones, is satisfyingly paranoid in atmosphere.

ABOVE Robert Redford as Bill McKay in *The Candidate*, 1972.
LEFT Jane Fonda as Bree Daniels in *Klute*, 1971.
OPPOSITE John Boorman directing Jon Voight, with bow and arrow, on location for *Deliverance*, 1972.

"WHO'S GOING TO SEE THIS MOVIE?"

A LITTLE OF THE LUDWIG VAN

After *Lolita* in 1961 Stanley Kubrick lived in England and made the rest of his films there. His 1971 work *A Clockwork Orange,* from a novel by Anthony Burgess, foresaw a dystopian Britain, a police state where people live in terror of the vicious thugs who maraud unchecked. The central figure is a young gang leader (Malcolm McDowell), a Beethoven-obsessed rapist and murderer. He and his followers dress in bizarre white outfits with black derby hats and giant plastic codpieces, sip milk cocktails, and converse in Nadsat, a weird intermingling of Russian and English. After a brutal murder he is incarcerated and subjected to a horrifying mental therapy process that purges his violence and with it his spirit of life. Kubrick was so appalled by the British reaction to the film's violence that he asked the studio to ban all further showings there until his death. Such was Kubrick's stature that his wish was observed.

His next film, *Barry Lyndon* (1975), from a lesser novel by Thackeray, starred Ryan O'Neal as an Irish adventurer in the eighteenth century, who fights for the English in the Seven Years' War then joins the Prussian army. An unrestrained social climber, he beds, duels, and gambles his way into the aristocracy toward his inevitable downfall. Kubrick filmed much of it like eighteenth-century paintings, even insisting that certain interior sequences be lit only by candles.

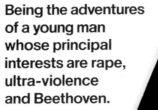

Being the adventures of a young man whose principal interests are rape, ultra-violence and Beethoven.

STANLEY KUBRICK'S CLOCKWORK ORANGE

A Stanley Kubrick Production "A CLOCKWORK ORANGE" Starring Malcolm McDowell • Patrick Magee • Adrienne Corri and Miriam Karlin • Screenplay by Stanley Kubrick • Based on the novel by Anthony Burgess • Produced and Directed by Stanley Kubrick • Executive Producers Max L. Raab and Si Litvinoff • WARNER BROS

OPPOSITE Scenes from *A Clockwork Orange,* 1971; the "Droogs" who dress in bizarre white outfits with black Derby hats and giant plastic codpieces.
ABOVE Stanley Kubrick at work directing on the set of *A Clockwork Orange.*
ABOVE RIGHT One sheet poster art for the film.

STANLEY KUBRICK
Another world

Born in 1928 in Manhattan and raised in the Bronx, New York, Stanley Kubrick was a middle-class Jewish boy whose father, a doctor, encouraged his hobby of photography. His pictures made young Stanley a star of his high-school magazine. In 1945, on his way to school, he spotted a news vendor surrounded by headlines announcing Roosevelt's death, and whipped his camera out to snap him. He sold the picture to a New York tabloid and it was reproduced around the world. *Look* magazine gave him a staff job, not initially realizing he was only seventeen. He became an accomplished photojournalist, and in 1950 shot a movie documentary about a boxer, *The Day of the Fight* (1951). Others followed, and in 1953 his first low-budget feature, *Fear and Desire*, on money borrowed from a network of relations garnered a supportive review in the *New York Times*. *The Killing*, a story of a racetrack heist that goes wrong, gave him critical attention, followed by the highly praised *Paths of Glory*, an indictment of World War I military hypocrisy.

He replaced Anthony Mann on the epic *Spartacus*, and went to England to make *Lolita* from Nabokov's black comic

novel. There he stayed, preferring the atmosphere and distance from studio executives, and his next two films, the nuclear apocalypse comedy *Dr. Strangelove, or How I Learned to Stop Worrying and Love the Bomb* and the epic science-fiction journey to discover the secret of the cosmos, *2001: A Space Odyssey*, defined him as a unique director who resided on his own planet, his mystique seemingly invulnerable to the constraints that hampered others.

From his nightmare vision of dystopia, *A Clockwork Orange,* onward, his films were released by Warner Bros., the intervals between them ever-lengthening. At the time *Barry Lyndon* seemed too much effort exerted on an insignificant Thackeray novel, in *The Shining* the supernatural spookiness of the Overlook Hotel expanded the Old Dark House to its ultimate limits, *Full Metal Jacket* followed drafted Vietnam marines into an exploration of the obsessive futility of war, and his last, the puzzling, paranoid and sexually confused *Eyes Wide Shut,* which took an unusually long time to shoot, was released posthumously in 1999 to mixed reviews. But time has always been on Kubrick's side and appreciation for his work continues to grow. A vigorous polymath and meticulous, laborious planner, his handful of films displayed dazzling craftsmanship and technical brilliance. In Britain he expended years of energy on massive projects, some of which were never made. He was built up by the press as a reclusive eccentric. The truth was that as a deliberate maverick he preferred not to travel or give interviews.

4 OSCARS

BARRY LYNDON

a film by
STANLEY KUBRICK
"RYAN O'NEAL "MARISA BERENSON"
PATRICK MAGEE · HARDY KRUGER · DIANA KOERNER · GAY HAMILTON
Produced by Executive JAN HARLAN
Warner Bros. A Warner Communications Company

LEFT One-sheet poster art for *Barry Lyndon,* 1975. ABOVE Stanley Kubrick and Ryan O'Neal (as Barry Lyndon) and other crew members on location for *Barry Lyndon.* OPPOSITE A contemplative moment for Stanley Kubrick during the making of *A Clockwork Orange.* OVERLEAF A stunning landscape scene from *Barry Lyndon,* filmed at the gardens at Stourhead in Wiltshire, England.

ABOVE Advertising art for *McCabe and Mrs. Miller*, 1971, featuring
Warren Beatty and Julie Christie. OPPOSITE TOP Warren Beatty as John
McCabe on location in "a savage, primitive, dirty developing township."
OPPOSITE BELOW Richard Harris in *Man in the Wilderness*, 1971.

FRONTIER ORDEALS

Robert Altman, like Stanley Kubrick, was an idiosyncratic director with a singular vision. Unlike Kubrick he did not limit his output by spending years in preparation, but maintained a fairly constant, if uneven, flow. In *McCabe and Mrs. Miller* (1971) he offered a frontier western that attempted to dislodge the conventional myths. His place is a savage, primitive, dirty, developing township in the wintry Pacific Northwest. McCabe (Warren Beatty) arrives to set up a whorehouse, with the encouragement of Mrs. Miller (Julie Christie), whose experience as a madam will make their fortunes in spite of his lack of business acumen. Altman's striking film is one of his best. In Richard C. Sarafian's *Man in the Wilderness* (1971), the brutal side of the early pioneering era is grimly portrayed, with Richard Harris as guide for a hunting expedition in the 1820s who is mauled by a bear and left to die by the expedition's leader (John Huston). Against the odds, and with terrible wounds, Harris survives in a superhuman feat of endurance, even though his rifle has been taken from him. Unsurprisingly he develops a taste for revenge.

Robert Redford is a gutsy early nineteenth-century mountain man in Sydney Pollack's outdoors paean *Jeremiah Johnson* (1972), making peace with the Indians and surviving against the odds in the wilderness. It hardly matters where he comes from, it is the legend he is to be that counts. Duke Callaghan's cinematography captures the unparalleled magnificence of Utah's scenery.

Robert Redford as *Jeremiah Johnson*,
filmed on location in Utah, 1972.

"WHO'S GOING TO SEE THIS MOVIE?"

LOVE THAT DARES NOT SPEAK ITS NAME

Made at Cinecittà in Rome, Luchino Visconti's *The Damned* (1969)—his epic account of a Krupp-like industrial dynasty in 1930s Germany making the painful adjustment to the ascendancy of the Nazis—was distributed by Warner Bros. It was followed by his version of Thomas Mann's novella *Death in Venice* (1971), with its protagonist changed from a writer into a composer. The British actor Dirk Bogarde, who had also been in *The Damned,* played the central figure Aschenbach to look like Gustave Mahler. Recovering from stress, he forms an unspoken passion for a beautiful young man (Bjorn Andresen) who is visiting the Venetian Lido from Poland. This leads to a fatal decision to remain when other visitors have fled from a cholera epidemic. With the majestic strains of Mahler's Third and Fifth Symphonies surging on the soundtrack, Venice has never seemed more photogenic, and while Visconti reduced some of Mann's subtleties, he obtained from Bogarde an emotionally remarkable performance.

WARNER BROS. presents
A film by
Luchino VISCONTI

Dirk BOGARDE
in
DEATH IN VENICE

with   and introducing
Mark BURNS · Bjorn ANDRESEN

Guest starring   Screenplay by
Silvana MANGANO   Luchino VISCONTI · Nicola BADALUCCO   Produced and Directed by
                           From the novel by Thomas MANN   **Luchino VISCONTI**
Associate   Music by GUSTAV MAHLER
Executive Producer Robert Gordon EDWARDS   Executive
                           PANAVISION®   TECHNICOLOR®   Producer Mario GALLO

OPPOSITE TOP Bjorn Andresen as Tadzio. OPPOSITE Dirk
Bogarde as Aschenbach (at left) contemplates the scene
on the beach in *Death in Venice*, 1971. ABOVE One-sheet poster
art for the film.

COMIC TURNS

Peter Bogdanovich, a critic before he became a filmmaker, had made his name with the valedictory *The Last Picture Show,* indicating his love of Hollywood's golden past. For *What's Up, Doc?* (1972) he turned his sights toward classic screwball comedy. Ryan O'Neal plays an absorbed musicologist, not so very different from Cary Grant's paleontologist in *Bringing Up Baby,* in San Francisco for a conference. Barbra Streisand plays a kooky young woman who, in a mix-up over bags, comes into collision with him and more or less wrecks his life. The basic screwball ingredients are all there: a chaotic banquet scene, a hotel corridor with doors popping open and shut with perfect timing, a pie fight, a chase involving a Chinese dragon, an out-of-control courtroom, and an aggrieved, hysterical fiancée

(Madeline Kahn in an auspicious debut). It worked, and was one of the year's top-grossing films.

Madeline Kahn also made a notable appearance in the hilarious Mel Brooks gross-out comedy *Blazing Saddles* (1974), brilliantly parodying Marlene Dietrich singing in a western saloon. The new sheriff, Cleavon Little, stupefies the townsfolk by being black and hiring an over-the-hill drunken gunman, the Waco Kid (Gene Wilder), to take on the land sharks and robber barons who are driving the railroad through. At its climax the fourth wall literally disintegrates, with the entire cast brawling and breaking their way into a musical being shot on the next stage, featuring a legion of camp chorus boys in white tie and tails who delightedly join in. None of Brooks's subsequent films would ever match its box-office performance.

OPPOSITE Barbra Streisand and Ryan O'Neal in *What's Up Doc?*, 1972. RIGHT Director Mel Brooks consults Gene Wilder while making *Blazing Saddles*, 1974. BELOW Cleavon Little as Bart and Gene Wilder as Jim wear bogus Ku Klux Klan robes in *Blazing Saddles*, 1974.

"WHO'S GOING TO SEE THIS MOVIE?"

FOR THE HELL OF IT

In *Badlands* (1973) Sissy Spacek is a baton-twirling South Dakota fifteen-year-old who meets a twenty-five-year-old garbage collector played by Martin Sheen. In her limited imagination she becomes infatuated because she thinks he looks like James Dean, but her strict father (Warren Oates) disapproves highly and to reinforce matters shoots her dog. When Sheen, almost casually, kills him she meekly abets, and embarks with her causeless rebel on a murderous journey across the state, yet remembering to take along her schoolwork.

Eventually the law catches up with them. He is condemned, but she is given probation. The director Terrence Malick is interested in the empty, apathetic void these two young people inhabit, and their indifference to normal emotions. Spacek narrates their tale in a dull monotone as if describing a boring shopping expedition, and

Malick dedicates his camera to the topography of the western landscape. Based on a real-life case, of Charles Starkweather and Caril Fugate in 1958, it makes a virtue of its obsessive fascination in banality.

EXIT THE MASTER

If one man could originate an entire movie genre it would have to be Bruce Lee. He was born in 1940 in San Francisco's Chinatown as Lee Jun Fan. The name "Bruce" was applied by an American nurse, and although he was born a U.S. citizen and remained so for the rest of his life, his parents took him to Hong Kong in his first year, where he lived until he was eighteen. He became a child actor and appeared in a score of Hong Kong films. Returning to the U.S., he studied philosophy at the University of Washington, and sought to perfect the martial-arts skills he had learned as a teenager, appearing in demonstrations, as well as teaching kung fu techniques to Steve McQueen and James Coburn. In 1964 he was spotted in a Long Beach Karate tournament and given the role of Kato, the sidekick of *The Green Hornet* in a TV series. He was in the film *Marlowe* (1969) with James Garner, but feeling that

Hollywood was predisposed against casting an Asian performer in leading roles he returned to Hong Kong where, in 1971, Raymond Chow featured him in Golden Harvest martial-arts action adventures, beginning with *Fists of Fury* (1973). Suddenly Lee was the leading Asian star. It was followed by *The Chinese Connection* (1973), which turned out to be an even greater box-office success. Warner Bros. beat other Hollywood studios in signing him, although to take no risks with western audiences they had John Saxon co-starring in *Enter the Dragon* (1973). Before the film's release Lee died very suddenly, apparently from an allergic reaction to a medicinal tablet.

Lee was an ascetic and a mystic, a perfectionist at his craft who preferred to perform his leaps, chops, and kicks without camera trickery. His death provoked anguish among his fans on the scale of the passing of Valentino and Dean and pallbearers at his Seattle funeral included McQueen and Coburn.

OPPOSITE TOP In *Badlands,* 1973, Martin Sheen walks into the sunset, recalling James Dean in *Giant.* OPPOSITE Sissy Spacek as Holly Sargis and Martin Sheen as Kit Carruthers, personifying Dean. ABOVE Bruce Lee, "an ascetic and a mystic" in *Enter the Dragon,* 1973, produced with Golden Harvest.

"IT'S A FIRE, MISTER, AND ALL FIRES ARE BAD"

A cycle of disaster movies raged in the 1970s, exploiting new techniques in special effects to simulate ocean liners turning turtle, cities ruined by earthquakes, volcanoes spewing molten destruction. Warner Bros. joined forces with 20th Century Fox to make one of the most spectacular, *The Towering Inferno*, in which the opening-night party at the world's tallest sky-scraper in San Francisco is marred by fire breaking out, the consequence of sub-standard wiring bought cheaply by Richard

Chamberlain. It quickly engulfs the middle floors while oblivi-ous guests attend the inauguration above. The register includes Fred Astaire, Faye Dunaway, Jennifer Jones, Robert Vaughn, O.J. Simpson and Susan Blakely with Paul Newman as the frantic architect, William Holden the owner, and Steve McQueen the fire chief who finds a whole new array of problems to confront. John Guillermin's film, with a script by Stirling Silliphant merged two novels (which each studio had optioned separately) into a formulaic progression of mangled bodies, exploding elevators, sickening death plunges, hairsbreadth escapes and daring res-cues. Its box-office popularity was unprecedented and having cost $14 million to make it grossed $119 million in the U.S.

ABOVE Steve McQueen as fire chief and Paul Newman as architect, as his new skyscraper combusts on its opening night, *The Towering Inferno*, 1974. OPPOSITE TOP In *The Exorcist*, 1973, Linda Blair as Regan MacNeil faces the statue of the demon, Pazuzu. BELOW Max von Sydow as Father Merrin arrives to perform the exorcism.

TALK OF THE DEVIL

William Peter Blatty's bestselling novel of demonic possession, *The Exorcist* (1973), based on an actual case he heard about while he was studying at Georgetown University, was turned into a controversial film, with his screenplay directed by William Friedkin. Ellen Burstyn plays a divorced actress aware of disturbing behavioral traits in her twelve-year-old daughter (Linda Blair). Jason Miller is a priest dealing with a terminally ill mother who is beginning to question his faith. The girl becomes possessed. She levitates, objects fly around the room, her speech becomes filthy, and she exhibits superhuman strength. Medical examinations and treatments are useless. The priest is convinced of the Devil's presence and calls in an old and feeble but experienced cleric (Max Von Sydow). Together they face unspeakable horror, as fountains of green bile spew from the girl's mouth, her head turns completely around on her neck, foul obscenities in a horrific voice are hurled as

they carry out a terrifying exorcism that is like a sixteenth-century vision of hell. In spite of protests from religious organizations, censorship cuts, and in some places outright bans, it is the most financially successful horror movie of all time.

1975–79

* Kubrick's *Barry Lyndon* wins four Oscars, 1975

* Clint Eastwood bases *Malpaso* on the Burbank lot, 1975

* Watergate exposé film *All the President's Men* wins four Oscars, 1976

* The U.S. celebrates the bicentennial of Independence, 1976

* Kidnapped heiress Patty Hearst is sentenced to seven years for bank robbery, 1977

* Jimmy Carter defeats Gerald Ford for the presidency, 1977

* Elvis Presley (forty-two) and Charlie Chaplin (eighty-eight) die, 1977

* Warner Bros. donates archives to the University of Southern California, 1977

* Christopher Reeve makes his debut as *Superman*, 1978

* In *Capricorn One* a manned flight to Mars is faked by NASA, 1978

* Jack L. Warner dies, aged eighty-six, 1978

ABOVE Patty Hearst, with a machine gun, stands in front of the symbol of the Symbionese Liberation Army, 1974.

SUMMER IN THE CITY

Sidney Lumet's *Dog Day Afternoon* is based on a real story, in which a pair of inept robbers (Al Pacino and John Cazale) hold up a bank in Brooklyn. The motive of the Pacino character is to use the money to finance his partner's (Chris Sarandon) sex-change operation. The robbery is a total failure with the police quickly surrounding the building, and the wretched pair take everyone hostage and prepare for a siege. Spectators and TV news teams, looking for a summer diversion from routine, converge outside. Pacino's sudden elevation to celebrity goes to his head, and the fever even affects some of the hostages, who seem thrilled to be the center of media attention. The crowd outside is for Pacino until his bisexualism becomes known, and then it is the turn of the gay community to come out and root for him. Lumet's film is a satisfying black comedy, although the consequences restore a sense of seriousness.

OPPOSITE Al Pacino in Sidney Lumet's *Dog Day Afternoon,* 1975, negotiating for the hostages. ABOVE Lumet and crew on location in Brooklyn for *Dog Day Afternoon.*

"DYIN' AIN'T MUCH OF A LIVIN', BOY"

Clint Eastwood took over *The Outlaw Josey Wales* (1976) from the writer of the screenplay, Philip Kaufman, who was originally scheduled to direct. He plays a farmer whose wife and son are killed, and his home burned to the ground by Union renegades toward the end of the Civil War. Bitterly he joins a Rebel guerilla group that fights on after the Appomattox surrender. As an outlaw he is bent on exacting vengeance, and with a price on his own head, he hunts down the killers for a bloody confrontation. The camera work of Bruce Surtees gives this epic western a compositional splendor reminiscent of nineteenth-century photography.

RIGHT AND BELOW Clint Eastwood in *The Outlaw Josey Wales*, 1976.

CITY LIFE

Herbert Ross directed Neil Simon's original screenplay *The Goodbye Girl* (1977), which he later turned into a Broadway musical and it was one of the most successful romantic comedies ever. Marsha Mason plays an ex-dancer with a ten-year-old daughter (Quinn Cummings) whose partner has skipped, subletting the New York apartment to a young actor played by Richard Dreyfuss. Having no alternative, she reluctantly agrees to share and it takes time for the odd couple to sink their differences. He is gentle, sleeps naked, and plays a guitar. She is abrasive and suspicious, bearing the pain of multiple rejections. The daughter is, of course, the catalyst for concluding the war. Dreyfuss was the first actor under thirty to win the Best Actor Oscar.

ABOVE TOP Richard Dreyfuss and Marsha Mason in *The Goodbye Girl,* 1977.
ABOVE Neil Simon and his wife, and star of the movie, Marsha Mason, with producer Ray Stark on set of *The Goodbye Girl,* produced with MGM.

SURF'S UP

When *Big Wednesday* first appeared in 1978 it was regarded as an expensive self-indulgence by its director and co-writer John Milius, who it seemed was engaging in sentimental recollections of his life in the early 1960s riding the Malibu surf, hanging out, and facing the Vietnam draft. Later it became regarded as the film that most encapsulated the Surfing U.S.A. years, a cult item for those who lived them. It is the story of three buddies (William Katt, Gary Busey, and Jan Michael Vincent) who dream of the big swell that will take twelve years eventually to materialize—the "big Wednesday" of the title. In the meantime Vietnam intervenes, and their lives are all irrevocably changed. The surfing scenes are magical, especially when the camera (cinematography was by Bruce Surtees) travels along within the great crescent of arching water.

ABOVE Jan Michael Vincent as Matt, catching the wave in *Big Wednesday*, 1978. BELOW Gary Busey as Leroy, Jan Michael Vincent as Matt, and William Katt as Jack, go surfing U.S.A. OPPOSITE The iconic poster art for *Big Wednesday*.

NO PARTICULAR PLACE TO GO

What was immediately apparent in *Mean Streets* (1973) was how well the young director Martin Scorsese knew the milieu. This was the Little Italy neighborhood in New York where he grew up, and he perfectly understands how the environment exerts pressures on his lowlifes (Harvey Keitel, Robert De Niro), who live surrounded by violence and degradation as the natural order. De Niro, who, like the director, makes his name in this film, is an irresponsible hothead. Keitel is his friend, a minor hood who suffers Catholic guilt and wants better, but stays around to rescue him. With a sure hand, Scorsese constructs some of his scenes in *verité* style, and incorporates apt rock music.

In Scorsese's *Alice Doesn't Live Here Any More* (1974), Ellen Burstyn won an Oscar for her portrayal of an insolent new widow journeying with her twelve-year-old son from New Mexico toward California, hoping for happiness. She flees a relationship in Phoenix with Harvey Keitel, who turns out to be married and dangerous, has a run-in and forms a friendship

with Oscar-nominated Diane Ladd, a foul-mouthed waitress in Tucson, and meets a nice rancher, Kris Kristofferson. Feminists hailed the film for presenting a self-sufficient woman, but were less pleased with the outcome. Scorsese skillfully captures the rootlessness and insecurity of the penniless in the Southwest.

OPPOSITE TOP Martin Scorsese directing Ellen Burstyn and Alfred Lutter III, in *Alice Doesn't Live Here Any More*, 1974. OPPOSITE BELOW In *Mean Streets*, 1973, Harvey Keitel as Charlie. RIGHT A confrontation between Robert De Niro as Johnny Boy and Harvey Keitel as Charlie. BELOW Robert De Niro, who made his name in *Mean Streets*, directed by Martin Scorsese.

MARTIN SCORSESE
Good Fella

Born in New York in 1942, Martin Scorsese, son of a Sicilian, was raised in the Little Italy section of Manhattan around Mulberry Street. It was then a tough neighborhood, but due to asthma he was not able to participate in the youth gangs, and was spared the path to delinquency and criminality that befell many of his contemporaries. His original destiny was the priesthood and for a while he was in the seminary. He dropped out to enroll in the film school of New York University and was a star student, making a number of shorts that showed signs of originality and daring. His first feature, *Who's That Knocking at My Door* was, like many of his later films, based on his background. He worked on the editing of Michael Wadleigh's *Woodstock* and gained critical attention with *Boxcar Bertha*, a low-budget crime film produced by Roger Corman.

Little Italy was the setting of *Mean Streets*, with his friend Robert De Niro as a hotheaded hood, protected by Harvey Keitel. Critical approval announced a new talent and his next, *Alice Doesn't Live Here Any More*, found favor at the box office. With *Taxi Driver*, again with De Niro, his success was assured. In *Raging Bull* De Niro played boxing champion Jake LaMotta in an uncompromising account of his downfall.

Scorsese endured the wrath of the church with *The Last Temptation of Christ* for suggesting the fallibility of Jesus, and *Goodfellas* brought him back to the underworld of gangsters and Mafiosi. He attempted period gentility with his version of Edith Wharton's *The Age of Innocence* and period criminality with *The Gangs of New York*. In *The Aviator* he pursued the strange career of the mega-rich Howard Hughes, and *The Departed* looked at the plight of two Boston youths who grew up to be on opposite sides of the law. Until recently Scorsese distanced himself from Hollywood, preferring to be seen as a New York filmmaker. His allegiance to cinema nevertheless runs deep and he has been industrious in campaigns to preserve film culture and to resurrect forgotten filmmakers. His devotion to British cinema of the 1940s surpasses that of the British themselves. Every frame of a Scorsese film reflects his love and passion for the medium, which he addresses with greater dedication than any other American director.

OPPOSITE Martin Scorsese on the set of *Mean Streets:* "Every frame of a Scorsese film reflects his love and passion for the medium." ABOVE Michael Wadleigh director, and editors Martin Scorsese and Thelma Schoonmaker working on *Woodstock,* 1970, under the eye of W. C. Fields.

CONTENDERS

Dustin Hoffman began directing *Straight Time* (1978) but yielded to Ulu Grosbard. As a released habitual offender Hoffman looks set for a quick return to prison, having fallen foul of an unfriendly parole officer (M.Emmet Walsh), and is heavy going for a middle-class girl (Teresa Russell) who believes in rehabilitation. Hoffman convinces as a hopeless loser who needs no encouragement from the corrupt to reoffend.

For a while in the late 1970s Burt Reynolds reigned at the box office, appealing to audiences with his blend of swaggering confidence and laid-back derision. In *Hooper* (1978) he plays a Hollywood stuntman (as were director Hal Needham and Reynolds in reality before they made *Smokey and the Bandit*). Past his prime and beset by rivals, especially the new contender Jan Michael Vincent, the ace must perform one last feat—a car leap across a 325-foot collapsed bridge. Sally Field is there to worry.

Affection for Warner Bros. movies of the double-bill era is the basis of *Movie Movie* ((1978), in which two mock features are welded by Stanley Donen to make a program. In *Dynamite Hands*, George C. Scott is an old boxing manager who spots the gifts of an unknown (Harry Hamlin) with a sick sister in need of an operation in Vienna, and pushes him to success while shielding him from corruption. In *Baxter's Beauties of 1933,* Scott is a Broadway producer with a month to live who has to put on a show to die for, an excuse for a clever Busby Berkeley parody with kaleidoscopic shots of rotating chorus girls. There is no heavy-handed satire, only a fondness for old movies and an understanding of why they were so entertaining.

CLINT DEFIES THE KNOW-ALLS

Clint Eastwood turned to comedy in *Every Which Way But Loose* (1978), directed by James Fargo, to the consternation of those who advised against it, and to the distaste of the critics who universally panned it. A frenetic, dumb comedy—in which a beer-guzzling, bar-room fighting trucker whose best friend is an orangutan called Clyde—it was loved by audiences, was a gigantic financial hit, and proved perfectly William Goldman's celebrated dictum on filmmaking: "Nobody knows anything," except in this case, Clint Eastwood.

OPPOSITE TOP Dustin Hoffman in *Straight Time,* 1978. BELOW Burt Reynolds in *Hooper,* 1978. ABOVE Rebecca York in the "Baxter's Beauties of 1933" segment of *Movie Movie,* 1978, produced with ITC Films, Inc. BELOW Clint Eastwood and Clyde in *Every Which Way But Loose,* 1978.

BREAKING OUT THE BREAK-IN

One of the most celebrated feats of investigative reporting in the twentieth century was the unraveling of the Watergate conspiracy that eventually led to the resignation of Richard M. Nixon from the presidency. The bestselling book *All the President's Men,* by Carl Bernstein and Bob Woodward of the *Washington Post* describes the events that led to it. William Goldman adapted for the screen and Alan J. Pakula directed. It is an absorbing story in spite of the fact that for much of the time the reporters, played by Dustin Hoffman and Robert Redford, talk mysteriously on the telephone or make assignations in a dark underground garage with their shadowy but knowledgeable informant known as "Deep Throat," an identity that remained unrevealed until 2005. Their editor, Ben Bradlee, is played by Jason Robards, seriously enough to win the Best Supporting Actor Oscar, and the *Post* newsroom was meticulously recreated in Burbank, as attempts to film in the real location became too artificial, with editorial staff recruited as actors far too self-conscious to be convincing. It manages to represent the working press much more authentically than is usual in films, demonstrating that great journalism is not achieved by Hildy Johnson histrionics, but as a consequence of interminable, patient toil.

ABOVE Robert Redford as Bob Woodward in *In All the President's Men,* 1976. OPPOSITE TOP Redford with Dustin Hoffman as Carl Bernstein work up their Watergate exposé. OPPOSITE BELOW The editorial team at the *Washington Post,* from left to right, Hoffman, Redford, Jason Robards as executive editor Ben Bradlee, Jack Warden as Harry Rosenfeld, and Martin Balsam as Howard Simons.

THE CASTING OF
CHRISTOPHER REEVE
AS SUPERMAN,
THE COMIC BOOK
SUPERHERO DEVISED
BY JERRY SIEGEL
AND JOE SHUSTER,
WAS **SERENDIPITOUS**.

A MAN CAN FLY

Superman had appeared in earlier films and on television, but for his generation of movie-goers, Christopher Reeve set the standard. It was as if he were born to play the "Man of Steel," who came from the faraway doomed planet Krypton to be raised in Smallville by the doting Kents, and to grow up to be his alter ego, Clark Kent, a mild-mannered, bespectacled reporter for the Metropolis *Daily Planet.*

In *Superman* (1978), directed by Richard Donner, Clark is smitten with sparky fellow reporter Lois Lane (Margot Kidder) who, in turn, is in love with Superman without realizing they are one and the same. The superhero takes on the arch-villain Lex Luthor (Gene Hackman) who, from a subterranean lair, plots the severing of the San Andreas Fault and the dispatch of California's largest cities into the Pacific. Marlon Brando appears briefly in a cameo role as Superman's father on Krypton. The film's success spawned several sequels, although Richard Lester replaced Donner for *Superman II* and *III.* In 2006, the franchise was reintroduced with *Superman Returns,* directed by Bryan Singer, with the hero played by newcomer Brandon Routh.

GEORGE PERRY

PREVIOUS PAGE Superman (Christopher Reeve) returns the American flag to the White House in *Superman II.* ABOVE Superman walking into a fire in a chemical factory in *Superman III.* LEFT Lee Quigley as Baby Kal-El and Marlon Brando as Jor-El. OPPOSITE *Superman Returns,* 2006, Brandon Routh as Superman standing in the Fortress of Solitude.

"WHO'S GOING TO SEE THIS MOVIE?"

CHAPTER

6

"WONDER IN OUR EYES"

RICHARD SCHICKEL

ON THE SATURDAY MORNING AFTER A WARNER BROS. PICTURE OPENED TERRY SEMEL KNEW HE HAD A HIT WHEN HE SAW THE RED LIGHT ON HIS ANSWERING MACHINE BLINKING FURIOUSLY AND OBSERVED THE NUMBER OF CALLS IT HAD PICKED UP—"PEOPLE CALLING TO CONGRATULATE THEMSELVES" IF THE FRIDAY BOX-OFFICE NUMBERS HAD BEEN GOOD. IF THE MACHINE WAS MUTE HE KNEW "WE WERE IN TROUBLE."

This is how life has been for studio bosses for the last thirty years or so, when everything is staked on a picture's opening weekend performance. To a certain degree, Semel was shielded by the fact that he shared executive responsibility with someone else, Robert Daly. Their arrangement was at that time unique in movie history in that, as co-presidents, they were absolutely equal partners in the management of the studio, sharing credit for its successes, blame for the flops, and, according to both men, not a single angry word crossed between them over the twenty years they worked together. Lots of times they simply agreed on whether or not to green light a project or launch some other business venture. If they did not, then the man who had the most passion for the idea would take charge of it and the other would never criticize the results.

In some ways they were an odd couple. Daly was older, hiding a tough mind under an avuncular manner. He had come out of television, and he was the man in charge of building up that side of the business. Semel was a Warner Bros. lifer, up out of motion-picture sales, a little more briskly articulate than Daly, though in truth their differences were in manner, not substance. When they took over at the studio in 1980, they recognized that, though the Ashley regime had been profitable, it had also been vulnerable to the hit-or-flop cycle of movie production. Television, they thought, was the key to financial stability with a hit show—something like *ER, Friends,* or *The West Wing* (all Warner Bros. productions) capable, literally, of generating as much as a billion dollars in revenue, far more than the biggest hit movie could ever take in. When they acquired Lorimar, a mighty TV operation specializing in adult series like *Dallas,* that side of the business really took off.

But they also thought there were other businesses that could help in that regard—theme parks, studio stores, and, perhaps most important, overseas movie theaters, many of which were of pre-World War II vintage and were shabby and unattractive. Over the years they built and rebuilt hundreds of theaters, greatly enhancing Warner Bros.' bottom line. Indeed, in general, the foreign markets became increasingly important to them until, midway in their regime, revenues from abroad exceeded the domestic box-office take. And that says nothing about the DVD revolution, which because the discs were cheap to produce and were designed more for sales than for rental (the opposite of the video-tape market) became a huge profit center for Warner Bros., not least because it held basic patents on the process, generating royalties on every disc produced by all the studios.

All of this vastly expanded the studio's revenue. Daly says that counting their regime and its successor the studio has only once failed to raise its annual revenues. Alongside the revived Walt Disney company, Warner Bros. consistently became either the number one or number two studio in the world. In film production their primary focus was, as Semel puts it, "making entertainment for the masses of the world, movies that spoke to everyone." Curiously enough, it didn't start out that way for them. Their first big hit was a pick-up, 1981's *Chariots of Fire,* a period piece about Olympic foot-racing, anti-Semitism, and the triumph of simple human decency. 20th Century Fox had rather unenthusiastically acquired it and was thinking of a modest art-house release. Semel (in particular) and Daly saw something more in it and offered the producer, David Puttnam, the money to buy it back from their rival, which was happy to see it go—until the reviews came in and the Best Picture Oscar was awarded. Daly remembered his people squeezing past billionaire oil man Marvin Davis, who then owned Fox, as they went to retrieve their prize and Davis muttering that he was going to fire everyone at his studio the next day.

PREVIOUS PAGE A distorted moment from *The Matrix,* 1999, produced with Village Roadshow Pictures.
OPPOSITE British Olympic athletes run along a Scottish beach to the Vangelis score in Hugh Hudson's Oscar-winning *Chariots of Fire,* 1981, produced with the Ladd Company and Goldcrest Distributors Ltd.

But *Chariots* was the exception to the rule at Warner Bros. in the eighties and nineties. The model was already established by *Superman,* to which the studio made two sequels. Daly and Semel wanted more such popular success, and through most of their first decade in command they kept nursing the notion of doing a film on another comic book hero, *Batman.* Many failed scripts ensued, until Tim Burton brought his sly, dark, slightly twisted sensibility to the enterprise. His two *Batman* films were, in effect, the anti-*Superman.* The lighting was anything but cartoonish (though, curiously, Burton had begun his career as an animator), and his pictures hinted at deep civic corruption and a certain bleakness about human nature in general. But the action was well staged, the dialogue minimal, both crucial factors in the international market, and the studio now had another "tentpole," as people increasingly referred to such movies—big, scary bets that could pay off not merely in the immediate gross, but in their merchandising and sequel potential.

Daly and Semel were cool with that. "Always pay for what you break," Semel quoted Steve Ross as saying. "If you're not willing to take the risk, don't do the job," which meant in practice taking responsibility for your failures and moving on as quickly as possible. Around this time (the late eighties) *Superman*'s director, Dick Donner, and producer Joel Silver, came up with a funny take on the cop-buddy genre—a staid family man (Danny Glover) and a wild-man wise guy (Mel Gibson) driving him crazy as they bicker their way through a case that offered plenty of fireball opportunities. *Lethal Weapon* (1987) was not inordinately expensive, became a not-too-surprising, genially lowball hit, and spawned three essentially pre-sold sequels—and a legendary act of largesse. When the second film made a ton of money the studio naturally wanted another, which was not necessarily something its key people wanted to do. Daly and Semel hosted a celebratory luncheon for them at the studio. When it was over, they went outside where eight new Range Rover cars were parked. Daly reached in his pocket, pulled

out a handful of keys and told their guests to pick the car they liked, with the thanks of a grateful studio. The press picked up on it—as a typically excessive Hollywood gesture. To which Daly's response was that for an investment of less than $350,000 they got their third *Lethal Weapon,* which went on to gross well over $100 million.

That's the way it went at Warner Bros. in those years. Another of Steve Ross's sayings was that movies were the only business where your chief assets—the people who created films—walked out the door every night. From this it followed that you treated them generously and forgivingly, and forged tight relationships with them. This worked particularly well for Daly and Semel, with two men who could not have been more antithetical, Clint Eastwood and Stanley Kubrick. The former liked to make at least one movie a year, sometimes two. He was famous for his frugality ("I treat the money as if it were my own," was something he was fond of saying) and for shooting fast; he liked the roughness and reality slightly under-rehearsed actors brought to their work. And he was famous for the quiet good humor that prevailed on his sets, on letting actors very largely work out their own interpretations, with only minimal guidance from him. People loved working for him and he loved working for Daly and Semel.

His bungalow office was just a few steps from the executive building, and he was wont to amble over to discuss projects with his bosses. There was always a lot of give and take in these conversations. During the worst crisis of Steve Ross's career, the collapse of Warner Communications' once-profitable video-game division, Atari, in

OPPOSITE Tim Burton directs Michelle Pfeiffer as Catwoman in *Batman Returns,* 1992. ABOVE Mel Gibson as Martin Riggs and Danny Glover as Roger Murtaugh, a successful police partnership in *Lethal Weapon 4,* 1998.

1984, Clint told Bob Daly to tell Steve Ross that he'd be happy to make another Dirty Harry film—he was loathe to continue that series, feeling it was played out—if that would help the company out. This *beau geste* proved unnecessary, though later Eastwood did one last Dirty Harry when an audience pool revealed to his employers that there was still a popular hunger for the aging cop. That said, they were prepared to do Eastwood favors in return, when for example he wanted to do one of his passion projects, *Bird,* Semel told him it was bound to lose money, then told him to go ahead and make it "and we'll sell the shit out of it." In short, this was about as good a long-term relationship as existed in modern Hollywood, and it has persisted—without benefit of long-term contract—for thirty-seven years and counting, which is truly unparalleled in our times.

Unless, of course, you count the many years Kubrick worked for the studio. Daly and Semel had inherited this relationship and nurtured it in a way that was entirely different from the one with Eastwood. Kubrick, of course, was everything Eastwood was not. Refusing to fly, he lived a sequestered life in his home outside London, leaving it only occasionally, usually when he was preparing or shooting a picture, which occurred only twice in Daly and Semel's two decades at the studio. He was not, however, a recluse; he kept in touch with a worldwide network of friends and colleagues via (in those pre-Internet days) phone, fax, and teletype, which he used without respect for the time zones. Working with Kubrick on *A.I. Artificial Intelligence* (2001), Steven Spielberg finally had to move the fax line exclusively dedicated to Kubrick out of his bedroom, since it tended to ring at all hours of the night. The way Kubrick worked with Daly and Semel was typical of him. The two executives would fly to London, wait in their hotel room for hand-delivered scripts (Kubrick was paranoid about them falling into the wrong hands), read them while the messenger (his brother-in-law) waited, turn them over, and await the invitation to join the director at home for discussions. Both men recalled keeping their overcoats on during these talks, because Kubrick refused to turn up the furnace.

Slow to develop his projects, he was also slow to shoot them. He was a director who would not hesitate to do as many as thirty takes of a shot, never once telling the actors what, exactly, he wanted. When he saw it, he would recognize it. Matthew Modine, starring in *Full Metal Jacket* (1987), was offered a part in another film, had to turn it down when Kubrick's shoot ran over, then watched as the other film was completed and released while he was still trapped in Kubrick's web. And the world knows about the two years Tom Cruise and Nicole Kidman devoted to *Eyes Wide Shut* (1999). One can't help but think that a kind of Stockholm Syndrome developed on Kubrick's pictures, with his cast and crew prisoners slowly abandoning resistance to their captor and becoming his loving collaborators. Yet this, too, must be said: Kubrick was a very lovable man. He may have been an autodidact, but he was a hugely intelligent one. Moreover, his almost lustful curiosity for information was omnivorous and delightful; you never felt better about yourself than when you were in his presence, answering his endless questions. A master of misdirection, he was always making movies that seemed to reside safely inside genre bounds, then breaking free of them to force an audience's contemplation of large existential issues in contexts of breathtaking visual beauty. He may have been an eccentric, but he was never a nut job. And mostly his pictures made money—enough to justify the cost and occasional annoyance of doing business with him. Daly would recall visiting the Warner office in Stockholm and being told by a young woman in the marketing department that she had no time to spend with the head of the studio. Why, Daly wondered. Because she was awaiting a call from Kubrick to discuss the art on the VHS box of one of his movies that was soon to be released in that territory. So it went with him: he would check every print going out on the first release of a picture, keep picture files of every theater it was playing to make sure the atmosphere was correct for his work. Once he ordered the interior of a major New York theater repainted the night before an opening, because he judged the present color unsuitable.

These, then, were the north and south poles of the Daly-Semel artistic world, and you could argue that their nurturing of these two filmmakers alone would secure their place in the production boss hall of fame. But because they were determined to roughly double the number of pictures the previous regime had annually released, they were not their sole concern. Eastwood aside, the duo tended to make more big-budget releases than the studio had in the past, mainly on topics with very broad popular appeal, some of which had merits well beyond their popularity. One such was George Miller's wild, crazy, cheekily violent *The Road Warrior* (1981), which made Mel Gibson a star. Another was Ridley Scott's visionary *Blade Runner* (1982), futuristic LA *noir,* which was not a huge hit in its initial release, but which has since developed a large cult following. They found a new star—Tom Cruise—with the low-budget, raunchy teen comedy, *Risky Business* (1983), which had to be slightly re-shot to give it a happy ending, which is what test audiences devoutly wished.

So it went. There were Spielberg pictures and Scorsese pictures, with the former testing his desire for seriousness with such aspiring works as *The Color Purple* (1985) and *Empire of the Sun* (1987), and the latter testing the ratings board with what the director described as "a rollicking road movie," *Goodfellas* (1990). The famous scene in which Joe Pesci polishes off an abducted rival gangster in the trunk of a car put X-rated thoughts in the minds of the motion-picture rating board. Daly and Scorsese kept cutting the sequence one or two frames at a time and re-screening it. Eventually, of course, the ratings people became addled and sick of the whole business, and granted the picture an R. This was a pretty typical executive performance for the loyal and patient Daly.

Probably Daly and Semel's most typical such performance was with Eastwood's Oscar-winning masterpiece, *Unforgiven.* He had acquired David Webb Peoples' script in the early eighties and everyone at the studio

ABOVE Stanley Kubrick directs on location, *Full Metal Jacket,* 1987.

agreed with the star-director that it was a great screenplay, and since Clint was enduring a so-so patch at the box office at the time, they kept urging him to make the film. He, however, thought he needed to age a bit before doing it. Daly—hint, hint—told him the world was ready for a western and Eastwood agreed. Great, Daly thought, we'll finally get *Unforgiven.* Instead Clint gave them *Pale Rider* in 1985—which was no bad thing, a western *cum* ghost story, but still not *Unforgiven,* which Eastwood said he thought of "as a nice little gold watch in my pocket," a reassuring talisman against the inevitable ups and downs of anyone's career. Like everyone else, he recognized its potential, though even he was surprised by the instant acclaim *Unforgiven* received when it opened in the summer of 1992. By then a lot of people were beginning to sense that he was on the way to greatness as a director, but this dark, brooding film about the costs of violence had about it a moral seriousness (and ambiguity) that he had not previously explored and it opened the way to his splendid late career, which has included the likes of *Mystic River, Million Dollar Baby, Flags of Our Fathers,* and *Letters from Iwo Jima*—perhaps the greatest run in movie history by a director in his seventies, an age when most careers dwindle and falter.

So it was not always tentpoles and franchises at Warner Bros. Indeed, it could be argued that in the eighties and nineties the financial record was stronger than it had ever been and that it was achieved with very little loss of eclectisism. If within a decade you are making *The Fugitive, Ace Ventura, Pet Detective, L.A. Confidential, Driving Miss Daisy, The Matrix* you must be doing something right. There is in that list—which could be extended—a range of costs, of subject matter, of audience appeal that is arguably superior to that of any competing studio. It may no longer be possible to speak of a Warner Bros. DNA guiding what the studio did, no longer easy to see how a certain kind of class consciousness binds together the studio's pictures. But still, it maintains a certain grittiness, a certain

OPPOSITE Clint Eastwood as the gunfighter William Munny in *Unforgiven,* 1992. ABOVE Eastwood as the boxing trainer Frank Dunn with Morgan Freeman as Eddie "Scrap Iron" Dupris, in *Million Dollar Baby,* 2004, produced with Lakeshore Entertainment.

lack of easy sentiment—setting aside something like *Driving Miss Daisy,* which had a certain liberal sentimental-ity about it—that is pretty consistent. And we have to remember that Warner Bros. acquired that picture when every studio in town had passed on it, the result being Academy Awards and astonishing grosses.

Yet conditions were changing for the studio. In 1990, Warner Communications and Time Inc. completed the merger that made Time Warner the world's biggest media company. It was presented to the world as an acquisition of Warner by Time, though in fact many insiders felt the governance plan for the merger favored the show folks over the more aristocratic and stolid Ivy Leaguers from Time. It was a resounding clash of corporate cultures, which largely undermined the synergistic hopes that were often expressed at the time. It also initiated a rivalry between the studio executives and those in charge of Time's modern-age jewel, HBO, the pay cable outlet whose leaders harbored big dreams of making movies outside the studio's aegis. Steve Ross might have charmed these birds into residing happily in the same nest, but he was dying of the cancer that carried him off in 1992. This was an irreplaceable loss to Daly and Semel, and in 2001 when the Internet giant AOL merged with Time Warner (in what turned out to be the most disastrous deal in modern American corporate history), Daly and Semel were no longer there, having retired from Warner Bros. in 1999. Daly, in particular, felt he had lost much of his fire for the business and wanted to retire (though, in fact, he accepted a position running the Los Angeles Dodgers baseball team for a while). Semel, who was younger, accepted another high-profile corporate post, as CEO of Yahoo, the Internet search engine, which started well and ended badly for him. They turned over the Warner Bros. reins to Barry Meyer and Alan Horn in 1999.

They left the company in good shape. They had produced the first visually exciting—even visionary—*Matrix* picture, which would in turn produce two profitable sequels, and they had acquired the rights to the *Harry Potter* series, a franchise with which the studio has been very successful. They also left behind Clint Eastwood, who became publicly unhappy with the new studio management, which he thought reacted unenthusiastically to *Mystic River* and *Million Dollar Baby.* Both pictures turned out to be highly profitable and critically successful, with the latter winning multiple Oscars. So Eastwood remains on the lot, and the mood between him and the execu-tives is reconciliatory. Also at the studio is George Clooney, "the last movie star" as *Time* magazine recently char-acterized him. He had begun at Warner Bros. in the series *ER,* then moved on to *The Perfect Storm* and the cheeky *Ocean's Eleven* franchise (and the mighty hit). He then made the seriously attended *Good Night, And Good Luck,* about Edward R. Murrow's fight against Joseph McCarthy—a picture that certainly harkened back in spirit to the old liberal days of the studio (it was even shot in black and white, and in a penny-pinching manner that would have pleased Jack Warner himself). Since then, he has, as an actor, put his starry clout behind two good and very serious films, *Syriana,* about highly dubious CIA machinations in the Middle East, and *Michael Clayton,* about a hard-pressed lawyer forced to choose between loyalty to his firm and his growing knowledge that its defense of a major corporation in a class action law suit is fatally compromised. These are both morally serious and narratively complex movies and a credit to a man who often presents himself as someone who does not take himself too seri-ously. That's certainly true of him. But, equally obviously, there is another more intriguing side to his nature.

In short, the studio continues to be profitable, if somewhat less innovative than it was in the thirties and forties. I don't mean that to be a reflection on Meyer and Horn. Indeed, the pair have led the company to industry records at the box office, expanded the breadth of the roster of filmmakers the studio works with and enjoyed a great number of successes, both expected (think *Harry Potter, Batman Begins*) and unexpected (*300, March of the Penguins*). While neither man could be called flamboyant or a showman, their understated leadership is guiding the company through changes in movie-going and technology not imagined by any of their predecessors. While there have been some admitted missteps, Meyer and Horn overall have managed to consistently produce films

OPPOSITE TOP LEFT Laurence Fishburne as Morpheus in *The Matrix.* OPPOSITE TOP RIGHT Daniel Radcliffe as Harry Potter in *Harry Potter and the Prisoner of Azkaban,* 2004. BELOW George Clooney directs *Good Night, And Good Luck,* 2005, produced by Participant Productions and Warner Independent Pictures. OVERLEAF One-sheet poster art for *Michael Clayton,* 2007, produced with Samuels Media Entertainment.

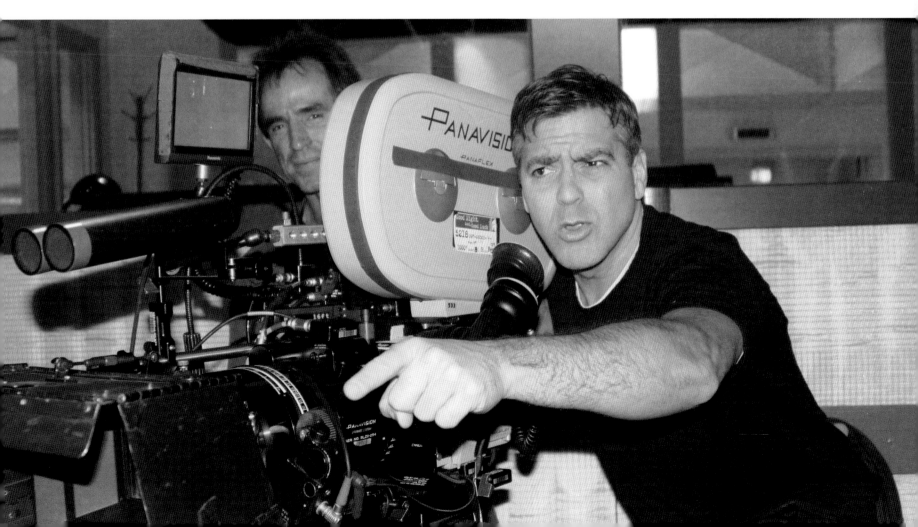

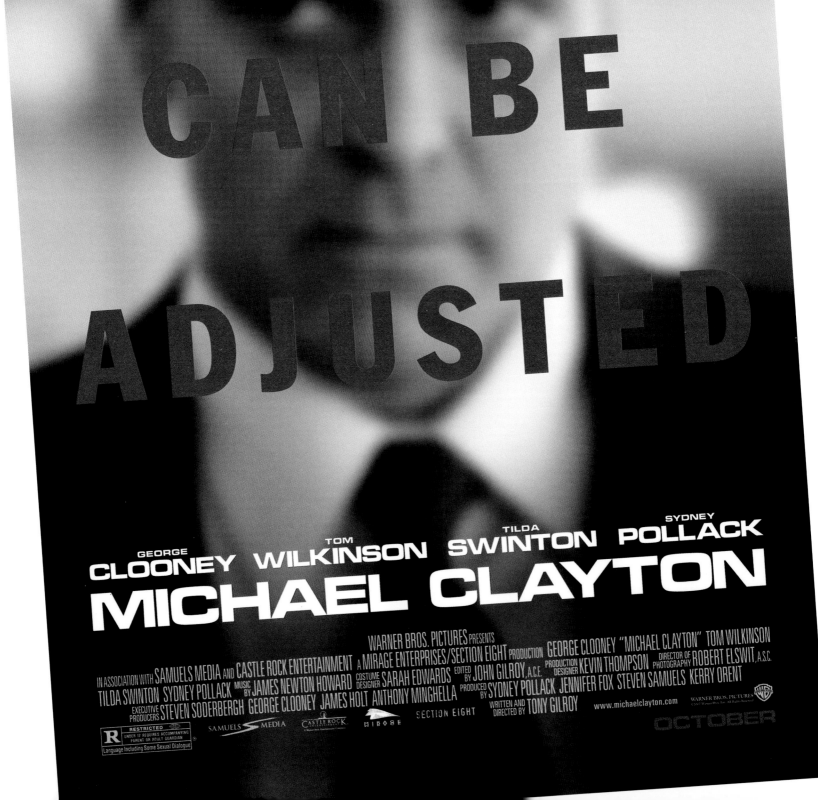

that click with audiences, play well overseas and make enough money to keep the studio well in the black and the parent company in New York happy.

Today as in the 1930s, studio bosses must always play the cards they are dealt, and movies in general are much more cautious and impersonal than they formerly were. It is hard nowadays to name an auteur whose status is comparable to that once enjoyed by Bergman or Kurosawa. Or Hitchcock or Hawks. Similarly, no studio has the definable character that Warner Bros. had in the thirties and forties. Or the anything-goes spirit that more or less ruled there in the last three decades of the twentieth century. (It's possible that Steve Ross was the modern incarnation of Jack Warner—considered better natured, less interfering, infinitely more likeable, but equally in love with movies and equally driven.) Be that as it may, his spirit—Jack's spirit—is not widely observed anywhere in Hollywood nowadays. We're also lucky to have units like Warner Independent Pictures working within the system to make smaller budget, but larger spirited, films than the blockbuster mentality can encompass. This is particularly true in an era when every major studio is a subsidiary of a distant and faceless conglomerate, which does not want Crazy Aces like Jack Warner running its movie operations—especially as they enter upon the new digital world, the dimensions of which no one fully perceives or understands.

This is not to say that the Warner brothers were in the movie business to establish a legacy. They were in it, like everyone else, to make money and to assert themselves in a hostile, anti-Semitic world. Nor is it to say that they were benign rulers of a sun-splashed empire. A case could be made that theirs was the most fractious of all the studios, a place that was fully capable of driving its talent crazy with their cheapness and occasional incomprehension. But a case could also be made that the tensions the brothers generated, among themselves, among their often angry underlings—the rub and scratch and occasional frenzy of the operation—were what energized it, forged its unique character, and perhaps animated its spirit long after the last Warner brother finally left the studio. Somehow, not entirely consciously, a legacy was, after all, created. The studio has never been a lightsome place, or one much interested in the purely fantastic or the purely chucklesome. You don't look to Warner Bros. for the classics of romantic comedy; there has often been a touch of bleakness even in many of its musicals. That's because it attracted to it talent that has, to this day, been a little more realistic, a little more willing to allow a touch of darkness to color its offerings. It seems to me not entirely accidental that the studio that once gave us *The Public Enemy* and *I Am a Fugitive From a Chain Gang,* later gave us *White Heat* and *Bonnie and Clyde* and *Unforgiven.* Maybe I am romanticizing a studio that I have admired more than any other since I first started going to the movies. But so be it. It is this studio, more than any other, that has drawn to it the talent that is in touch with its dark side—and ours.

In his dotage, someone suggested to Jack Warner that it must be a relief to lay down the burdens of day-to-day studio management. He replied: "Once I ran a studio. Now I'm just a rich old Jew." It's a telling statement—slightly vulgar, slightly shocking, but like the best Warner Bros. pictures, brutally truthful. And touchingly human. Movies are an accidental art, which from their very beginnings those connected with financing them have wanted to make more predictable, more rational. That has never worked out very well. It's likely that the natural state of film's creation is chaos, producing in equal measure triumphs and disasters. If that's the case then the Warner brothers, their heirs and assigns, have built better than they knew. In the end, this book and the television series from which it derives, celebrate not the arrival of those new technologies and marketing stratagems that are the engines that have driven broad scale, even revolutionary, industrial change over the course of movie history but those particular films—from *Wild Boys of the Road* to *Goodfellas, The Searchers* to *Unforgiven, Baby Face* to *Cool Hand Luke*—that have taken up permanent residence in our memories (and often enough in our hearts). Which says nothing about the dozens of lost jewels—*Heroes for Sale, The Hard Way, The Damned Don't Cry*—that await our delighted rediscovery. If movie history is to live, not as the property of cults, but as a living, stirring part of our cultural history, we need to approach it with wonder in our eyes, the belief—more ironic than cynical—in our minds that things will almost never work out the way we think they will, and the expectation in our souls that that's the ideal condition for making something that approximates art. In life. Or on a sound stage in Burbank, California.

RICHARD SCHICKEL

1980–84

* The United States boycotts the Moscow Olympics, 1980

* Stanley Kubrick's *The Shining* stars Jack Nicholson, 1980

* Ronald Reagan wins the presidency from Jimmy Carter, 1981

* *Chariots of Fire* is the Best Picture Oscar, 1981

* Ridley Scott's first film made in America is *Blade Runner,* 1982

* Warner Bros. releases the Ladd Company's *The Right Stuff,* based on Tom Wolfe's book about the space program, to win four Oscars, 1983

* Woody Allen's mockumentary *Zelig* is produced by Orion, released by Warner Bros., 1983

* *Gremlins* is co-produced with Amblin, 1984

* Soviet Russia and fourteen Eastern Bloc countries boycott the Los Angeles Olympics, 1984

ABOVE At his birthday ball in February 1981 at the White House, President Reagan cuts in on Frank Sinatra to dance with the First Lady. RIGHT Goldie Hawn in *Private Benjamin,* 1980. OPPOSITE Bette Midler sparkles in *Divine Madness!,* 1980, produced with the Ladd Company.

COMEDY DIVAS

Goldie Hawn had emerged in 1968 in the comedy TV program *Laugh-In* in which as an airhead blonde in a bikini she regularly fluttered her eyes, fluffed her lines, and dissolved into hopeless giggles, rendering the loquacious hosts Dan Rowan and Dick Martin temporarily speechless. Her film career began with *Cactus Flower* (1969) and included Steven Spielberg's *The Sugarland Express* (1974).

Renowned for her ditsy blondeness, Hawn scored a substantial hit with *Private Benjamin* (1980), directed by Howard Zieff, in which after sudden widowhood and falling for a glib line by Harry Dean Stanton, an army recruiter, she finds herself enlisted as a rookie. Much of the first part's

humor deals with the plight of a Jewish American princess being made to clean the latrine area with an electric toothbrush. Eileen Brennan as her captain leans on her hard, ostensibly to make her into a soldier. Once her anguish has subsided she begins to enjoy herself, achieving a posting to Europe and romantic possibilities with a handsome Frenchman.

Shrewder than she looked, Hawn was executive producer on *Private Benjamin,* which grossed over $100 million, and sparked a television series spin-off.

The singer Bette Midler's energy, versatility, and raunchiness was captured by Michael Ritchie in his concert film *Divine Madness!* (1980), in which she runs the gamut of her repertoire from "Boogie-Woogie Bugle Boy" to "The Rose." Ritchie employs camera techniques such as elaborate crane shots that are more usual in studio-bound musicals than live performances, ensuring that the typical glimpses of camera crews are not to be seen. As a record of Midler at her career peak it holds up well.

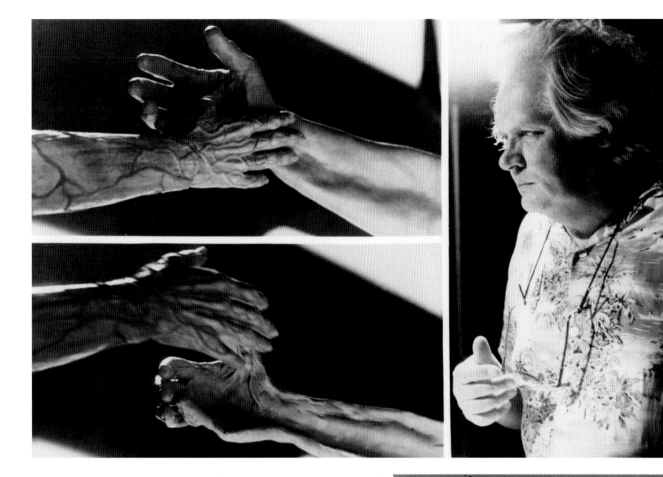

ALL YOU NEED IS LOVE

For *Altered States* (1980) Paddy Chayefsky adapted his own
novel, using the partial pseudonym Sidney Aaron (his first
two names), and Ken Russell, replacing Arthur Penn, directed
William Hurt in his debut. Hurt plays a psychologist engaged
in dangerous sensory-deprivation experiments, giving Russell
plenty of scope to visualize his hallucinogenic theories, especially when he simultaneously uses the immersion tank and
Mexican drugs. The effects are ahead of their time, but Hurt's
imagined path backward through civilization to the dawn of
existence offers a not unusual explanation for the meaning of
life—all apparently boiling down to love.

ABOVE RIGHT Ken Russell directs *Altered States,* 1980. ABOVE LEFT Two
photos of an altered state. RIGHT One-sheet poster art for *Altered
States.* OPPOSITE TOP In *Chariots of Fire,* left to right, Nicholas Farrell
as Aubrey Montague, Ben Cross (seated) as Harold Abrahams and
Nigel Havers as Lord Lindsay. BELOW Nigel Havers and behind him Ben
Cross, run round Trinity Great Court, Cambridge. It was actually
Eton College because Trinity barred the filmmakers.

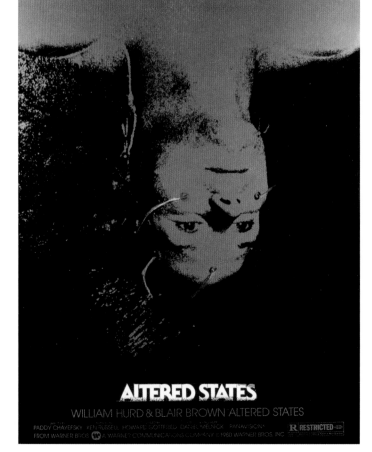

In the basement of a medical school Dr. Jessup floats naked
in total darkness. The most terrifying experiment in the history of science
is out of control . . . and the subject is himself.

ALTERED STATES

WILLIAM HURD & BLAIR BROWN ALTERED STATES

PADDY CHAYEFSKY KEN RUSSELL HOWARD GOTTFRIED DANIEL MELNICK PANAVISION®   R RESTRICTED
FROM WARNER BROS. A WARNER COMMUNICATIONS COMPANY ©1980 WARNER BROS. INC.

WET RUN

A British classic, produced by David Puttnam and directed with assurance by Hugh Hudson in his feature debut, the Oscar-winning Best Picture *Chariots of Fire* (1981) is based on two outstanding athletes, Harold Abrahams (Ben Cross) who was Jewish, wealthy, and Cambridge-educated, and Eric Liddell (Ian Charleson), a devout Protestant Scot from a missionary background. Both compete in the 1924 Paris Olympics, the one to combat class prejudice, the other to win God's approval. An obstacle—Liddell's refusal to compete on the Sabbath—nearly stymies the challenge, but a compromise results in events being swapped. A 1980's electronic score by Vangelis provided a stirring theme, memorably accompanying a slow-motion view of a squad of athletes on an early-morning training run, splashing along a wet, sandy beach.

WAR GAMES

Clint Eastwood directed *Firefox* (1982) and played a retired U.S. Air Force pilot brought back into service to go on a covert mission inside the Soviet Union. His task is to steal a secret Russian warplane that is radar invisible and loaded with high-tech equipment, including a thought-controlled weapon system, and capable of Mach 6 speeds—faster than anything in the West. Once he has surmounted the obstacles and gets into the Firefox's cockpit it is as though he is suddenly immersed in a video game, and an Arctic dogfight with a similar aircraft has a surreal quality.

ABOVE Behind the scenes on *Firefox,* 1982, directed by Clint Eastwood, who also played Mitchell Gant (RIGHT). OPPOSITE TOP The Mercury astronauts in *The Right Stuff,* 1983, produced with the Ladd Company. Left to right: Scott Paulin, Lance Henriksen, Charles Frank, Fred Ward, Scott Glenn, Ed Harris, and Dennis Quaid. OPPOSITE BOTTOM Scott Glenn gets confrontational as Charles Frank, Fred Ward, Ed Harris, and Dennis Quaid watch.

NEW KIND OF HERO

Tom Wolfe's lively bestseller on the birth of the space age was turned into a film, written and directed by Philip Kaufman, that seemed intent on creating a new mythology of pioneering heroes. *The Right Stuff* (1983) starts with the day Chuck Yeager, played by Sam Shepard, breaks the sound barrier in the X-1, and goes through to a grand celebration of the Mercury space program hosted by President Lyndon B. Johnson in the Houston Astrodome.

The first astronauts are shown not simply as courageous, highly trained professionals who risked their lives in the unknown, but also as media performers who were obliged to exhibit a public persona to satisfy a tax-paying electorate eager to know if the expense of it all has been worthwhile. They are played by capable actors, among them Scott Glenn, Ed Harris, Dennis Quaid, and Fred Ward, and the humor and occasional satire of Wolfe's original survives.

LONG TALE, NO SEE

Before it was released to American cinemas, Sergio Leone's last film, *Once Upon a Time in America* (1984), made after his twelve-year absence from the screen, lost eighty-five minutes of footage, drastically shortening the 229-minute original that had been acclaimed at the Cannes Film Festival.

The narrative structure was also reordered, eliminating the flashbacks, but there were so many gaping holes in the plot and references to unseen characters that, not, surprisingly audiences were bewildered, so the film failed. Fortunately it can be seen on DVD in the form Leone intended, and it has since become appreciated for its complex exposition of the forty-year relationship between childhood friends who grow up in a Jewish neighborhood on New York's Lower East Side to become career criminals. Robert De Niro and James Woods give magnetic performances in a lengthy, ambitious film, with Ennio Morricone's distinctive score working hard to cohere the intricate storyline.

ABOVE In *Once Upon a Time in America,* 1984, produced with the Ladd Company and Arnon Milchan, Robert De Niro walks the New York streets with James Woods.

"WAKE UP! TIME TO DIE!"

Ridley Scott's *Blade Runner* was based on Philip K. Dick's science-fiction novel *Do Androids Dream of Electric Sheep?* and is set in a future Los Angeles, its rain-sodden streets lined with semi-derelict buildings and gigantic moving advertising displays, while the sky is thick with airborne vehicles. At ground level the city has been claimed by the Third World and is overrun by the poor, the rich having retreated to impregnable fortresses. Harrison Ford is a particular kind of detective whose assignment is to track down and destroy the replicants, or super-androids, from another planet that have mutinied and made their way to Earth to mingle with the human population. A brilliant, stylish triumph of production design, it was initially received with wariness but soon attracted a cult following, assisted by the director's revised version of 1993, which stripped out Ford's voice-over narration.

RIGHT One-sheet poster art for *Blade Runner*, 1982, produced with the Ladd Company and Blade Runner Partnership, featured Harrison Ford and Sean Young. BELOW A spinner zips past an electronic billboard in Los Angeles 2019.

THE WARNER BROS. STORY

Harrison Ford as Deckard, the replicant hunter, hangs on precariously by his fingertips in *Blade Runner*.

ODDBALLS

John Irving's quirkily eccentric novel *The World According to Garp* (1982) was filmed by George Roy Hill from a screenplay distilling its essence by Steve Tesich, and featured Robin Williams in his first dramatic role as the calamity-beset hero whose weird life journey is followed. Glenn Close plays his unmarried mother, a strange nurse who becomes an active feminist, his wife is Mary Beth Hurt, and impressively, John Lithgow almost steals the film as a transsexual football player.

In *The Man With Two Brains* (1983), Steve Martin plays the world's most accomplished brain surgeon who can perform two operations simultaneously and has perfected a cranial screw-top technique that leaves the hair intact. He marries a beautiful woman (Kathleen Turner) only to find that she is a nymphomaniac gold-digger. A manic doctor in Vienna (David Warner) comes to his aid by allowing him to meet a disembodied yet live brain in a jar and with which he forms a tender relationship. The path to true love has never been so rocky in Carl Reiner's amiable spoof of mad-scientist films.

ABOVE John Irving referees in the screen adaptation of his novel, *The World According to Garp*, 1982, with Robin Williams in the lead role as T. S. Garp. OPPOSITE Steve Martin and his true love in a jar in *The Man With Two Brains*, 1983.

COPS AT COLLEGE

Hugh Wilson's *Police Academy* (1984) is a happy example of a silly idea for wild comedy, a campus for trainee cops that is run like a prep school. It proved so popular with the public that eventually six other films in a long-running series were made in a ten-year period. The rookies include Steve Guttenberg, Kim Cattrall, Bubba Smith, and Donovan Scott, and their mentor is the accident-prone G. W. Bailey. The saving grace is that this police academy could only exist in the imagination.

FROM A JUNGLE BOOK

Hugh Hudson's film *Greystoke: The Legend of Tarzan, Lord of the Apes* (1984), adapted from Edgar Rice Burroughs by Robert Towne, is the definitive version of the *Tarzan* legend on film, superbly photographed in Cameroon and in a huge indoor jungle on the biggest stage at Elstree Studios, London. The story is told from the beginning, with the shipwreck that maroons Tarzan's aristocratic British parents on the African coast. After his mother has given birth both parents die, and the infant is raised by apes. Years later the young man, played by Christopher Lambert, rescues a Belgian explorer (Ian Holm) who teaches him English. The most moving performance is that of Ralph Richardson, in his last screen appearance as Tarzan's grandfather, the 6th Lord Greystoke, who meets him in a joyous homecoming at the vast English ancestral home. Rick Baker's brilliant makeup effects make it hard to distinguish real apes from costumed actors.

OPPOSITE Graduation day at *Police Academy,* 1984, produced with the Ladd Company. RIGHT Christopher Lambert as Tarzan in *Greystoke: The Legend of Tarzan, Lord of the Apes,* 1984, and BELOW with Andie MacDowell as Jane.

"WONDER IN OUR EYES"

CHILD'S PLAY

Steven Spielberg produced the humorous fantasy *Gremlins* (1984) from a screenplay by Chris Columbus, with Joe Dante directing. It is a fusion of *It's a Wonderful Life* small-town homeliness and Hollywood monsters-on-the-rampage horror. A boy whose Christmas seems made by the gift of a cuddly, wide-eyed, sweet little creature finds that it turns into a nightmare when the warnings against late-night feeding and allowing it to get wet are breached. Multiplying gremlins overrun the neighborhood, creating swathes of destruction and terror among the residents who see their suburban dream imploding before their eyes. In the sequel, *Gremlins 2: The New Batch* (1990), the little fiends reach New York City.

Spielberg wrote the story and Columbus the script for *The Goonies* (1985), directed by Richard Donner, in which a bunch of kids in a small Oregon coastal town find a map of buried treasure and set out on a rapidly paced adventure that brings surprises and danger with almost every step. The possibilities of magical worlds lurking unseen in close proximity to the most mundane settings is a Spielberg trademark.

RIGHT "Mohawk" pops out of a candy container in *Gremlins 2: The New Batch,* 1990. BELOW Zach Galligan and Phoebe Cates with a gift box containing a Mogwai named Gizmo. OPPOSITE One sheet poster art for *The Goonies,* 1985.

They call themselves "The Goonies."

The secret caves.
The old lighthouse.
The lost map.
The treacherous traps.
The hidden treasure.
And Sloth...

Join the adventure.

STEVEN SPIELBERG Presents

THE GOONIES

A RICHARD DONNER Film

"THE GOONIES"

Story by STEVEN SPIELBERG   Screenplay by CHRIS COLUMBUS

Music by DAVE GRUSIN   Executive Producers STEVEN SPIELBERG

FRANK MARSHALL · KATHLEEN KENNEDY

Produced by RICHARD DONNER and HARVEY BERNHARD

Directed by RICHARD DONNER

READ THE WARNER PAPERBACK   Original Soundtrack Album on Epic Records and Cassettes

DOLBY STEREO
IN SELECTED THEATRES   AMBLIN ENTERTAINMENT   FROM WARNER BROS.
A WARNER COMMUNICATIONS COMPANY
TM & © 1985 Warner Bros. Inc. All Rights Reserved

PG PARENTAL GUIDANCE SUGGESTED
SOME MATERIAL MAY NOT BE SUITABLE FOR CHILDREN

379

1985–89

✻ Soviet President Gorbachev introduces *perestroika* and *glastnost* freedom reforms, and abandons the Brezhnev Doctrine, 1985

✻ Clint Eastwood's films include *Pale Rider*, 1985, *Heartbreak Ridge*, 1986, and *The Dead Pool*, 1988

✻ The first *Lethal Weapon* film stars Mel Gibson and Danny Glover, 1987

✻ Glenn Close and John Malkovich star in *Dangerous Liaisons*, 1988

✻ Pan Am 103 is downed by Libyan terrorists over Scotland, 1988

✻ Communism collapses in the Eastern Bloc

✻ Michael Moore's documentary *Roger and Me* attacks General Motors, 1989

✻ *Driving Miss Daisy* is Best Picture, its star, Jessica Tandy, wins Best Actress, 1989

✻ George H. W. Bush is elected 41st President, 1989

ABOVE George H. W. Bush, the 41st President, and wife Barbara at the inauguration, January 20, 1989.
RIGHT One sheet poster art for *The Color Purple*.

STRUGGLE AND SURVIVE

Steven Spielberg's film of Alice Walker's *The Color Purple*, a Pulitzer Prize-winning novel about the struggles of a black woman in the South in the early twentieth century, gave dramatic roles to two remarkable performers, Whoopi Goldberg, who had been doing a comic act in a San Francisco club, and Oprah Winfrey, a former TV reporter who had become the presenter of a national talk show originating in Chicago. Danny Glover took the male lead.

The film was superbly photographed by Allen Daviau, and received eleven Academy Award nominations.

OPPOSITE TOP Oprah Winfrey as Sofia and Whoopi Goldberg as Celie in Steven Spielberg's *The Color Purple*, 1985. OPPOSITE BELOW Laurence Fishburne, Margaret Avery, and Willard E. Pugh.

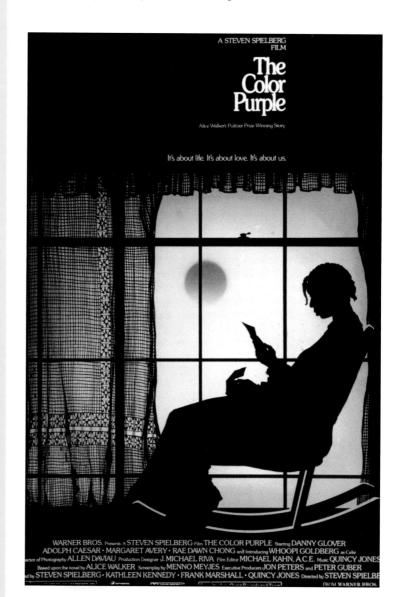

"WONDER IN OUR EYES"

THE WARNER BROS. STORY

Whoopi Goldberg as Celie leads children along a dirt road in *The Color Purple*, which received eleven Academy Award nominations.

SHANGHAI SON

Spielberg's next film, *Empire of the Sun*, from J. G. Ballard's autobiographical novel, was an account of a British boy in the wealthy international enclave of Shanghai in 1941. As the Japanese invade he is separated from his parents and interned, learning in his early teenage years the arts of self-sufficiency and endurance, with John Malkovich playing an important surrogate parent and mentor. At the end of the war the boy, in an accomplished performance by Christian Bale, is reunited with his parents. Although Spielberg was allowed three weeks to shoot scenes on the Bund waterfront in Shanghai, which in the 1980s still looked much as it had forty years earlier, the lush homes of the international settlement were represented by 1930s mansions in suburban Surrey and Berkshire, near London.

RIGHT AND OPPOSITE Christian Bale as Jim in *Empire of the Sun,* 1987.
BELOW Ben Stiller, Joe Pantoliano, John Malkovich, with other cast members.

"WONDER IN OUR EYES"

ABOVE Steven Spielberg on the set of *Empire of the Sun*.
RIGHT directing Whoopi Goldberg in *The Color Purple*.

STEVEN SPIELBERG
Dreaming

If success is measured in box-office gross—and in the business of entertainment there is nothing dishonorable in applying such a yardstick—Steven Spielberg has to be the most successful filmmaker of all time, responsible for such spectacular money-making works as *Jaws*, *Close Encounters of the Third Kind*, *Raiders of the Lost Ark*, *E.T.: The Extra-Terrestrial*, *Jurassic Park*, and others. Uniting them thematically is the power of the unknown, the forces beyond the limits of man's knowledge that can only be viewed with awe and a sense of wonder. The more somber side of Spielberg is represented in his comments on inhumanity—*Schindler's List*, *Saving Private Ryan*, *Munich*.

He was born in Cincinnati in 1946, moved to Phoenix, Arizona, and started making 8mm movies in his pre-teens. His parents divorced and he went to California with his father, eventually attending California State University Long Beach, until hired by Universal for television. His first feature, *Duel,* was a brilliant movie-of-the-week that was successfully released theatrically outside the U.S. It was *Jaws* that made him inviolably bankable, giving him the freedom to expand and exert influence. He quickly became a catalyst for talent, at his production company Amblin (named after the short film that earned him the studio job), fostering the careers of Bob Zemeckis, Joe Dante, Chris Columbus, Phil Joanou, and others. With Jeffrey Katzenberg and David Geffen he started DreamWorks in the 1990s. His association with Warner Bros. includes *The Color Purple, Empire of the Sun, AI: Artificial Intelligence, Gremlins, The Goonies, Innerspace,* and television's *Tiny Toon Adventures* and *Animaniacs*. Spielberg's imaginative contribution to film is enormous and wide-reaching, yet until *Schindler's List* in 1993 the Academy Award eluded him. He won Best Director then and for 1998's *Saving Private Ryan.*

APPLES FOR TEACHER

In *Stand and Deliver* (1988), from first-time director Ramon Menendez, a class of habitual losers at a high school in an East Los Angeles barrio is taken in hand by a dedicated, charismatic and unconventional math teacher. In spite of opposition and skepticism from his superiors he pushes them to compete in an advanced calculus test that notoriously has only a two percent pass rate, yet all his students succeed. Beyond probability? It is a true story, and Edward James Olmos is adept at capturing the curious, captivating mannerisms and innovative teaching style of the real-life Jaime Escalante. As one of the students, Lou Diamond Phillips is a standout.

John G. Avildsen's *Lean on Me* (1989) pursues a similar idea, with Morgan Freeman as the new principal of a dismal New Jersey high school where both students and staff are hopelessly demoralized. A driven, angry, prickly man, he is at first perceived as an imperious martinet who humiliates teachers in front of pupils, orders a mass expulsion of all the druggies, and leads paint parties to cover up the graffiti on the school walls. Yet somewhere there is an inspiring streak, and the tide turns as his energized students start getting good results. Not from great teaching, it would seem, but because they now feel good about themselves. It is another supposedly true story, but this man is education's Dirty Harry.

ABOVE Edward James Olmos portraying real-life teacher Jaime Escalante, in *Stand and Deliver*, 1988. OPPOSITE Morgan Freeman as a controversial high-school principal in *Lean on Me*, 1989.

"WONDER IN OUR EYES"

IN VIETNAM THE WIND DOESN'T BLOW IT SUCKS

BORN TO KILL

Stanley Kubrick's

FULL METAL JACKET

WARNER BROS PRESENTS STANLEY KUBRICK'S FULL METAL JACKET

STARRING
MATTHEW MODINE ADAM BALDWIN VINCENT D'ONOFRIO LEE ERMEY DORIAN HAREWOOD ARLISS HOWARD
KEVYN MAJOR HOWARD ED O'ROSS SCREENPLAY BY STANLEY KUBRICK MICHAEL HERR GUSTAV HASFORD
BASED ON THE NOVEL
THE SHORT-TIMERS BY GUSTAV HASFORD CO PRODUCER PHILIP HOBBS EXECUTIVE PRODUCER JAN HARLAN PRODUCED AND DIRECTED BY STANLEY KUBRICK

R RESTRICTED
UNDER 17 REQUIRES ACCOMPANYING
PARENT OR ADULT GUARDIAN
WARNER BROS A WARNER COMMUNICATIONS COMPANY
1987 Warner Bros. Inc. All Rights Reserved.

ABOVE One-sheet poster art for *Full Metal Jacket,* 1987
RIGHT ABOVE Kieron Jecchinis as Crazy Earl, and
BELOW Dorian Harewood as Eightball.
OPPOSITE In *Bird,* 1988, director Clint Eastwood works
with Forest Whitaker as Charlie "Bird" Parker.

KUBRICK'S BOOT CAMP

For *Full Metal Jacket* (1987), Stanley Kubrick—who resolutely refused to return to the United States to shoot his films—created the U.S. Marine Corps boot camp, Parris Island in Cambridgeshire, England, and the devastated Vietnamese city of Hue on the site of a gasworks due for demolition in East London. His film is an indictment of the war, but is also about the professional dehumanizing of military personnel to make them ready for combat. The first part of the film shows rigorous training, made realistic by the performance of a genuine Marine Corps gunnery sergeant, Lee Ermey, whose creatively obscene haranguing of his platoon is mesmeric. The second part, set in Vietnam, is filled with intense fighting sequences, especially in the city of Hue.

BIRD

Clint Eastwood's love of jazz is the force behind *Bird* (1988), his tribute to the iconic saxophonist Charlie "Yardbird" Parker, who pioneered bebop, and had a New York club—Birdland—named in his honor. He died in New York in 1955 aged thirty-four, but his body was so wasted by drug and alcohol abuse that the coroner mistakenly estimated him to be between fifty and sixty. Central to Eastwood's film is the extraordinary performance of Forest Whitaker as the self-destructive, yet intensely compassionate and gentle Parker, hooked from his teenage years with an addiction that became essential to his musical creativity.

Great technical skills went into remixing original recordings, separating Parker's solos and bringing in new musicians to accompany them. *Bird* is in shadowy muted color, and the narrative is fragmented. Diane Venora gives an outstanding performance as Chan, his white wife. Eastwood wisely allows the genius of Parker's music to dominate his film.

IRON CURTAIN RAISER

In the cynical Cold War comedy *Spies Like Us* (1985), directed by John Landis, Chevy Chase and Dan Aykroyd are talentless exam cheats who expect to be appointed as full-fledged CIA operatives, and are sent on assignment to the Pakistan-Afghanistan border without realizing that their purpose is to act as decoys, diverting Soviet attention away from the real mission. A running gag has well-known directors, including Joel Coen, Terry Gilliam, Constantin Costa-Gavras, and Michael Apted constantly popping up in cameos.

RIGHT In *Spies Like Us,* 1985, Chevy Chase, Bob Hope, Donna Dixon, and Dan Aykroyd on location. BELOW Dan Aykroyd and Chevy Chase experience G-force. OPPOSITE TOP RIGHT One sheet poster art for *National Lampoon's Vacation,* 1983. TOP LEFT An automotive nightmare in Monument Valley. BOTTOM Chevy Chase hallucinates in Death Valley.

ROAD-TRIP FARCE

Chevy Chase is the star of *National Lampoon's Vacation* (1983), directed by Harold Ramis, with Beverly D'Angelo as his bubbly wife. He is a Chicagoan who thinks it would be great to drive his family cross-country to California and visit the Walley World theme park. Every last detail has been carefully planned with great precision, and naturally anything that can go wrong on the journey does. John Hughes wrote the script based on his story "Vacation '58," published in *National Lampoon* magazine. This particular thread of NL comedies inspired three sequels.

FAITH IN THE WILD

David Puttnam produced Roland Joffe's film *The Mission* (1986) from a screenplay by Robert Bolt. It was made under arduous conditions on location in South America. Set in the 1750s, it stars Jeremy Irons as a pious Jesuit priest who establishes a mission for the Guarano Indians to protect them from the forces of imperialism. He is joined by a formerly ruthless slave trader, Robert De Niro, who has done backbreaking penance and undergone a conversion. Violence is a constant factor in a complicated story of inner and outer struggles, and the Oscar-winning cinematography of Chris Menges is often breathtaking.

TOP AND OPPOSITE In *The Mission,* 1986, produced with Goldcrest Distributors Ltd., Robert De Niro plays Rodrigo Mendoza. ABOVE Jeremy Irons as Father Gabriel, leading natives in a ceremony.

In *The Mission*, Daniel Berrigan as Sebastian observes Liam Neeson as Fielding and Jeremy Irons as Father Gabriel, greeting each other.

"WONDER IN OUR EYES"

PRIDE AND PREJUDICE

In *The Witches of Eastwick* (1987) directed by George Miller based on a script from John Updike's novel, Jack Nicholson is the devil in sprightly form, conjured up by three bored New England women (Cher, Michelle Pfeiffer, and Susan Sarandon) who want a perfect man. The capacity of Nicholson to enjoy himself is a pleasure to watch in an agreeable, absurdist fantasy.

Bruce Beresford's *Driving Miss Daisy* (1989), adapted by Alfred Uhry from his play, uses a racial theme as the basis for its comedy. Morgan Freeman is hired as chauffeur for an elderly Southern widow (Jessica Tandy) who can no longer control her ancient Packard, and in the period of the early 1960s when segregation is fighting its last trump, a tender dependency develops between them, confounding all prejudices. Dan Aykroyd, in a relatively straight part, plays her anxious son. Among its Oscars were Best Actress for Tandy, Best Adapted Screenplay for Uhry, and Best Picture, but Beresford was not even nominated.

OPPOSITE Jessica Tandy and Morgan Freeman in *Driving Miss Daisy*, 1989, produced with Majestic Films Ltd.

ABOVE In *The Witches of Eastwick*, 1987, a devilish Jack Nicholson stands behind Cher, Susan Sarandon, and Michelle Pfeiffer.

"WONDER IN OUR EYES"

1990–94

✴ Time Warner is formed from a merger with Time Inc., 1990

✴ Nelson Mandela is released after twenty-seven years' imprisonment, 1990

✴ The Soviet Union collapses, 1991

✴ Germany is reunited, 1991

✴ Operation Desert Storm starts the Persian Gulf War against Iraq, 1991

✴ Clint Eastwood's *Unforgiven* is Best Picture, 1992

✴ Frances Hodgson Burnett's *The Secret Garden* is filmed in England, 1993

✴ Joel and Ethan Coen's *The Hudsucker Proxy* is co-produced with Warner Bros., 1994

✴ Bill Clinton becomes 42nd President, 1993

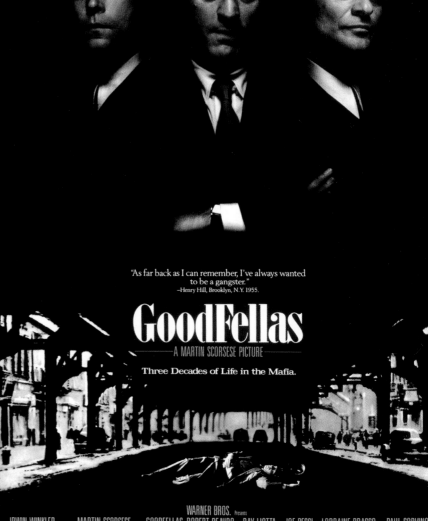

"WE WERE GOODFELLAS, WISEGUYS"

Martin Scorsese's adaptation of Nicholas Pileggi's book *Wise Guy: Life in a Mafia Family*, about the Brooklyn Mafia in the mid-twentieth century, is a tour de force. Ray Liotta, an Irish-Sicilian who has always wanted to be a gangster, achieves his wish, with chilling performances by Joe Pesci, Robert De Niro, and Paul Sorvino as denizens of the world he joins. Scorsese never balks at showing the ethos of violence that is often alarmingly casual, such as when Pesci shoots a

waiter for taking too long over the drinks. The Liotta character, Henry Hill, who is based on reality, ends up hidden with his Jewish wife (Lorraine Bracco) under the witness protection program.

OPPOSITE FAR LEFT At his inaugural party in January 1993, President Clinton blows up a storm. LEFT TOP One-sheet poster art for *Goodfellas*, 1990. LEFT BOTTOM Martin Scorsese directs *Goodfellas*. BELOW Left to right: Ray Liotta, Robert De Niro, Paul Sorvino, Martin Scorsese, and Joe Pesci.

CAT AND MOUSE

Michael Mann's *Heat* (1995) is long at 172 minutes, but given that Robert De Niro and Al Pacino are pitted against each other as thief and cop it has a mesmerizing association at its center. The gangster and the detective may be enemies, but they have an odd symbiotic kinship, their lives so barren that each depends on the other for the buzz that gets them through the day. This is summed up in a scene where Pacino, tailing De Niro, pulls him over and invites him for a cup of coffee, during which time they simply talk about their respective lives and how they know no other calling. Michael Mann based his script on a real-life drama that played out in Chicago between a tough cop and a hardened criminal, and came up with a brilliantly textured character study of the nature of criminality, with incidental violence.

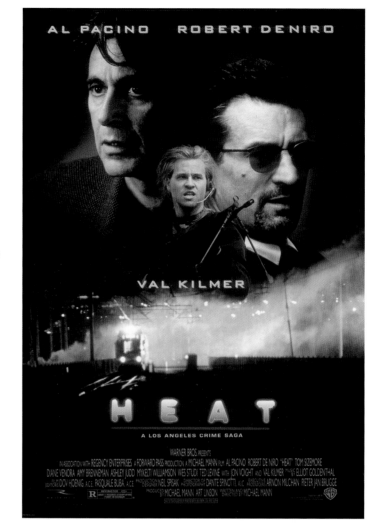

RIGHT One-sheet poster art for *Heat,* 1995, directed by Michael Mann, produced with Regency Enterprises. BELOW Al Pacino and Robert De Niro confront each other over coffee. OPPOSITE In *JFK,* 1991, produced with Regency Enterprises, Oliver Stone directs Kevin Costner in the courtroom sequence and, ABOVE, recreated the assassination in Dallas in 1963.

CONSPIRACY THEORIES

Whatever views are held with regard to the assassination of President Kennedy in Dallas in 1963, Oliver Stone's *JFK* (1991) is compelling filmmaking. Although it is well over three hours, it zips along at an exhilarating pace, never letting attention wander, a tribute to Stone and his editors, Joe Hutshing and Pietro Scalia.

Kevin Costner, heading a huge cast, plays the New Orleans district attorney Jim Garrison who is so dissatisfied with the conclusions of the Warren Report that he conducts his own investigation, and turns up evidence of not one but half a dozen or more conspiracy theories that disprove the thesis that Lee Harvey Oswald acted alone. There is no definitive answer and Stone came under fire, but his film is a brilliant submission to a continuing debate.

ROBBING THE RICH

Scott Turow's bestselling novel *Presumed Innocent* (1990) was filmed by Alan J. Pakula with Harrison Ford as a prosecutor investigating the murder in his office of a lawyer (Greta Scacchi). She has had a checkered sexual history and one of the scalps is his. He finds himself in the Hitchcockian nightmare of being seen as the main suspect. There are multiple twists in this claustrophobic courtroom drama.

In *Guilty by Suspicion* (1991), written and directed by Irwin Winkler, the dark days of the mid-century House Committee on Un-American Activities' hearings are recalled, with Robert De Niro as a prominent director called upon to name names. When he declines because it would implicate a friend he is quickly and effectively blacklisted, his career shredded. His wife, played by Annette Bening, rallies to him as many of his so-called friends evaporate. Martin Scorsese appears as another director who has chosen to continue his career in England, a part clearly modeled on Joseph Losey. A shameful period of Hollywood history is chillingly recapitulated.

The partnership of director Kevin Reynolds and actor Kevin Costner, kindled in *Fandango*, was revived in *Robin Hood: Prince of Thieves* (1991). Gone is the romanticism of the Michael Curtiz-Errol Flynn film of 1938, and in its place, a much grittier view of an England wasted by corruption.

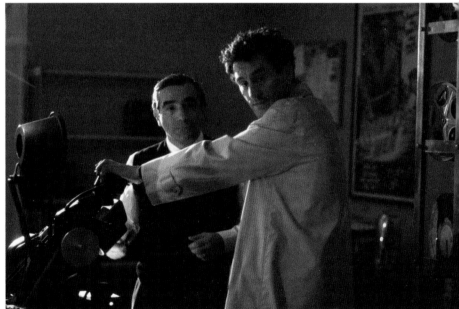

Rather surprisingly, Sir Robin of Locksley has acquired a black sidekick, a Moor with whom he was imprisoned by the Turks, played by Morgan Freeman. Mary Ann Mastrantonio plays Maid Marian, and Alan Rickman relishes his role as the villain of the piece, the Sheriff of Nottingham, adding humorous touches to the film.

LEFT One-sheet poster art for *Presumed Innocent,* 1990.
ABOVE Martin Scorsese made an appearance as a movie director, here with Robert De Niro, in *Guilty by Suspicion,* 1991.
OPPOSITE Kevin Costner as Robin of Locksley in *Robin Hood: Prince of Thieves,* 1991, produced with Morgan Creek Productions.

ONE LAST JOB

In 1985 *Pale Rider*, Clint Eastwood's first western after *The Outlaw Josey Wales* nine years earlier, follows a traditional line, the mysterious stranger who rides into a troubled community,

settles the wrongs, and moves on. In this instance land snatchers are ruthlessly exploiting a township of harassed miners. As their visitor, known as "Preacher," Eastwood inspires them to fight for their rights. Nobody knows who he is or where he came from, and although it is never explicit there is a suggestion of the supernatural. The ambiance is harsh and gritty, and the cinematography by Bruce Surtees avoids picturesque landscapes.

Eastwood's *Unforgiven* (1992) is the western he waited years to make. He plays a retired gunfighter driven to perform a last assignment by the need for money for his impoverished family. With his old associate (Morgan Freeman) he travels to avenge the brutal mutilation of a prostitute for a $500 reward, and encounters the most vicious sheriff in the West (Gene Hackman). Neither man has time on his side. A pulp novelist (Saul Rubinek) is ensuring that the mythology of the passing era is recorded. It won Oscars for Best Picture, Best Director, Best Editing (Joel Cox), and Best Supporting Actor (Hackman).

ABOVE AND BELOW Clint Eastwood in both roles as lead actor and director in *Pale Rider*, 1985. OPPOSITE One-sheet poster art for *Unforgiven*, 1992.

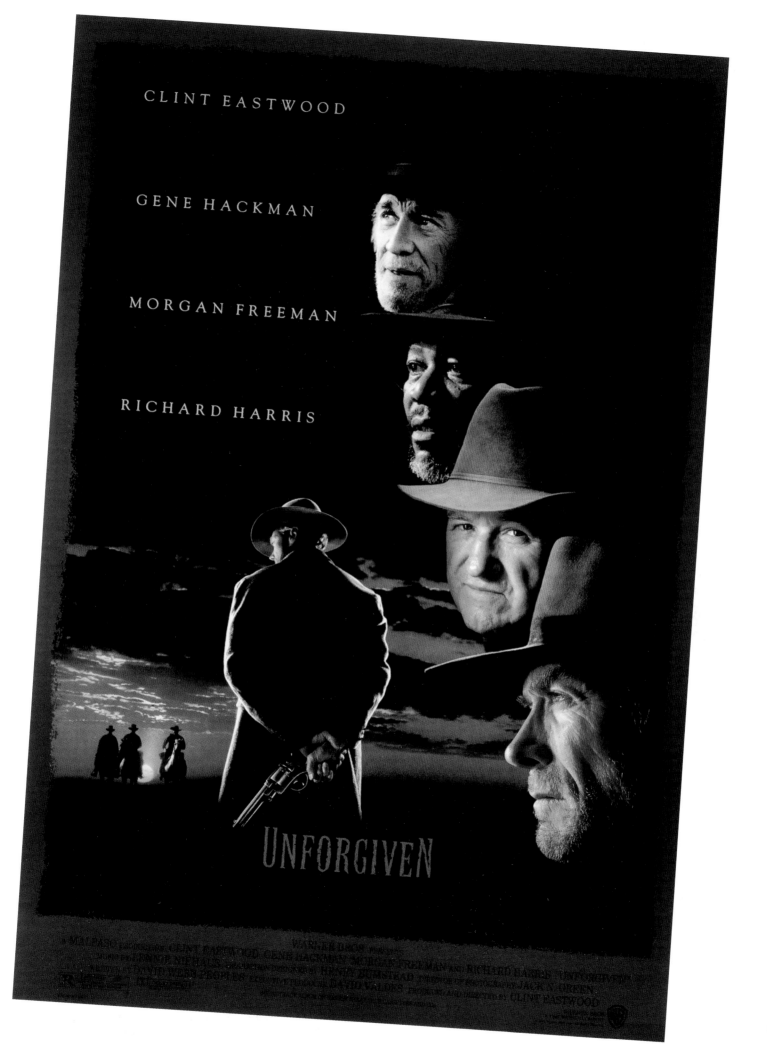

Clint Eastwood in his Oscar-winning movie, *Unforgiven*.

ON THE RUN

The 1979 Australian film *Mad Max*, shot on a low budget and starring a then-unknown Mel Gibson, was a sleeper in most parts of the world, which in spite of indifferent U.S. distribution (not by Warner Bros.) and dubbing into American voices, had sufficient impact to warrant a sequel.

Warner Bros. produced *The Road Warrior* (titled *Mad Max 2* in the rest of the world), which was set like its predecessor in an anarchic, oil-starved future, with a small desert community fighting to protect its gasoline stock from marauders, who swarm on motor cycles, in supercharged racers,

and gigantic semis and tanker trucks. The opportunities for spectacular clashes and crashes are plentiful and some of the stunts are among the most extravagant ever performed.

A third film, *Mad Max Beyond Thunderdome*, again with George Miller directing (with George Ogilvie) and Mel Gibson (with Tina Turner) starring, plunged further into the post-apocalyptic gas-depleted world, with Max pursuing his stolen camel train to a desert settlement ruled by Aunty Entity (Turner). She has him fight a behemoth in her arena but when he refuses to kill he is banished and rescued by feral children. The trilogy has a deserved cult following among science-fiction enthusiasts.

ABOVE *Mad Max Beyond Thunderdome,* 1985, Mel Gibson and Helen Buday with the Little Ones.

TOP Mel Gibson in *Mad Max Beyond Thunderdome*.
ABOVE Mel Gibson as Mad Max in *The Road Warrior*.

"WONDER IN OUR EYES"

TV FAVORITES

In *The Fugitive* (1993), directed by Andrew Davis, Harrison Ford plays a doctor wrongly convicted of his wife's murder. He makes a dramatic escape when a train hits the prison bus, and stays at liberty against astonishing odds in a cat-and-mouse tussle with Tommy Lee Jones as the federal marshal leading the manhunt. It is a classic nail-biter, based on a television series of the 1960s.

In *Maverick* (1994), directed by Richard Donner and scripted by William Goldman, Mel Gibson plays the role of the gambling conman who takes on the Old West with a card deck, and James Garner, who originated the role in the 1950s popular TV series, appears as a retired U.S. marshal. A befrilled, vampish Jodie Foster is the third member of the picaresque trio, who travel by stage, dealing with bandits, Indians, and runaway horses en route, toward a big coup at a poker tournament on board a river paddleboat. By the mid-1990s westerns of all descriptions had become rare, making this spoof all the more welcome.

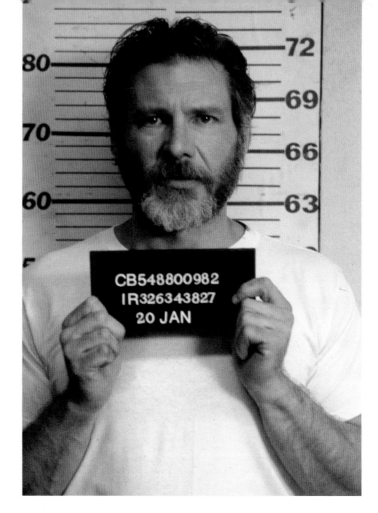

OPPOSITE ABOVE AND BELOW Harrison Ford is Dr. Richard Kimble, in prison and on the run in *The Fugitive*, 1993. ABOVE Mel Gibson, Jodie Foster, and James Garner (the original TV Bret Maverick), in *Maverick*, 1994.

"WONDER IN OUR EYES"

PARANOIA AT THE TOP

John Grisham's bestselling novels with a southern legal background resulted in three Warner Bros. films in the 1990s. In *The Client* (1994), directed by Joel Schumacher, an eleven-year-old boy (Brad Renfro) is in trouble with the law (represented by Tommy Lee Jones) and the Mafia because he knows too much, so he turns to a lawyer played by Susan Sarandon for help. The suspense is effective, and a tense story is deftly told.

Alan J. Pakula's interest in top-level conspiracies served him for his adaptation of Grisham's novel *The Pelican Brief* (1993). A bright law student (Julia Roberts) works out how two Supreme Court judges were assassinated, and when her theory becomes known, it is clear that someone in a high position wants her eliminated. She becomes a fugitive alongside investigative reporter Denzel Washington, and a trail of bodies piles up in this conventional thriller that even stages a menacing sequence in a covered parking lot. The performances of Roberts, Washington, Sam Shepard as her professorial boyfriend who is blown up for knowing too much, and Stanley Tucci as a wily killer, keep the action alive.

Grisham's first book was made into a film also directed by Joel Schumacher, *A Time to Kill* (1996) with Sandra Bullock, Samuel L. Jackson, Matthew McConaughey, and Kevin Spacey. In a small southern town a black man (Jackson) shoots the white trash who raped his ten-year-old daughter and goes on trial. A smart young lawyer (McConaughey) defends him, but uproar prevails. The Klan starts getting its robes out of the linen chest and the district attorney (Spacey) rages. An eager law student (Bullock) tries to help the overwhelmed lawyer. Grisham's plotting sets up a nightmare situation that will require nail-biting ingenuity to resolve.

ABOVE Susan Sarandon and Brad Renfro in *The Client,* 1994, produced with Regency Enterprises. RIGHT Julia Roberts and Denzel Washington in *The Pelican Brief,* 1993.

MEDIA-AGE BONNIE AND CLYDE

Oliver Stone's *Natural Born Killers*, from a story by Quentin Tarantino, is seemingly a satire on the media's ability to elevate colorful psychopaths to national celebrity status, and created an uproar with morality organizations. The plot involves two young marrieds, Woody Harrelson and Juliette Lewis, who go on a killing spree, leaving behind them more than fifty corpses. Their fame is assured by the host (Robert Downey Jr.) of a TV show called *American Maniacs*. Stone's technique is disturbing, with violent jump cuts, color splashes, switches from color to black and white, even changes of film stock, so that the narrative is the presentation, with the message punctuated by displays of dazzling filmmaking.

LEFT Samuel L. Jackson in *A Time to Kill*, 1996, produced with Regency Enterprises. BELOW Juliette Lewis and Woody Harrelson in *Natural Born Killers*, 1994, produced with Regency Enterprises.

FUNNY MEN

Nobody could do irascibility like Jack Lemmon and Walter Matthau, and in *Grumpy Old Men* (1993), directed by Donald Petrie, they play ice-fishing neighbors in wintry Minnesota, who have feuded for half a century with such dedication that their quarrelsome relationship has become a dependency in their lives. The incursion of the maturely beautiful Ann-Margret, a vivacious redhead who careens at a fast pace on her snowmobile, has a devastating effect, as first one then the other becomes smitten. There had to be a sequel, *Grumpier Old Men* (1995), which was directed by Howard Deutch. One of the curmudgeons had by then married Ann-Margret, but the other finds a new interest when Sophia Loren moves into the neighborhood and opens a restaurant in the old fish-bait shop. Burgess Meredith makes his last appearance as Lemmon's ninety-five-year-old father, and has some of the best lines.

With his portrayal of *Ace Ventura: Pet Detective* (1994), Jim Carrey moved from television, as a performer on *In Living Color,* to movie stardom. He had already appeared in a few films in lesser roles but as Ace he had his first major lead, grabbing the opportunity like a man in a burning building who has found a working fire hose. He plays an investigator who looks for missing animals and is hired by the Miami Dolphins to track down their kidnapped mascot. Throughout, Carrey is a gurning, elastic-limbed clown who never lets up. The film began his career as a star and within two years he was earning $20 million a picture, including the sequel *Ace Ventura: When Nature Calls*.

OPPOSITE BELOW Jack Lemmon and Walter Matthau in *Grumpier Old Men*, 1995 and (TOP) with Sophia Loren. ABOVE Poster art for *Ace Ventura: Pet Detective*, 1994, produced with Morgan Creek Productions.

THINGS FROM OUTER SPACE

Tim Burton's *Mars Attacks!* (1996) is a big-budget re-enactment of a 1950s sci-fi fantasy, in which hordes of aliens armed with blasters arrive from another planet to battle Earth people for possession. The Martians are small, bulbous-headed, wholly dangerous, and counter all peace initiatives with instant vaporization of the negotiators. In the big cast Jack Nicholson has two roles, as the U.S. President attempting by telecast to assure his fellow Americans that he can cope, and as a Las Vegas casino owner, with Annette Bening as his wife.

RIGHT Tim Burton on set directing *Mars Attacks!*, 1996.
BELOW Tom Jones with Annette Bening. OPPOSITE Jack Nicholson as President James Dale.

"WONDER IN OUR EYES"

TIM BURTON
Meat Pies and Chocolate

As he approaches fifty, Tim Burton still has the air of an enfant terrible, which is often reflected in his films where the hero is an outcast or at odds with the rest of society. Born in Burbank in 1958, he was an early fan of the movies of Roger Corman and especially those starring the grand eminence of horror, Vincent Price. He was awarded a Disney scholarship to the California Institute of Arts in Valencia and later worked at the Disney Studios as an animator. He then made a six-minute animated short, *Vincent,* about a young boy's fantasy that he is Vincent Price, and the actor himself narrated. It was followed by a live-action short, *Frankenweenie,* a Frankenstein story about a rejuvenated dog. Paul Reubens saw it and requested that Burton direct him in *Pee-Wee's Big Adventure,* which turned out to hugely profitable.

Even more so was *Beetlejuice,* made by the Geffen Company and Warner Bros., and starring Michael Keaton as a crazy ghost rescuing a house from its obnoxious new human owners. Burton was chosen to direct *Batman,* and did so in England, insisting that Keaton play the new caped hero, and it was a $400 million worldwide hit.

Warner Bros. passed on *Edward Scissorhands* with Johnny Depp as the tender, damaged title character and Vincent Price in his last screen appearance as his creator. Burton came back to Warner Bros. and Burbank, where he filmed the next *Batman* film *Batman Returns.*

Apart from the extended spoof *Mars Attacks!,* based on a series of trading cards, most of his subsequent films—such as *Ed Wood, Sleepy Hollow,* and the remake of *Planet of the Apes*—were made at other studios. However, the delightful reimagination of Roald Dahl's dark childhood fable *Charlie and the Chocolate Factory,* his fifth collaboration with Johnny Depp, was a Warner Bros. film made at Pinewood, London. His Academy Award nominated stop-motion animation film *Corpse Bride* followed, also made in England, and he went back to Pinewood for the crepuscular, gory horrors of *Sweeney Todd: The Demon Barber of Fleet Street*, a DreamWorks-Warner Bros. co-production, with Johnny Depp in the lead and Helena Bonham-Carter, Burton's romantic partner in real life, as his pie-baking associate.

Because Burton had achieved so much relatively early in his career there had been a concern that his singular talent would never last, but his two latter Pinewood films satisfactorily allay that fear.

OPPOSITE Tim Burton directing Michael Keaton as Batman, and Michelle Pfeiffer as Cat-woman in *Batman Returns*, 1992. ABOVE Burton on the set of *Batman Returns* and BELOW directing *Charlie and the Chocolate Factory*, 2005, produced with Village Roadshow Pictures.

1995–99

* Clint Eastwood is honored with the Irving G. Thalberg Award, 1995

* Time Warner acquires Turner Broadcasting System, 1995

* O.J. Simpson is acquitted of murdering his wife and her friend, 1995

* Warner Bros. and Tribune Company launch The WB Network, 1995

* Michael Mann's *Heat* co-stars Al Pacino and Robert De Niro, 1995

* Diana, Princess of Wales dies following a Paris car crash, 1997

* Kim Basinger wins Best Supporting Actress for *L.A. Confidential*, 1997

* *The Matrix* trilogy spin-offs include sequels, comic books, animations, and video games, 1998

* Oliver Stone's *Any Given Sunday* is an exposé of pro football, 1999

* Tom Hanks is a prison guard in Frank Darabont's *The Green Mile*, 1999

ABOVE Clint Eastwood receives the Irving G. Thalberg Memorial Award from Arnold Schwarzenegger in 1995.
In *L.A. Confidential*, 1997, produced with Regency Enterprises and Monarchy Enterprises, RIGHT TOP Guy Pearce and BELOW Russell Crowe. OPPOSITE Kim Basinger.

DISHING THE DIRT

Curtis Hanson's *L.A. Confidential* (1997) is a *film noir* set in the early 1950s, with the city's police department split between the corrupt and the straight, each side having sufficient ambiguity to hold the attention. Kevin Spacey, Russell Crowe, Guy Pearce, and James Cromwell are policemen pursuing their separate self interests; Kim Basinger is a call girl whose specialty is to look like Veronica Lake; and Danny DeVito edits a Hollywood sleaze magazine with no shortage of copy. James Ellroy's novel is long and complex, but Hanson and Brian Helgeland's distillation is excellently crafted.

LOVE FROM A STRANGER

Clint Eastwood starred in and directed *The Bridges of Madison County* (1995), adapted by Richard Gravenese from the novel by Robert James Waller. He plays a *National Geographic* photographer wandering the backroads of Iowa in the mid-1960s to shoot a story on the covered bridges of the area.

He meets an Italian housewife (Meryl Streep) living in an isolated farmhouse, with her husband and children away for days at the Illinois State Fair. She invites him to dinner and they talk and talk, and realize that they have fallen for each other. However, rather like David Lean's 1945 masterpiece *Brief Encounter,* they know that her husband will return, her visitor will move on and out of her life, and the romantic interlude will be over.

RIGHT, BELOW AND OPPOSITE In *The Bridges of Madison County,* 1995, Clint Eastwood directed and starred as a *National Geographic* photographer who meets an Italian housewife, played by Meryl Streep, in rural Iowa.

WORKING AS A PAIR

In *Lethal Weapon* (1987), directed by Richard Donner, Mel Gibson is a psychotic cop, more or less unhinged by his wife's death in an automobile accident, who is teamed with a stable, middle-aged family man, played by Danny Glover. When they plunge into hair-raising action the near-suicidal Gibson is prepared to take any risk, while Glover is motivated by the need to protect his family and find his kidnapped daughter. The partnership was hugely successful and three sequels followed, *Lethal Weapon 2, 3,* and *4,* each film outdoing the previous one in spectacle, violence, and exotic criminality.

MEL GIBSON Mad and Lethal

Mel Gibson, one of eleven children, was the son of an Irish-American railroad brakeman and an Irish-born woman, and had a grandmother who was an Australian opera singer. He was born in 1956 in Peekskill, New York, but raised in New South Wales after he was twelve—a duality of upbringing that would be of value to his career. He was a star student at the National Institute of Dramatic Art, and played Romeo to Judy Davis's Juliet. His break came when George Miller cast him to play the lead in the first *Mad Max* film, as a fired-up post-apocalyptic avenger, which was made in Australia on a low budget. Warner Bros. produced the second and third of the eventual trilogy. *The Road Warrior* and *Mad Max Beyond Thunderdome* were gigantic hits.

Gibson continued to make his name in Australia with *Tim* and Peter Weir's *Gallipoli*. He worked with Weir again on *The Year of Living Dangerously* and was Fletcher

Christian to Anthony Hopkins' Captain Bligh in *The Bounty*. In Richard Donner's *Lethal Weapon* at Warner Bros. he was cast with Danny Glover to play the unstable half of a Los Angeles cop team, and after its box-office success three sequels followed.

He won an Oscar for directing the Best Picture of 1995, *Braveheart,* a legend-making Scottish epic in which he also appeared in the leading role of the heroic William Wallace. Gibson excels in volatile roles, and his background gives him the ease to be as American or Australian as a character demands.

OPPOSITE TOP RIGHT One-sheet poster art for *Lethal Weapon,* 1987, featuring Mel Gibson and Danny Glover. LEFT Mel Gibson and Danny Glover in *Lethal Weapon 3,* 1992. BELOW *Lethal Weapon 2,* 1989. ABOVE On the set of *Lethal Weapon 4,* 1998, producer Joel Silver talks to Mel Gibson.

EXIT LINE

In March 1999, Stanley Kubrick screened his long-awaited film *Eyes Wide Shut* for Warner Bros.; four days later he died in his sleep at the age of seventy. Such dramatically timed finality was perhaps appropriate for one of the most idiosyncratic directors of all time. His film, appearing twelve years after his penultimate *Full Metal Jacket,* had been shot in secure conditions over four hundred days—an inordinate time. Although set in New York it was made entirely in England, where Kubrick shaped his locations carefully and built an approximation of Greenwich Village on the Pinewood backlot. It was even rumored that assistants had been sent to the real place to bring back garbage cans loaded with authentic Village trash.

His film compounded the strangeness of its reputation. Based on an Arthur Schnitzler novella and co-scripted with Frederic Raphael, its setting was transferred from 1920s Vienna to modern Manhattan, with Tom Cruise and Nicole Kidman as a wealthy, contented professional couple living stylishly by Central Park. A visit to a high-powered formal party leads to her being propositioned by a smooth Hungarian and to him being asked as a doctor to minister to a naked girl who has taken a drug overdose. Suddenly stimulated, an impulse for sexual adventure leads him to attend an orgiastic gathering in a country mansion, and the edifice of his life is threatened. The most sexually explicit of all Kubrick films, it attracted controversy and condemnation, and U.S. prints were digitally altered to conceal nudity in an orgy scene.

In *Eyes Wide Shut,* 1999, Tom Cruise plays Dr Bill Harford and Nicole Kidman his wife, Alice, in the last and most controversial film directed by Stanley Kubrick (RIGHT).

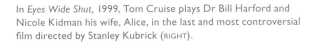

THE DARK KNIGHT

Bob Kane's comic book creation *Batman* had appeared in film serials, a television series, and a hasty 1966 feature. In 1989 Tim Burton moved the character up several notches with *Batman,* which was based at Pinewood Studios, London. Controversially his caped crusader was played by Michael Keaton, who was not by any measure an action hero, and was far better-known as an accomplished comedian. Keaton had scored considerable success as a zany spook in *Beetlejuice,* which had also been a big hit for Burton, giving him the power to become director of *Batman.* The casting of Jack Nicholson as the charismatic villain, the Joker, was seen as a considerable aid to achieving box-office success. The film proved to be immensely profitable in spite of the dark overtones that Burton had invested in the treatment, and proved to be very different in narrative and atmosphere from the *Superman* films, although both had originated in comic book form from DC Comics.

Burton and Keaton reprised their act for *Batman Returns,* which was made at Burbank, and was populated by a grotesque trio of opponents—Danny DeVito as the Penguin, Christopher Walken as the evil tycoon Max Schreck, and Michelle Pfeiffer as the slinky, latex-clad Catwoman. For the third film, directing duties passed to Joel Schumacher, with Val Kilmer taking on the lead role. Tommy Lee Jones played the villainous Two-Face and Jim Carrey the Riddler, with Nicole Kidman as Batman's romantic interest. Less successful was Schumacher's *Batman and Robin* with George Clooney as Batman and his alter-ego Bruce Wayne, Arnold Schwarzenegger as Mr. Freeze and Uma Thurman as Poison Ivy. The franchise was entertainingly revived in 2005 with *Batman Begins,* directed by Christopher Nolan, with Christian Bale showing how the wealthy Wayne came to adopt his strange nocturnal persona and become the scourge of criminals in Gotham City. Nolan directed Christian Bale again in the 2008 *Batman* blockbuster, *The Dark Knight,* with Heath Ledger reinventing the role of the Joker.

OPPOSITE Clockwise from top: Jack Nicholson as the Joker in *Batman,* 1989; Danny Devito as the Penguin in *Batman Returns,* 1992; Uma Thurman as Poison Ivy in *Batman and Robin*; Christian Bale as Batman in *Batman Begins,* 2005, produced with Legendary Pictures; Katie Holmes holding Jack Gleeson in *Batman Begins*; George Clooney as Batman in *Batman and Robin,* 1997, and Michelle Pfeiffer as Catwoman, on top of Michael Keaton as Batman, in *Batman Returns.*

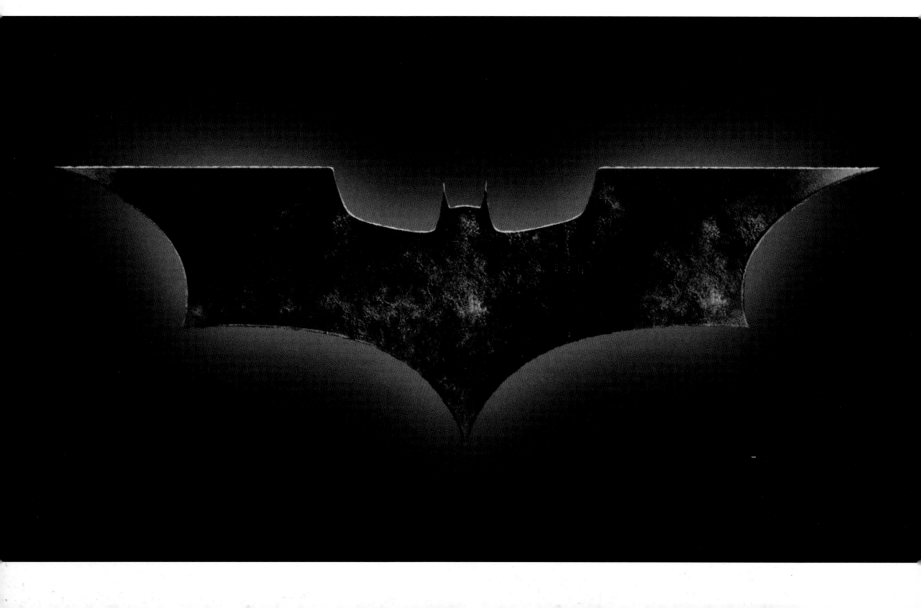

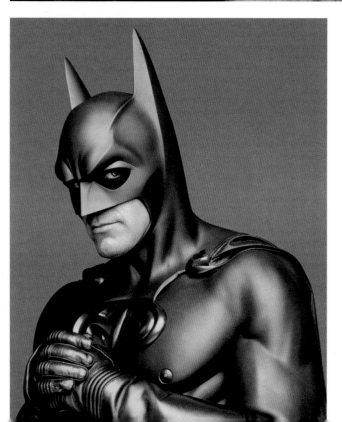

ABOVE One-sheet poster art for *Batman and Robin*, featuring Arnold Schwarzenegger, Chris O'Donnell, Alicia Silverstone, Uma Thurman, and George Clooney.
OPPOSITE One-sheet poster art for *Batman Begins*, with Christian Bale.

THE WARNER BROS. STORY

433

THE WARNER BROS. STORY

OPPOSITE Christian Bale in full flight in *Batman Begins*. OVERLEAF Bale as Batman confronts Heath Ledger as the Joker in *The Dark Knight*, 2008, produced with Legendary Pictures.

435

GHOST IN THE MACHINE

In the 1950s it was the growth of television that threatened the stability of the film industry, leading eventually to studios establishing secondary production divisions to make programs. By the millennium it was the Internet and the rapid development of computer game technology that provided the new challenges and threats. The use of computer graphics in filmmaking was becoming well established, often yielding spectacular results. *The Matrix* (1999), directed by Andy and Larry Wachowski, not only took these skills to the existing limits, but also suggested a situation where a hacker played by Keanu Reeves discovers that he has been subsumed into cyberspace and is a pawn in a gigantic game in a world controlled by computers. Much of the Wachowski brothers' screenplay is in arcane techno-speak, which is not easily understandable, particularly as it was ahead of its time in so many ways. The sequel, *The Matrix Reloaded* (2003), is more literal and features tremendous set pieces, a prolonged battle with hundreds of clones of Hugo Weaving, for instance, and the most terrifying freeway chase ever filmed (fortunately an exclusive section of highway was built specially for the sequence, which took three months to film and resulted in the write-off of 300 cars). The last film, *The Matrix Revolutions* (2003), jointly used the written word and access to elaborate set pieces, reaching for the same inventiveness as the first two *Matrix* films.

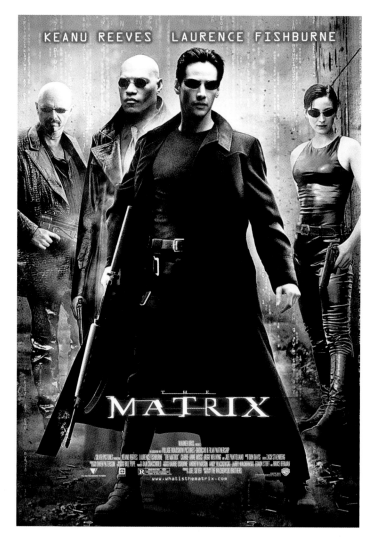

ABOVE AND LEFT Keanu Reeves in *The Matrix*, 1999. TOP One-sheet poster art.
OPPOSITE Conceptual art for the human embryo in the harvesting chamber from *The Matrix*, all Matrix films produced with Village Roadshow Pictures.

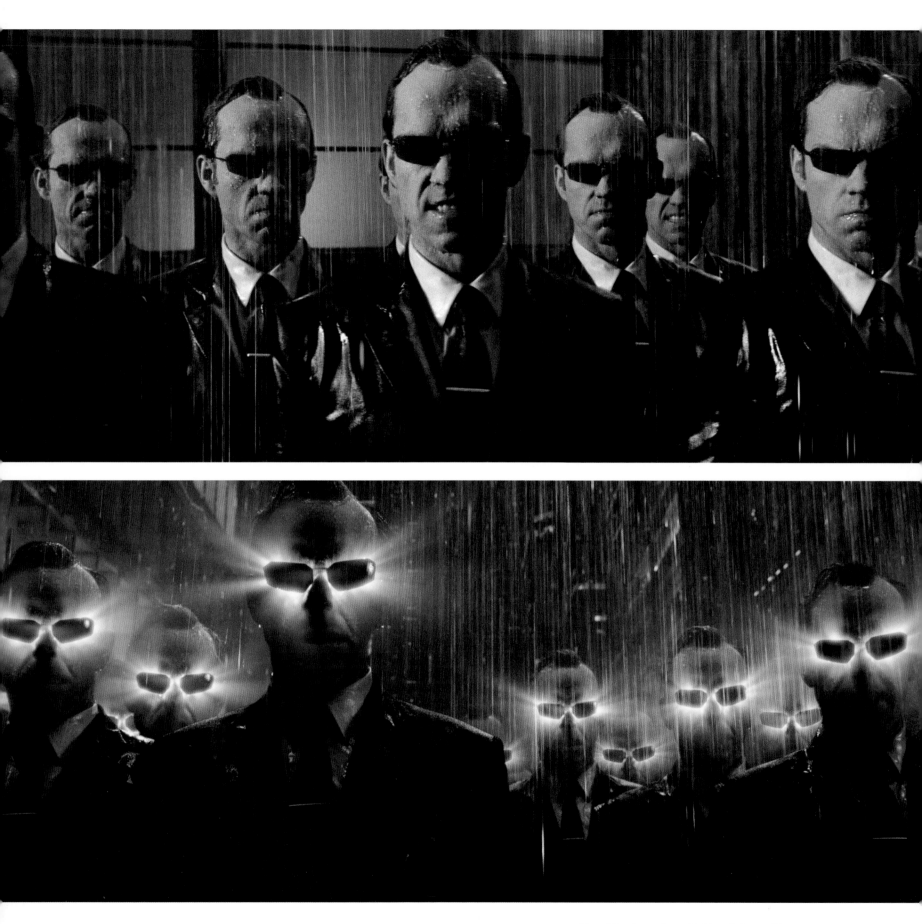

ABOVE Hugo Weaving as Agent Smith and clones, *The Matrix Revolutions*, 2003. OPPOSITE Carrie-Anne Moss and Keanu Reeves in front of racks of guns and weapons. OPPOSITE ABOVE Keanu Reeves fights Hugo Weaving.

2000–08

∗ The Time Warner merger with AOL becomes the biggest in corporate history, 2001

∗ After a close finish, George W. Bush defeats Al Gore to become 43rd president, 2001

∗ Warner Bros. releases the first of the *Harry Potter* films, 2001

∗ The World Trade Center in New York is destroyed by terrorists and a plane is deliberately crashed into the Pentagon, 2001

∗ Iraq is invaded by the U.S.-led coalition forces and Saddam Hussein is toppled from power, 2003

∗ *Million Dollar Baby* wins Best Picture and Clint Eastwood Best Director at the Oscars, 2004

∗ Martin Scorsese's *The Departed* is Best Picture, 2006

∗ Clint Eastwood directs *Flags of Our Fathers* and *Letters from Iwo Jima* back-to-back, 2006

∗ Tilda Swinton wins Best Supporting Actress for *Michael Clayton,* 2007

ABOVE Ground Zero, September 11, 2001. RIGHT Jude Law as Gigolo Joe, and Haley Joel Osment as David Swinton, in Rouge City, *AI: Artificial Intelligence,* 2001, produced with Dreamworks SKG. OPPOSITE TOP the undersea world of the Blue Fairy. BELOW director Steven Spielberg discusses a scene with Haley Joel Osment.

DREAM TEAM

For many years Stanley Kubrick talked with Steven Spielberg about his adaptation of Brian Aldiss's science-fiction short story *Super Toys Last All Summer Long.* After Kubrick's death Spielberg went ahead with directing the film as an homage to his friend. That both great filmmakers should have put their stamp on an ambitious film led to heightened expectations. *AI: Artificial Intelligence* envisions a future in which the Arctic has melted, engulfing New York so that deserted skyscrapers poke up from the sea, and New Jersey has reverted to primitive rain forest. Scientist William Hurt and his team have perfected a cyborg child that can experience love and other human emotions and a couple (Frances O'Connor and Sam Robards) adopt it as their own. The boy (magically played by Haley Joel Osment) is a version of Pinocchio, yearning to be real. Abandoned in the woods, he is befriended by another cyborg (Jude Law) and they embark on their journey to seek the mysterious Blue Fairy.

"WONDER IN OUR EYES"

ON TOP OF OLD SPARKY

Frank Darabont followed *The Shawshank Redemption* (1994), his classic film of a Stephen King novella, with another Stephen King prison drama, *The Green Mile* (1999), which he adapted into a huge box-office hit. Tom Hanks is a kindly Louisiana chief guard in the Depression era, whose responsibilities include making sure that the electric chair is maintained in full working order. The title refers to the sitter'vs last walk to it along a green linoleum floor. A new condemned prisoner—a mountainous, simple-minded man (Michael Clarke Duncan)— seems far too gentle to have committed his terrible crimes, and turns out to have miraculous powers of healing and the capacity to alter people's lives. The horrific details of death by electrocution are forcefully presented in a lengthy assault on the emotions, in what is essentially a spiritual metaphor for the power of goodness to prevail in an evil world.

BEAUTY QUEENS

In *Miss Congeniality* (2000), directed by Donald Petrie, Sandra Bullock plays a tough FBI agent who has been beating up boys since childhood. Her assignment is to go undercover to find a terrorist, a task that requires her also to become a contestant at the Miss United States Pageant. The transformation from tomboy feminist to curvaceous beauty queen is entrusted to Michael Caine, who delivers an exotic performance as a campy consultant as he embarks on the seemingly hopeless task. Both are accomplished stars who seem to be taking a break, and having fun in a throwback to screwball comedy that proved popular enough to warrant a sequel in 2005.

OPPOSITE top In *The Green Mile,* 1999, Tom Hanks plays the chief guard. BELOW With David Morse, escorting the psychic Michael Clarke Duncan. Produced with Castle Rock Entertainment. ABOVE Benjamin Bratt and Sandra Bullock in *Miss Congeniality,* 2000. Produced with Castle Rock Entertainment.

"WONDER IN OUR EYES"

TOP SHOGUN

Edward Zwick is the director and co-writer of *The Last Samurai* (2003). Tom Cruise, as restless and charged with energy as ever, plays a U.S. Army captain with a Civil War and Indian fighting background who is hired to train Japanese imperial soldiers into a fighting army against the last samurai warriors. Western methods turn out to be no match for the samurai tradition, and his men with rifles are routed by bows and arrows. He is taken prisoner by his proud enemy— superbly played by Ken Watanabe. As mutual respect develops, the men bond and Cruise is indoctrinated, coming to understand the code of honor and the subtleties of Japanese ideology, a culture that regards discipline, loyalty, and a "good death" as the path to fulfillment.

Brad Pitt plays Achilles in *Troy* (2004), the expensive ($200 million) adaptation of Homer's *Iliad* in which thousands of soldiers engage in battles of hideous savagery. Orlando Bloom as Paris sparks it all by stealing Helen (Diane Kruger) from Menelaus (Brendan Gleeson), giving Agamemnon (Brian Cox) the cause to fight. In Wolfgang Petersen's breathtaking epic the gigantic spectacles are overwhelming and a fine cast is well-displayed, particularly Peter O'Toole as Priam, the king of Troy who makes his appeal to Achilles' conscience.

RIGHT Tom Cruise in *The Last Samurai,* 2003.
BELOW Brad Pitt in *Troy,* 2004.

JOURNEY BEYOND YOUR IMAGINATION

From the Academy Award winning team of Tom Hanks and director Robert Zemeckis, *The Polar Express* (2004) is an inspiring adventure based on the beloved Caldecott Medal children's book by Chris Van Allsburg about a doubting young boy who takes an extraordinary train ride to the North Pole on Christmas Eve. He embarks on a journey of self-discovery that shows the wonder of life never fades for those who believe. Combining classic storytelling with cutting-edge filmmaking, *The Polar Express* debuted a highly advanced version of motion-capture technology developed and tailored to meet Zemeckis' uncompromising vision and was the first feature ever to be shot entirely in his format.

LEFT AND BELOW Composite shots taken from *The Polar Express*, 2004, in which Tom Hanks plays the conductor and four other parts including Santa Claus; produced with Shangri-La Entertainment and Castle Rock Entertainment.

DENZEL
WASHINGTON

ETHAN
HAWKE

TRAINING
DAY

The only thing more dangerous than the line being crossed, is the cop who will cross it.

WARNER BROS. PICTURES PRESENTS

IN ASSOCIATION WITH VILLAGE ROADSHOW PICTURES AND NPV ENTERTAINMENT AN OUTLAW PRODUCTION DENZEL WASHINGTON ETHAN HAWKE "TRAINING DAY" SCOTT GLENN CLIFF CURTIS DR. DRE
SNOOP DOGG EDITED BY CONRAD BUFF A.C.E. PRODUCTION DESIGNER NAOMI SHOHAN DIRECTOR OF PHOTOGRAPHY MAURO FIORE MUSIC BY MARK MANCINA CO-PRODUCERS DAVID WISNIEVITZ SCOTT STRAUSS DAVID AYER
EXECUTIVE PRODUCERS BRUCE BERMAN DAVIS GUGGENHEIM WRITTEN BY DAVID AYER PRODUCED BY JEFFREY SILVER BOBBY NEWMYER DIRECTED BY ANTOINE FUQUA

VILLAGE ROADSHOW PICTURES
www.trainingday.net America Online Keyword: Training Day
Soundtrack Album on Priority Records

WARNER BROS. PICTURES
AN AOL TIME WARNER COMPANY
©2001 Warner Bros. All Rights Reserved

September 21

LEARNING ON THE JOB

Denzel Washington won the Best Actor Oscar for his performance in *Training Day*, directed by Antoine Fuqua, as a seasoned Los Angeles Police Department narcotics detective who is assigned a rookie (Ethan Hawke) who wants to be a drug enforcer. His task is to indoctrinate him into procedures. Although Washington's record for busts is exemplary, Hawke soon realizes that his methods for obtaining them are corrupt, brutal, and illegal, and that he is the lynchpin of a reign of terror on the streets. Hawke then finds that he is being initiated into the slimy world Washington inhabits and that resistance is not a survivable option. In the space of one working day he must progress from being a bright-eyed idealist to a toughened fighter who will have to use resources he never knew he had to stay alive.

ABOVE One-sheet poster art for *Training Day*, 2001, produced with Village Roadshow Pictures, Ethan Hawke and Denzel Washington. OPPOSITE *Oceans Eleven*, 2001, produced with Village Roadshow Pictures. ABOVE, George Clooney and Brad Pitt. BELOW left to right, back row, Andy Garcia, Brad Pitt, Don Cheadle; front row, George Clooney, Julia Roberts, Matt Damon.

JACKPOT TIME

The 1960 Las Vegas caper film *Ocean's Eleven* enjoyed a classy remake in 2001, which, apart from the basic situation of an assortment of specialists convening to pull off a casino super-heist, bore little resemblance to the original. George Clooney is the ringmaster in Steven Soderbergh's film, Andy Garcia is the owner of three casinos and his target, whose liaison with his ex-wife (played by Julia Roberts) supplies the motive. Sequels followed—*Ocean's Twelve,* in which the sights are extended to Paris, Rome, and Amsterdam, and *Ocean's Thirteen,* in which a casino is attacked to make it lose money on a prodigious scale.

WIZARD RAISING

J. K. Rowling's youthful bespectacled wizard Harry Potter first appeared in 1997 in the novel *Harry Potter and the Philosopher's Stone*. That and the six successive Harry Potter books have sold well in excess of 385 million copies worldwide.

In 1999 the film rights for the first of the *Harry Potter* titles were sold to Warner Bros. Since that time *Harry Potter* has proven to be the most successful film franchise in history, with the first five releases grossing over $4.5 billion to date. In order to remain true to the vision of J. K. Rowling's stories, the films were made in the United Kingdom with predominantly British casts. They have followed the sequence in which the novels were published, each representing a year in Harry's life at Hogwarts School of Witchcraft and Wizardry, where young wizards are taught by a faculty of experts in magical disciplines and led by the wise headmaster Albus Dumbledore. Initially Richard Harris played Dumbledore, but after the

actor's death Michael Gambon took over the role. Throughout the films Harry Potter has been played by Daniel Radcliffe. Emma Watson and Rupert Grint have portrayed Harry's best friends Hermione Granger and Ron Weasley respectively, and all of them have grown through their teenage years at the pace of the characters they play. Each movie has progressed the story, moving Harry ever closer to his destiny of confronting the evil Lord Voldemort, who killed his parents many years earlier. The first two films, *Harry Potter and the Sorcerer's Stone* and *Harry Potter and the Chamber of Secrets*, were directed by Chris Columbus, the third, *Harry Potter and the Prisoner of Azkaban* by Alfonso Cuarón, *Harry Potter and the Goblet of Fire* by Mike Newell, and *Harry Potter and the Order of the Phoenix* and the penultimate story *Harry Potter and the Half-Blood Prince* by David Yates. All of the films have been produced by David Heyman, with Stuart Craig as production designer throughout.

Although there is continuity of narrative, the tone differs from film to film, with some much darker and more frightening than others. Spectacular deployment of digital special effects, and a rotation of distinguished actors including Ralph Fiennes, Maggie Smith, Gary Oldman, Julie Walters, Alan Rickman, Robbie Coltrane, Emma Thompson, Jason Isaacs, Imelda Staunton, Helena Bonham Carter, Kenneth Branagh, Richard Griffiths, enhance their appeal to broad-ranging audiences.

In *Harry Potter and the Sorcerer's Stone*, 2001, LEFT Daniel Radcliffe as Harry Potter, Emma Watson as Hermione Granger, and Rupert Grint as Ron Weasley. ABOVE Robbie Coltrane as Rubeus Hagrid. OPPOSITE TOP Daniel Radcliffe as Harry Potter, Rupert Grint as Ron Weasley, and Emma Watson as Hermione Granger. In *Harry Potter and the Prisoner of Azkaban,* 2004, RIGHT Michael Gambon as Albus Dumbledore. OVERLEAF Harry Potter (Daniel Radcliffe) defending Sirius Black (Gary Oldman) from a swarm of attacking Dementors.

"WONDER IN OUR EYES"

TOP Daniel Radcliffe as Harry Potter in *Harry Potter and the Order of the Phoenix*, 2007. ABOVE Ralph Fiennes as Lord Voldemort in a graveyard battle with Harry Potter in *Harry Potter and the Goblet of Fire*, 2005. OPPOSITE One-sheet poster art from *Harry Potter and the Sorcerer's Stone*, 2001.

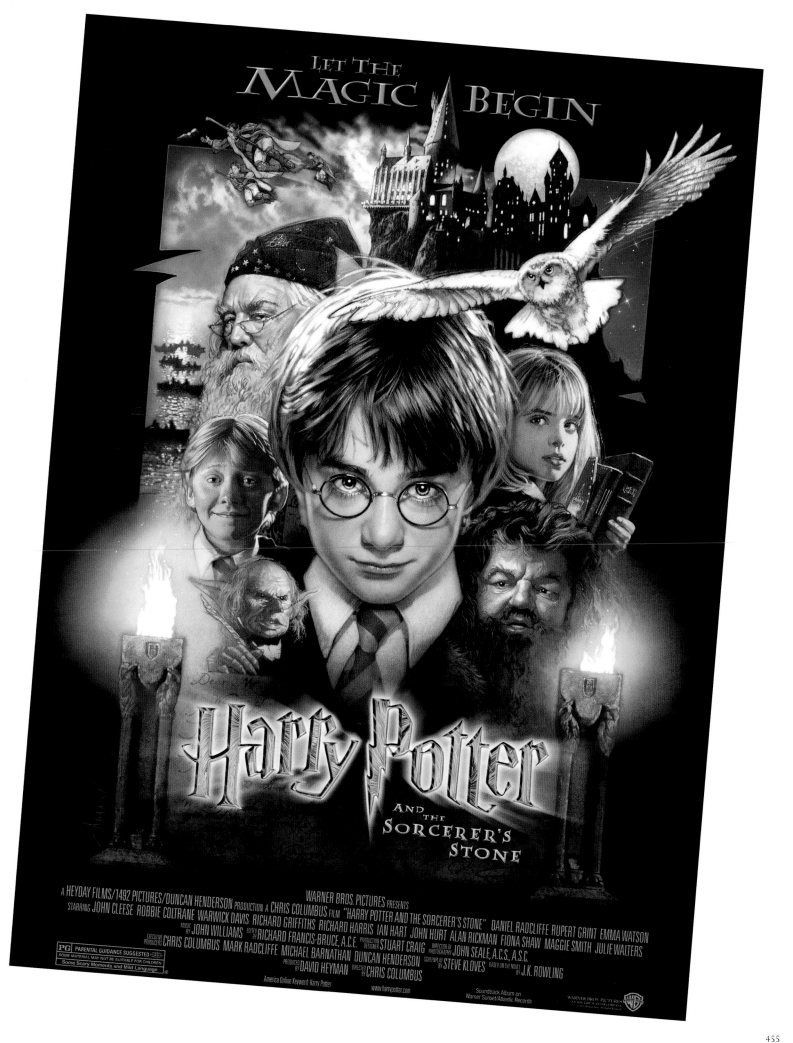

"WONDER IN OUR EYES"

MATURE REFLECTION

Clint Eastwood's association with Warner Bros. began with *Dirty Harry* in 1971, and from 1975 Malpaso, his production company, has been based in a 1926 Spanish-style bungalow on the Burbank lot. At a time when most septuagenarians would be happier reclining in the sun, his output as producer, director, and actor has flowed and the quality has been as consistently high as at any period in his long career.

Sean Penn and Tim Robbins won Oscars for their roles in the Boston working-class neighborhood saga of past conflicts and scars in *Mystic River*, which was also nominated for Best Picture with Eastwood as Best Director. The following year, 2004, he won Best Director for *Million Dollar Baby*, which also won Best Picture. It was the 25th film he had directed, and he played an aging boxing manager persuaded to take on as a fighter a poor but determined and talented young woman (Hilary Swank, who won an Oscar for her performance), leading to a tragic outcome. He then made two films back-to-back, looking at a crucial and intensely bloody battle of World War II from opposing points of view. In partnership with

DreamWorks, *Flags of Our Fathers* used as its basis the famous Iwo Jima flag-raising photograph by Joe Rosenthal, and the subsequent exploitation of the Marines involved. The other, *Letters from Iwo Jima*, saw the battle from the Japanese perspective, with Ken Watanabe as a C.O. fighting to the death. In Japanese, with subtitles, it is a classic among war films and was nominated for Best Picture and Best Director Oscars.

OPPOSITE TOP Sean Penn in *Mystic River*, 2003, produced with Village Roadshow Pictures. BOTTOM Clint Eastwood playing the piano on the set of *Mystic River*. TOP Clint Eastwood, Morgan Freeman, and Hilary Swank in *Million Dollar Baby*, 2004, produced with Lakeshore Entertainment. ABOVE AND RIGHT Clint Eastwood directing two very different movies, *Mystic River* and *Letters from Iwo Jima*—with RIGHT Ken Watanabe. ABOVE RIGHT The iconic planting of the Stars and Stripes in *Flags of Our Fathers*. OVERLEAF Japanese soldiers in *Letters from Iwo Jima*. Both *Flags* and *Letters* produced with DreamWorks SKG.

COLD CALLING

A superb French documentary, *March of the Penguins* (2005), directed by Luc Jacquet, reveals the extraordinary trek made annually across frozen Antarctic wastes by Emperor Penguins to their breeding grounds, where the males remain, keeping the eggs warm with their feet, while the females go back to fetch food. The dignified stoicism of these strange flightless birds was seen by some as an inspirational message on the meaning of existence, and although Morgan Freeman's commentary is sentimental at times, the American version, which won the Best Documentary Feature Oscar, is superior to its French original, which adopted a comical anthropomorphic approach with the penguins speaking in dubbed human voices.

Taking anthropomorphism further was *Happy Feet* (2006), the Academy-Award winning animated feature made in Australia, directed by George Miller, featuring the voices of Elijah Wood, Robin Williams, Brittany Murphy, Hugh Jackman, Nicole Kidman and Hugo Weaving. In this story, Emperor

Penguins attract their soul mates by singing, but young Mumble is the worst singer in the world. He is, however, a fabulous tap dancer. When a catastrophic fish famine is blamed on Mumble, he is banished from his home. Meeting up with a bunch of Latino penguins, he learns the importance of being true to himself, and this beautiful, immensely cinematic film starts to impart a powerful ecological message for all mankind.

OPPOSITE The reality of life in the Antarctic, with scenes from *March of the Penguins*, 2005. ABOVE One-sheet poster art from the animated adventure about a tap-dancing penguin, *Happy Feet*, 2006, produced with Village Roadshow Pictures.

BLOOD FROM A STONE

In another age, Edward Zwick's *Blood Diamond* (2006) would have been a Rider Haggard-style adventure yarn, but instead it is turned into a political eco-message. In war-ravaged Sierra Leone a South African arms dealer, Leonardo DiCaprio disguised by a thick accent, and a humble fisherman (Djimon Hounsou) are thrown together in the search for the fabulous pink diamond the fisherman has hidden. The white man wants it as a means for getting out of the arms business, the other to regain his son, kidnapped by vicious rebels who raided his village. Jennifer Connelly is a beautiful foreign correspondent trying to piece together a story on "conflict stones." The performances are strong, the carnage horrific.

RIGHT AND BELOW In *Blood Diamond,* 2006, Leonardo DiCaprio and Djimon Hounsou are thrown together in the hunt for a fabulous pink diamond, produced with Virtual Studios.

ZAP, POW, SPLAT!

Zack Snyder's *300* (2007) turns Frank Miller's graphic novel on the Battle of Thermopylae in 480 BC between 300 well-motivated Spartans and the Persian hordes of King Xerxes into a vivid, blood-soaked film, liberally relying on computer effects. Considering it was shot in a warehouse in Montreal, the fact that the scope and splendor of Miller's dusty, dry mountainous vistas was captured onscreen is all the more amazing. Gerard Butler leads the brave Spartans in an entertaining, epic tale.

BELOW Gerard Butler as King Leonidas in *300,* 2007, produced with Legendary Pictures and Virtual Studios. BOTTOM Michael Fassbender as Stelios.

ON OPPOSITE SIDES OF THE LAW

Martin Scorsese's *The Departed* (2006) is set in Boston, and is a loose remake of the Hong Kong police thriller *Infernal Affairs*. Jack Nicholson is a crime boss who has succeeded in planting his mole, Matt Damon, in the Massachusetts State Police, and Leonardo DiCaprio, whose shady family upbringing makes him eminently suitable, is the Boston police's underground representative on Nicholson's team. The aim is to nail the number one, but the double game of the two young men has many twists. Scorsese's brilliant sense of camera, with cinematography by Michael Ballhaus, the fine editing of Thelma Schoonmaker, the screenplay by William Monahan, and a large cast that also includes Martin Sheen, Mark Wahlberg, and Ray Winstone make it one of the best of the director's films.

BELOW Martin Scorsese directs *The Departed,* 2006, advising actors on set in the bar scene with Leonardo DiCaprio (RIGHT AND OPPOSITE BELOW). OPPOSITE TOP Jack Nicholson. Scorsese won his first Oscar for Best Achievement in Directing (one of four awarded to the film).

CLOONEY DELIVERS

George Clooney is one of the few stars to have translated his popularity on television into a prestigious movie career, appearing in a succession of leading roles for some of the best directors in Hollywood. Born in Lexington, Kentucky, in 1961, his father the television anchorman Nick Clooney, his aunt the late chart-topping singer and actress of the 1950s, Rosemary Clooney, he was a journalism major at Northern Kentucky University.

He went to Los Angeles and spent a struggling decade working in television and in such low-budget films as *Return of the Killer Tomatoes,* but in 1994 the handsome and self-assured actor was cast as Dr. Doug Ross in the enormously successful Warner Bros. series *ER*, a part he played until 1999. Although he made films while still on the show, his big-screen career did not ignite until 1998's *Out of Sight,* directed by Steven Soderbergh. He continued making quality films for such distinguished directors as Soderbergh, Terrence Malick, David O. Russell, and the Coen brothers. Wolfgang Petersen's *The Perfect Storm*, in which he played the captain of a doomed fishing vessel, proved to be a big hit, as was his second collaboration with Soderbergh in 2001, a stylish, all-star reshaping of the Rat Pack's Las Vegas heist thriller of 1960, *Ocean's Eleven.* It was followed by two sequels, *Ocean's Twelve* and *Ocean's Thirteen,* all produced with Village Roadshow Pictures.

Of all the contemporary stars whose work has been concentrated at Warner Bros. George Clooney has proved to be both versatile and consistently attractive to his audiences. He has moved into direction, first with *Confessions of a Dangerous Mind*, the entertaining story of a trash-TV entrepreneur who claimed to be an agent for the CIA, and then the sure-footed *Good Night, And Good Luck*, for Warner Independent Pictures, in which the distinguished commentator Edward R. Murrow (played very tellingly by David Strathairn) is instrumental in breaking the notorious witch-hunting anti-communist Senator Joseph McCarthy. Clooney has also been executive producer of a number of films, including *Syriana*, an oil-industry intrigue written and directed by Stephen Gaghan, in which he plays a CIA man in the Middle East, an old hand who has begun to question the agency's motives. His performance earned him the Best Supporting Actor Academy Award.

After *The Good German*, a foray into military intrigue in postwar Berlin, directed in a black-and-white 1940s' noir-style by Soderbergh, he again reprised the Danny Ocean role for him in *Ocean's Thirteen*. He was then nominated for an Oscar for his fine work in *Michael Clayton,* directed by Tony Gilroy, in which he plays a weary attorney who has become a fixer—a highly experienced but shadowy figure who uses his skills to clean up difficult situations for a high-octane law firm.

Clooney's versatile track record shows him to be one of the most successful and durable modern star/directors.

RIGHT George Clooney in *Ocean's Eleven,* 2001. OPPOSITE TOP Acting and directing in *Good Night, And Good Luck,* 2005, produced with Participant Productions. OPPOSITE BELOW In *Syriana,* 2005, produced with Participant Productions.

Tilda Swinton and George Clooney in *Michael Clayton,* produced with
Samuels Media Entertainment. Swinton won the Oscar for the Best
Performance by an Actress in a Supporting Role, 2007.

COWARD'S WAY OUT

The title ensures that there are no surprises in *The Assassination of Jesse James by the Coward Robert Ford*. As written and directed by Andrew Dominik, the well-known story with its inevitable consequence unwinds at a deliberate pace throughout its 160 minutes, shot by Roger Deakins in the expansive open spaces of western Canada.

Brad Pitt plays Jesse James, the nationally famous leader of a declining band of bank and train robbers, and in 1881 very near the end of his run, aching to retire to his patient wife and children. Casey Affleck is his hero-worshipper, a young follower who attaches himself leechlike to the outlaw, rather like a rock-star's groupie. The film does not end with the killing, but looks at the fate of the killer, as he tries to exploit his own tarnished celebrity for as long as the public takes an interest.

RIGHT *The Assassination of Jesse James by the Coward Robert Ford*, 2007, produced with Virtual Studios, with Brad Pitt and Casey Affleck. BELOW Brad Pitt, guns drawn, at the last train robbery. OPPOSITE Will Smith, the last man on Earth, in *I Am Legend*, 2007, produced with Village Roadshow Pictures. OPPOSITE TOP RIGHT One sheet poster art.

GOING SOLO

Richard Matheson's novel visualizing a post-apocalyptic future had been filmed twice as *The Last Man on Earth* and *The Omega Man*. The most recent incarnation, *I Am Legend*, directed by Francis Lawrence, outshone both, not just for the advent of computer-generated imagery and other digital means making the possibility of how Manhattan might look three years after its total abandonment by the human race seem horrifyingly realistic, but with the acting of Will Smith who, for the majority of the running time, is obliged to perform a solo act. He is a military biologist, the sole survivor after a virus that began as a cure for cancer has wiped out the rest of humanity. He lives in a Washington Square brownstone with a well-stocked refrigerator (where the electricity comes from is not revealed) and hunts deer along Fifth Avenue in his Shelby Mustang. And of course, as he will discover, he is not alone.

CUTTING EDGE

Stephen Sondheim's gory musical *Sweeney Todd: The Demon Barber of Fleet Street* was filmed in partnership with Dream-Works by Tim Burton, who for the sixth time cast Johnny Depp as his film's leading character. He is a vengeful barber falsely sentenced and transported from eighteenth-century London to Australia by a vicious judge (Alan Rickman) who has designs on his wife and daughter. In the opening sequence, having escaped, he returns up the Thames in the persona of the ghastly Sweeney, his face deathly pale, his black hair streaked white like a badger. He resumes his old haunts and in partnership with Mrs. Lovett (Helena Bonham Carter) he is slitting throats as his victims recline in an adapted barber's chair, which is like an ejector seat to hell. Their cadavers are then ground up and used as the basis for Mrs. Lovett's succulent meat pies—soon the most sought-after delicacies in London, with none of the satisfied customers knowing why. The images of London squalor as visualized by Dante Ferretti are an Oscar-winning triumph of art direction, and both Depp and Bonham Carter sing undubbed, with Sacha Baron Cohen as a villainous Italian adding his full voice.

GEORGE PERRY

ABOVE Tim Burton directs Johnny Depp in *Sweeney Todd: The Demon Barber of Fleet Street*, 2007, produced with Dreamworks SKG.
RIGHT Johnny Depp as Sweeney Todd with Helena Bonham Carter as the sinister pie-maker Mrs. Lovett.

"WONDER IN OUR EYES"

ACKNOWLEDGMENTS

We are in deep gratitude to many executives of Warner Bros. and in particular to Leith Adams whose unfailing support, wise counsel and oracular knowledge of Warner history has made so much of this book possible. We pay tribute to our old friend and colleague Clive Hirschhorn who trod this path long before us (*The Warner Bros. Story,* 1979), and to the authors of many other books on the Studio, especially Nick Roddick (*New Deal in Entertainment: Warner Brothers in the 1930s,* 1983); Rudy Behlmer (*Inside Warner Bros. 1935-1951,* 1986); Cass Warner Sperling and Cork Millner (*Hollywood Be Thy Name,* 1998). We have also consulted for the checking of facts: James W. English (*The Rin Tin Tin Story*), Michael Birdwell (*Celluloid Soldiers, Warner Bros. Campaign Against Nazism*), A.M. Sperber and Eric Lax (*Bogart*), Anne Edwards (*Early Reagan: The Rise to Power*), Scott Eyman (*The Speed of Sound: Hollywood and The Talkie Revolution, 1926-1930*), and Jack L. Warner (*My First Hundred Years in Hollywood*).

We are immensely grateful to the executives of Running Press and especially to the unwavering encouragement given us by Cindy De La Hoz, while marveling that one of her generation can have so much sensitive erudition and passion for Hollywood history. And most of all, without the guiding hand and labors of Colin Webb and his dedicated team at Palazzo who achieved miracles within the tightest of time frames, this book would not have happened. GP

At Lorac Productions Inc.: Doug Freeman as co-producer, Faith Ginsberg and Bryan McKenzie, the former as editor, the latter as editor and post-production supervisor.

At Warner Bros.: Julie Heath, Linda Cummings, Lisa Janney, Jeff Stevens, Michael Arnold, Jeff Briggs, Geoff Murillo, Steven Bingen, Steve Sonn, Arturo Nunez, Maria Garza, Pat Kowalski, Scott Gaba.

PICTURE CREDITS

The Warner Bros. Corporate Image Archive has provided all images with the exception of those on the following pages:
Courtesy of the Academy of Motion Picture Arts and Sciences: 422
Corbis: 238 (Bettmann), 264 (Bettmann), 268 (Bettmann), 272 (Bettmann), 276 (Ted Streshinsky), 284 (NASA/ Roger Ressmeyer), 302 (Bettmann), 332 (Bettmann), 364 (Bettmann), 380 (Wally McNamee), 400 (Reuters), 442 (Peter Turnley).
Getty Images: 95 (Time Life Pictures), 261 (Popperfoto).
The Kobal Collection: 56, 80, 112, 133, 141, 154-155,165, 180, 181, 188, 194, 197, 234, 235, 243, 274.

INDEX

Page numbers in italics indicate illustrations